GODDESS ENERGY

GODDESS ENERGY

Awakening the Divine Feminine
✦ through Myth and Magick ✦

GABRIELA
HERSTIK

A TarcherPerigee Book

tarcherperigee
an imprint of Penguin Random House LLC
penguinrandomhouse.com

Most TarcherPerigee books are available at special quantity discounts for bulk
purchase for sales promotions, premiums, fundraising, and educational needs.
Special books or book excerpts also can be created to fit specific needs.
For details, write: SpecialMarkets@penguinrandomhouse.com.

ISBN 9780593330883

Printed in the United States of America
1st Printing

Book design by Laura K. Corless
Text photographs by Alexandra Herstik
Images pages 64 and 178 courtesy Clipart.com

This book is dedicated to the Goddess

CONTENTS

CONTENTS

5
The Dark Goddess

6
Embracing the Goddess Within

LIST OF RITUALS AND PRACTICES

1: The Goddess Is (Re)Awakening

+ Ritualizing Goddess Energy: Setting Up the Space, Grounding and Centering, and Closing and Grounding
+ Creating a Goddess Grimoire and a Consecration Ritual for Your Goddess Grimoire
+ Forming a Relationship with the Divine Feminine
+ Leaving Offerings for the Goddess
+ Journal Questions
+ A Meditation to Commune with the Goddess
+ Affirmations
+ A Tarot Spread for Meeting Goddess Energy

2: The Goddess of the Earth

+ The Goddess as the Elements
+ More Goddesses of the Earth
+ Creating an Altar to the Earth Goddess
+ Journal Questions
+ Affirmations
+ A Tarot Spread for Grounding into the Powers of the Goddess

3: The Goddess of Protection and Healing

+ Ways to Connect to the Goddess of Protection and Healing
+ Goddesses of Protection and Healing
+ Creating Energy Signatures for Protection and Healing
+ Journal Questions
+ Affirmations
+ A Tarot Spread to Receive Healing from the Goddess

4: The Goddess of Love

+ Cultivating a Relationship with the Goddess of Love
+ Goddesses of Love
+ Crafting Prayers to the Goddess of Love
+ Sex Magick 101
+ An Aphrodite/Venus Glamour Spell to Attract Love, Lust, and Desire
+ Journal Questions
+ Affirmations
+ A Tarot Spread for Invoking Your Inner Love Goddess

5: The Dark Goddess

+ Connecting to the Dark Goddess
+ Faces of the Dark Goddess
+ A Shadow Magick Ritual for Embracing the Dark Goddess Within

GODDESS
ENERGY

The Goddess Is (Re)Awakening

The earth, alive. The Sun and Moon, shining, dancing, revealing. The way the birds sing. The way flesh on flesh feels in the early morning. Love, lust, magick, devotion, to all that is or was. The fierce protection of the heart, of the beloved. The cries of rage and passion, a holy sacrament. The desire to bleed until it's all gone. *This is the Goddess, awakening, inspiring, calling.* She is as old and wise as the earth, but Her myriad faces transcend age and time.

Welcome, beloved, to the wild world of Goddess energy. I am so glad you are here, ready to embody new expressions of yourself and your heart.

Unlike the religions many of us grew up with, the religion of the Goddess isn't one separated from nature, from the body, from the creative and life-giving energy of sexuality. Goddess *is* the earth. She *is* the body. She *is* transformative carnal power. Many of us were taught that the body is sinful and separate from "God," yet this is the antithesis of the Goddess religion, the oldest religion on earth. Instead of spending your life transcending, or working toward the goal of leaving your body behind on this earthly plane, the Goddess is about immanence; finding a direct connection to the Divine through the self and the physical world.

The Goddess isn't separation. She isn't some old judgmental woman up in the clouds. She is the sacred and the mundane, seen in piles of trash and in holy places. *The Goddess is in everything.*

The Goddess is everywhere, and She is constantly expressing Herself to you. The Goddess evolves, as you do. The Goddess is not static. She has not remained unchanged for the thousands of years She's been worshipped. The Goddess is reflected in the cultures that worship Her, in those who revere Her, in Her devotees who span age and time. She's definitely not human, and yet She evolves alongside us, often depicting Herself in a familiar light to those who honor Her so they more easily recognize Her.

The way you worship the Goddess will look different from the way your ancestors did, but isn't that the point? Don't you want to pray to a deity who accepts all your twenty-first-century magick? We may not have as many temples and sacred sites as we once did, but now you can worship with a coven that spans the globe. Surely, the Goddess must be here for the ease of honoring Her, no matter where or when you live.

So why the Goddess? Why now? And what or who is the Goddess, truly, anyway?

Like the gender binary, the definition of the Goddess is a bit blurry these days. Each practitioner will have their own definition of *what* the Goddess is. Your own understanding will allow you to relate to Her more intimately, too. The Goddess does not exist in black and white, and She is not solely expressed through gender or biology.

More than anything, the Goddess is love. She is the living expression of the Divine Erotic, the potencies of sexuality, of death and

**She is all-encompassing—a vibration,
a frequency that every person on Earth
has access to. This is Goddess energy,
and *Goddess energy is for everyone.***

rebirth, of destruction and creation. The Goddess is consciousness, immanence, intuition, and the cyclical. She is the love that links everything, that brings the whole world into creation. The Goddess is form; She is the alive-ness of the universe. She is best known and felt through the heart.

The Divine Feminine is the counterpart to the Divine Masculine, which sits as the center of all that is, the logical and chronological force of the universe. These two energies are opposites, which just means they are extremes of the same thing. As the pillars of this polarity, every sort of energetic configuration exists between them, and any divine expression may take form on the spectrum of these energies. What I'm saying is, you don't have to be a woman, or cisgender, or straight to work with the Goddess. The Goddess accepts all Her children, as they are all expressions of Her magick. You are welcome here. All you have to be is willing to begin the journey.

The Goddess doesn't adhere to the same structures or beliefs so many of us have thrown onto "God." The Goddess doesn't punish you for your imperfections, but rather celebrates self-expression, magick, creativity, sensuality, and ecstatic experiences. She is not trying to cut you off from yourself; instead, She is guiding you to your most abundant expression. The Goddess doesn't smite you to atone for "sins" or supposed wrongdoings, nor does She see sexuality or sexual energy as shameful or evil; all acts of love and pleasure are Her rituals.

To honor the Goddess means to live in a state of flow, of surrender. This requires a conscious reprogramming of our internalized capitalist mindsets. While the Divine Masculine is expansive, active, and outward facing, the Divine Feminine is the integration that happens after, that allows you time to process, absorb, and rest. The Goddess doesn't exist in a state of constant production to prove Her worthiness; She requires stillness and gestation, too. It's all about balance, baby. This can mean allowing yourself to rest and not to have to constantly be "on." It is a spiral dance, one that you will learn as you continue walking this path.

Again, the Divine Masculine and the Divine Feminine are energies, and this isn't dictated by biology or the toxic binaries the patriarchy feeds us. God/dess expands past this.

The power of the Goddess doesn't come from anything external; not from a god or a man or a lover. It is Her consciousness, *Her existence*, that infuses the universe with life. To work with Goddess consciousness is to acknowledge the ecstasy of being. It is to find the vibration of the Divine in everyone and everything. It is to step onto the pathless path, the tantric path. Everything is an expression of the Goddess. Everything is sacred and profane. This dissolves the barrier of the self and others and invites in empathy. You are of the Goddess, and so is everyone else. Remembering this is heart changing.

This formulation of the Divine isn't new either. Before there was monotheism and patriarchy and war and genocide, there was Her. It's hard to imagine that there was a time before, but it wasn't until the Bronze Age, which began about 3500 BCE, that historians see evidence of war, so we're talking about a *return*. A return to Goddess means honoring the earth and all her children, not just Her human ones. It is a return to the corporeal, to the sacred and chaotic Feminine. It is a return to the most profound, creative, sexual, powerful, receptive, and inspired parts of yourself.

Magick and the Goddess have much in common, and if you are called to explore either one, that's reason enough to begin.

Are you ready?

A SHORT HISTORY OF THE GODDESS

As humans who live in a paradigm of linear time, it can be hard to imagine that our ancestors weren't steeped in monotheism, or fearful of a faraway, punishing God. Weeks and months were tracked by the Sun and Moon. Sexuality was sacred in its own right, and rituals and celebrations of life and death were communal. Matriarchal societies meant that all people were equals, with property and the family name passed through the mother. Before there was monotheism, there was the Goddess.

Consider: instead of seeing your life as a straight line from birth to death, Goddess time means witnessing it as a spiral moving upward. When time is nonlinear, you reach the same point again and again, but each time, you arrive wiser, more present, more grounded. To live with the Goddess means recognizing that you can swing the pendulum from our unjust and poisonous patriarchy back to an existence based on community, perception, and the interconnectedness of death and life.

When I say that the Goddess religion is the first religion, that is a literal statement. There is evidence of worship of the Great Mother Goddess since the Paleolithic era, which lasted from about 35,000 to 10,000 BCE. The well-known handheld statues of Goddesses, exuberant in their curves, from France, Austria, the Czech Republic, and Spain date to this period—the most famous being the Venus or Goddess of Willendorf, from 20,000 to 18,000 BCE. These effigies, made from clay and often covered in red ochre (perhaps symbolizing the red blood of renewal) were likely used in ritual. They are mostly found in caves, representing the sacred womb of the Goddess and the entrance to the underworld.

More sacred symbols of the Goddess have emerged from Paleolithic time, especially surrounding Her association with birds and snakes. Through the bird, She is transcendent of this earthly reality, and the snake signifies life force and regeneration. Both symbols appear in many cosmologies: the snake being sacred to the Goddess of Crete, integral to the story of Adam and Eve, and represented in the East as sexual energy called Kundalini. In the cosmology of ancient Egypt, Osiris, Isis, and Thoth are associated with birds, including kites, falcons, and ibises.

The Neolithic era, or Middle Stone Age (8000–2700 BCE), generated a new relationship to the Goddess. As agriculture was invented, societies became anchored in specific places, different from the nomadic hunters and gatherers of the Paleolithic, who had to follow animals during their migrations. And when this happened, art was birthed. Spirals and labyrinths—symbols that represent, among other things, the curving, serpentine energy of the Goddess—began to show up on decorative and ritualistic objects like vases.

A society's relationship to a divine being, whether the Goddess, God, or a prophet like Jesus, is reflective of its circumstances. As the Neolithic people grew and harvested their own food, they began to worship a Goddess of Vegetation, who has since appeared in the Greek Goddess Demeter and the Egyptian Goddess Isis, among others. Here, She embodied fertility and self-renewal, and sculpted figures at the time include masculine and feminine elements (for example, a long, phallic neck on a vase).

All was good and swell for the Goddess and her devotees in Old Europe for two thousand years, until invaders known as the Indo-European (or Kurgan) people brought their Gods of the heavens and skies and settled where the Goddess was being worshipped. They married their Gods to local Goddesses, which marked the beginning of the end. Slowly but surely, those Gods came to adopt the features the Great Goddess was known for, and She fractured into many more faces.

With more permanent settlements came the need to protect and defend them, which morphed into violence and war. The Great Goddess became the Great Protector, seen in such examples as Inanna/Ishtar in Mesopotamia and Athena in Greece. Blood sacrifice, animal and human, also became part of certain religious practices.

By the Iron Age (about 1200 BCE), the Goddess had again mutated, now into the dragon or darkness to be slain, as exemplified in Goddess Tiamat of Babylon, who represented the creative potencies of chaos and needed to be killed to keep order in the world. As we learned to dominate nature, we also felt the need to control the divine disorder of the Goddess. And as that was rejected, so was Her totality. With the transfer of power to one Supreme God came a corresponding shift from matrilineal to patrilineal descent, or from the partnership to the dominator model. (In mainstream Abrahamic practice, God seems to exist perfectly fine without a Goddess. Yet mysticism tells another tale. Jewish Kabbalah holds up the Shekinah, or the feminine form of the God Yahweh/YHVH. In gnostic Christianity, Sophia is the wisdom Goddess and feminine creatrix. And in Islam, the "three daughters of Allah" exist in Al-Lat, Al-Uzza, and Manah.) A partnership model rejects hierarchy. There's no king or ruler with more power than everyone else; equitability and community reign supreme. Meanwhile, in a dominator paradigm, there is a nonconsensual established power dynamic and a constant tug-of-war of resources. It's the difference between a pyramid and a circle.

But don't forget, to work with the Goddess is not to separate yourself from the Divine Masculine, but to bring back a sense of balance to the way you see the world. We couldn't survive without the Sun or the Moon, and to work with the Goddess is not to abandon the God. Every Goddess-based religion *also* includes a God. To return to a place of divine order and justice, the pendulum must swing from the side of oppression of the feminine and those who exist outside the male/female binary. When you commit to exploring the Goddess within, you are committing to honoring the whole of life that is expressed through Her creation.

※

Before we dive in, there are a few things to keep in mind to help initiate your relationship to the Goddess.

The purpose of this book is not to provide an all-encompassing history of the Goddess nor to tell you about all the Goddesses in every pantheon ever. (Many of the books in the Bibliography at the back of the book are more thorough and specific.) My goal is to help you understand, embody, and activate the Divine Feminine within; this book is a catalyst in your relationship with the Goddess, in reframing what it means to be Her devotee, and in beginning on this path with an open heart.

I'm especially interested in sharing the importance of the Goddess here and now, in this new millennium, and how you can weave Her magick into your day-to-day life through ritual, meditation, and spellwork. I want to remind you of your unending capability to turn your life into a magnificent offering to Her.

I'm not here to convince you the Goddess is real; She can do that on Her own. What I hope, however, is that by coming to this book with honesty and vulnerability, you feel Her intensity, love, splendor, vision, creativity, and eros for yourself. The practices here are offerings from my heart to help you do just that. These rituals have deepened my relationship to the Goddess and have supported the creative, erotic, magical life I have always dreamed of.

We need the Goddess; we need the numinous and sacred; we need to remember the life-giving force we all carry. As we continue moving through this period of patriarchal oppression, we each can play a part in the return of partnership and matriarchy. When we move back to the Sacred Feminine, we return to the understanding that the individual experience is fractals of the collective. The Goddess religion is based on the idea that every human, plant, and animal is a separate piece of one Divine entity. We have lost our sense of community, reverence, and relationship, both in the ways in which we dominate the land and one another. To return to equilibrium, the pendulum must swing to the side of the Goddess before it can return to the holiest of truths, that life is an endless cycle of the God and Goddess, Sun and Moon, death and rebirth.

Welcome home, beloved.

─────────) ❭ ◐ ● ◑ ❬ (─────────

APPRECIATION, NOT APPROPRIATION

To write about the Goddess and to worship Her many faces means comparing mythologies and stories about how humans have interacted with the Feminine Divine for millennia. If, like me, you are inspired by Goddesses who are not part of your religion or your culture, let's start by bringing our awareness to this.

Appropriation is when a cultural or religious belief or practice is taken out of the original context, especially when someone from a dominant group borrows it from an unacknowledged minority culture. This can mean adopting the beliefs of a closed religion (one that you must be initiated into), or wearing or displaying its signifiers (such as a bindi or a ceremonial headdress). Many of us have crossed this line without realizing it; recognizing it is certainly something I am still learning.

As a witch, I am committed to evolving to serve my highest purpose, and that means holding myself accountable. In my first book, *Inner Witch*, I wrote about working with Oshun and Yemaya, whom I defined as Goddesses of Love. I now know that I was wrong on a number of fronts, including that Santeria is a closed religion, meaning that those who are not a part of the religion shouldn't be working with these beings, and that Orishas aren't considered Goddesses, but more akin to ancestral spirits. In the first printing, I also incorrectly used the term *smudging* as a synonym for "smoke cleansing," when smudging refers to a specific ritual practiced by Indigenous Americans. I also advocated the use of white sage, a sacred herb that is overharvested due to its recent popularity. I recognize how my past actions were appropriative; take responsibility for these mistakes; and am doing my part to learn and grow from them, including editing my books when possible.

Still, a respectful comparative mythology reveals the way religions and faces of the Divine Feminine overlap through time and space. In the Hindu Goddess Kali, we see the black formlessness of the void and the destruction of the ego. We might compare Her to Babalon, the ancestress of the Holy Whore from the book of Revelation and a Goddess of Unconditional Love and Lust, who, like Kali, requires ego annihilation. You likewise see parallels between the Hindu Goddess Lakshmi, the Roman Venus, Greek Aphrodite, Egyptian Hathor, and the Aztec Xochiquetzal. These overlaps illuminate how we are all trying to make sense of the same things. As my brilliant rabbi father says, "We are all holding on to a different piece of the elephant thinking we have the whole elephant."

Learning about different perspectives not only helps us cultivate compassion and understanding, but also expands the very notion of whatever it is we're learning about—such as the faces of the Goddess. Part of the work is determining which beliefs are your own. Others can guide you, but it's not their responsibility to do the work—it's yours. Learning about the context, cultures, attitudes, and beliefs shared by those who worship different Goddesses is key, and allowing this to guide you with reverence is what makes all the difference.

RITUALIZING GODDESS ENERGY

In the following sections, we delve into rituals and spells that follow a specific order, beginning with setting up the space, followed by grounding and centering, the ritual, and then being called to close and ground. These steps are the same throughout this book.

Setting Up the Space

The first step in any spell or ritual is ensuring that your physical space is ready with all the tools and supplies you'll need. Be sure you're wearing something appropriate for the ritual (meaning something comfortable that you can sit and move in with ease), and set the lights; light candles or incense; put your phone on silent; and ensure that any pets, children, or roommates are taken care of and know not to disturb you. Gather your supplies, set them up, adjust your altar, and do anything you need to ensure you can be present and without worry. I refer to this step as "setting up the space."

Grounding and Centering

After you've set up your space, but before you begin any ritual or practice, I suggest you ground and center. This is a practice to anchor you in your body, to connect you to the heavens above and earth below, and to protect you. I will share my personal practice, but if you have a version that serves you, please continue to use that.

Find a comfortable position, preferably sitting up, although you can lie down, too. Breathe as you find your way back to your body, yourself. With each inhale, feel drawn into a sense of expansion; with each exhale, feel yourself releasing all worries, anxieties, and tension from the day. When you're ready, visualize the heavens above you as pure, white light that exists for all of infinity. Pull this into your body, through the crown of your head and down your spine, filling every inch with this healing, protective, and cleansing light. Feel held by the heavens and then, as this energy gathers at the base of your spine, visualize roots growing down into the earth. These roots move through the base of the building or ground you're sitting on, through caverns and rock, into the core of the earth and pull up grounding, healing white light that moves up the roots, up your spine, and into your body. The energy from the heavens and the earth meets at your heart center, and now you breathe into it and expand it outward, like blowing a bubble. This bubble expands past your chest, stretching in each direction, forming a sphere that encompasses you, including the space you'll be using for the ritual. This is your witch's circle, your sphere of protection. Only that which serves your highest good and that which dwells in 100 percent Divine light may penetrate this barrier. From here, perform any magick, ritual, journaling, or tarot that you wish. I refer to this visualization as "grounding and centering."

Closing and Grounding

When you're ready to end a ritual or spell, reverse the previous steps. Feel the energy from the earth inside your body before sending it back down your spine and the roots you grew, into the earth. Visualize the roots dissolving into light, rejoining the energy of the underworld. Then feel the heavenly energy in your body moving up your spine, through the crown of your head, back into the cosmos, where it dissolves into light. Feel your sphere of protection. Breathe into it as you pull it back into your body so it shrinks with each inhale. Finally, breathe it into your heart, and allow it to dissolve into a seed of light. I refer to this practice as "closing and grounding."

CREATING A GODDESS GRIMOIRE

Building a relationship with the Goddess requires faith and devotion, time and dedication. And it requires the time and space to center these things, alongside support systems that allow you to grow and unfurl in a way that feels inspiring and not diminishing. An effective aid here is a Goddess Grimoire.

A grimoire, or book of shadows, is a magickal diary or journal in which to record reflections, rituals, tarot spreads, affirmations, journal questions, and downloads. This is your space to explore, and it can be a $1 composition book, a Google Doc, a custom leather journal, a Moleskine, or whatever calls to you. What matters is that the format makes sense for your practice and that you enjoy recording your experiences there.

Enliven your grimoire with Goddess energy by consecrating it, or dedicating it to your pilgrimage with the Goddess. This transforms the journal into a talisman enriched with magick and consciousness.

A Consecration Ritual for Your Grimoire

You will need: your grimoire; water (Moon, Florida, rose, spring, or tap); a lighter or matches; herbs to burn (like lavender, mugwort, rose, or ethically sourced palo santo); a shell, cauldron, or fireproof bowl; and a pen or pencil.

STEP 1: SET UP THE SPACE,
GATHER SUPPLIES, GROUND AND CENTER
Follow the instructions on page 12 to set up the space and ground and center. You may meditate with the Goddess or call upon Her in your own words.

STEP 2: CLEANSE THE GRIMOIRE

Feel the power of the Goddess moving through you, clearing any old energies from your journal. Dip your fingers in water, and lightly sprinkle it on the grimoire, making sure it doesn't stain the pages or mess up your computer. As you sprinkle the water, say the following, rewriting or adapting as you feel called:

> *Goddess of the sacred waters of the heart*
> *Goddess of the sacred waters of love*
> *Goddess of the sacred waters of healing*
> *I call upon you now to cleanse and bless this grimoire*
> *I call upon you now to create a sacred space upon these pages*
> *May all energy herein be cleared for you and our sacred journey*
>   *through and through*
> *And so it is*

STEP 3: CONSECRATE THE GRIMOIRE

Feel the feral flame of the Goddess as it courses through you. Light your herbs and then blow them out so they smoke, and pass the grimoire through the smoke, letting it infuse the journal with Goddess energy. Say the following, rewriting or adapting as you feel called:

> *Goddess of sacred flame*
> *Goddess of the Divine Erotic*
> *Goddess of the underworld, of death and rebirth*
> *I call upon you now to consecrate and infuse this grimoire with*
>   *your consciousness*
> *I call upon you now to create a sacred space upon these pages*
> *May all energy herein be devoted to Goddess energy*
> *And so it is*

STEP 4: INFUSE THE GRIMOIRE WITH YOUR LIFE BREATH

Take a deep breath and hold it until you feel like you can't hold it for even a second longer. With your Goddess Grimoire between your hands, forcefully exhale all the air in your lungs onto it. Say the following, rewriting or adapting as you feel called:

> *With my sacred breath, with the breath of the Goddess, I create*
> *A vessel for the Divine Feminine consciousness to flow*
> *From the highest above*
> *To the lowest below*
> *As aligned with my True Will*
> *For the highest good of all involved,*
> *I have now cleansed and consecrated this Goddess Grimoire*
> *As an offering from my heart*
> *And so it is!*

Optional: At this point, you may write a prayer or the blessing above in your Goddess Grimoire. You can also record the date, phases of the Sun and Moon, and any other pertinent information.

STEP 5: GROUND AND CLOSE

Thank the Goddess and yourself, and ground and close (page 13). You may leave an offering of fruit, wine, or flowers or burn incense.

OFFERINGS

An offering is an energetic exchange, an homage, a petition, or a way of nourishing the Goddess. Offerings show reciprocity. Many cultures and religious traditions integrate offerings into their spiritual practices, and there is no right way to do it. What matters is that it comes from your heart.

Consider burning incense; offering fruit, blood, baked bread, sweets, milk, honey, candy, water, wine, liquor, tobacco, or flowers; sharing a poem; saying a prayer; singing a song; creating art; dancing; picking up litter or trash; volunteering; or donating money as a Goddess offering. As you work with the Goddess in Her many faces, She will tell you what She likes. A sense of reverence is what transforms a mundane object or act into an offering.

Your offering feeds the Goddess with whatever you want to receive. If you are doing a ritual for creativity, you could burn incense in a bright citrusy scent or perform a song or dance. If you are honoring the Dark Goddess, you could offer menstrual blood, blood from a prick of your fingertip, or dragon's blood or opium incense. If you are performing a working for love, you could leave roses on your altar or read a poem by a love mystic like Rumi.

For food offerings:

+ Leave food in a specific dish or plate (if you wish) on your altar. After it goes bad, dispose of it as follows: Hold your palms above the offering, sending it all your remaining gratitude and reverence. Let the Goddess know, either mentally or out loud, that this offering is complete, and send Her the rest of the life-force energy within the offering through your palms. Thank the Goddess and throw out the offering. You also can use this method to dispose of nonconsumables, such as a candle or spell, in a garbage can at a three- or four-way intersection— the modern witch's crossroad.

✦ Offer food to the Goddess, and consume it in Her honor, taking the offering within, to feel yourself as the Goddess.

In the next few chapters, we will meet Goddesses from around the world: Love Goddesses, Goddesses of the Earth, Goddesses of Protection and Healing, Dark Goddesses, and everything in between. Later, I will share how to plan and structure a devotional practice and how to weave Her magick into your life. My hope is that there's a Goddess or two who piques your interest, so by the time you reach the last chapter, you have at least one in mind with whom to build a relationship.

THE GODDESS IN MYTH

To embody the Goddess means weaving Her magick into your life, seeing each stage of your odyssey as personal mythos. You are the ancient Goddess, moving through the underworld and the dark night of the soul, coming out stronger than you could have ever envisioned. To be devoted to Her path means knowing how Her splendor can transform your life. There will still be pain, trials, and tribulations. That's just life, baby, and that's part of the Goddess's path. But the Goddess can help you find faith, insight, and gnosis, even during the most intense ordeals. She is the cocoon.

Myth is integral because it's a reflection of the experiences and attitudes of a certain period that awaken something in the collective unconsciousness. By learning the myths of the Goddess, like those in this book, you can understand the way this frequency has been woven throughout history, and you can also begin to see yourself within this story.

Archetypes of the Goddess

One of the sources of immediate connection you have with the Goddess is through Her symbols and archetypes. Psychoanalyst Carl Jung, who proposed the idea of archetypes, describes them as the "magnetic energy field at the core of our being." They are reflections of the cultural beliefs that we all carry in a "collective unconscious." You have your individual subconscious and unconscious, and we also share truths and images. These archetypes are abundant, whether you recognize them or not: the mother, the queen, the good girl, the slut, the superhero, the bad boy, the king, and the fool, to name a few.

The potency of archetypes is that they are already awake within you. To begin refamiliarizing yourself with these parts of your truth, grab a notebook (or your Goddess Grimoire, see page 15) and ask yourself: *When I think of the Goddess, what characteristics come to mind? Is She a Goddess of battle, assertive and unapologetic? Does She have what it takes to slice through the bullshit of patriarchy? Is She soft and loving, an embrace of all-encompassing compassion? Does She exemplify a devoted and caring mother? What does She feel like, and what reminds me of Her?*

The point isn't to make you conform to one aspect of the Goddess, but to help you realize that She already exists within you in numerous incarnations. Whatever archetype you most relate to—whether that's as a warrior, mother, trickster, or slut—is worthy of exploration. Sometimes the Goddess will reflect the part of yourself you may not feel so comfortable with (aka your shadow). But by exploring even Her scariest and fiercest archetypes, you can find a way to honor and integrate these aspects of yourself. Notice what you already resonate with, or, if you want a challenge, work with an archetype you don't feel aligned with at all.

One of the most profound aspects of my devotional relationship came when different Goddesses began expressing new archetypes of Themselves to me—ones I had never seen or heard about. First came Venus of the shadow, Dark Venus, the subversive expression of the Goddess of Love who showed Herself to me as a poised and demanding dominatrix. She became my guide in living my sexuality and has been a huge part of my exploration of erotic witchcraft and kink. Dark Venus is counterpoint to Venus, one of the Goddesses I am devoted to, and She reminds me of the potency of the shadow, especially in love and even more so in lust. After that came Babalon, Goddess of Unconditional Love and Non-Duality, Destruction and Creation, in Her face of solar radiance as Golden Babalon. Golden Babalon emerged while I was working with the solar sphere on the Qabalistic Tree of Life, or Tiferet, which means "beauty." Golden Babalon is so bright that Her radiance protects those who worship Her. She guides me in owning every crevice of my heart and is an emblem of the Holy Whore in Her power and light.

The Goddess has many faces, and She may express a side of Herself to you that you haven't seen or read about. She may shock you by showing you new sides of Her truth. Trust in your heart to guide you, and allow Her to unveil new aspects of your magick as you do so.

A Note on the Goddesses in This Book

The Goddess cannot be contained by neat and tidy containers; She is too extensive and powerful for that. The overlap between Goddesses is there, and these chapters and divisions are made not to confine Her, but simply so you can see Her faces more clearly. Some Goddesses, like Inanna/Ishtar, are Goddesses of Love but placed in the chapter on the Dark Goddess. This is intentional, as a way of showing you one of Her faces, and is not meant to contain Her. Keep in mind that the Goddess often breaks boundaries our human minds put on Her, and this is one of Her gifts.

The Triple Goddess

One of the earliest archetypes of the Goddess had three faces. Many of us are unknowingly familiar with the Triple Goddess through the Holy Trinity in Christianity, with the Holy Spirit being the immanence of all life—the Goddess hiding in plain sight. The Triple Goddess emerged in Anatolian society in the first-known urban center of Çatalhöyük in the seventh millennium BCE. Her three phases line up with the human life cycle: the first is the virgin or maiden, the second is the life-giving mother, and the third is the old woman or crone. Western standards may make you think that these aspects are tied to a linear timeline for those who are physically able to give birth, but let's observe them outside this rigid separation.

The virgin or maiden has a lust for life, a yearning to experience all there is. Although modern thinking equates virginity with chasteness, the ancients saw the virgin as an archetype of independence, as represented by Goddesses like Vesta, Diana, and Athena. The maiden aspect represents the fertility of wonder and play that allows you to turn your whole life into a garden of reverence, joy, magick, and awe.

Then comes the mother, who is about nurturing something and cultivating it. She is the archetype of that which sustains and transforms, of fecundity, of the rich possibilities you hold to tend to something, whether that's being a parent of a child or pet, or through the creative and artistic projects you bring into this world. The mother also can bring the masculine force into form through birth and rebirth. (What if you don't connect to motherhood, even in this holistic way? Instead, think of the link between maiden and crone as the Queen—the sovereign holder of the legacy, the matriarch, who uses both head and heart to make decisions. I invite you to instead work with the maiden/queen/crone triplicity if it speaks to you.)

The most underappreciated of the Triple Goddess faces is the crone because as a society, we still reject death and aging, especially for women. For those of us who bleed, the crone represents a transition through menopause. She is a Goddess of Wisdom because she keeps her wise lunar blood rather than releasing it each month. The crone has lived as maiden and mother/queen and carries their knowledge with her. She is the wisest, the elder, the living ancestor. The crone is unapologetic and fierce because she's been through some shit. She is not scared of death because she knows when it comes, it will be a transition, and not an end.

The maiden, mother/queen, and crone are within each of us at all times, and you can work with these aspects of self whenever you need to, disconnected from where you may be physically in this human voyage.

The Triple Goddess is also known as the Triple Moon. One of the modern symbols of the Goddess depicts a waxing crescent Moon on the left, a full Moon in the middle, and a waning crescent on the right. The waxing Moon, or when the light grows between the new and full Moon, is associated with the maiden on her journey to expansion and self-realization. The full Moon is the most fertile aspect of the cycle and is associated with the mother. This is when birth is near, when the month and seasons of preparation have come to a climax and it's time to birth something new. In the darkening waning Moon, between the full and new Moons, you are in the stage of the crone, reminded of the inevitability of death, of the fact that to be born in a body means the eventual end of living—but that this, too, is just a transition, leading to rebirth.

Meanwhile, the Greek Goddess Hekate, the Goddess of Witches, Crossroads, and the Underworld, is often seen in her three-faced form with one head looking at the past, one at the present, and one at the future. Instead of representing the Triple Goddess throughout time, she becomes time itself. Hinduism, meanwhile, features the triad of Parvati/Durga/Kali. Here, the faces of the Great Goddess are in Her embodiments of spiritual growth (Parvati), protection (Durga), and creation and destruction (Kali). In Celtic myth, the Dark Goddess Morrigan has the three faces of Babd/Macha/Morrigna: a fertile maiden, the cauldron of life, and Mother Death or the Great Queen of Phantoms. In Greek mythos, the Triple Goddess is represented by the three Fates, the Moirai, the weavers of life and death: Clotho, the spinner of time; Lachesis, the measurer of time; and Atropos, the cutter of the thread of life.

When I began on the Goddess path, and up until a few years ago, I believed that you could be devoted to only one Goddess or have a single Matron Goddess. Venus was my first, but I later felt called to Isis (or Auset) and Babalon as well. My devotion to these three Goddesses has transformed all aspects of my life. Isis ties me to the heavenly realm and my angelic self, to my sexual sovereignty, magick, and healing. Venus links my heart and body to the earth as the Patroness of my glamour, sensuality, and self-expression. Babalon guides me in sacred subversion through kink and taboo sexuality, toward my shadow, into the tantric belief that everything is everything. They have become my own triple Goddess of Love.

All this is to say that you can work with the idea of triplicity in your own way, with Goddesses who complement each other. You can be devoted to more than one Goddess, and you can honor multiple Goddesses without pledging yourself to one. Finding an expression of the Divine Feminine that works for you is everything. We will go through examples of possible frameworks, but there is one in particular that changed my magickal practice, and I want to share it with you.

The oldest recorded myth is about Inanna, the Sumerian Goddess of Love and War, known as Queen of Heaven and Earth, and Her descent into the underworld. The story tells of how Inanna descends into the realms of Her sister Ereshkigal, passing through seven gates and forced to remove an article of clothing or talisman at each. When She arrives, She is naked, human, and no longer adorned with all that brings Her authority. Ereshkigal, meanwhile, represents the power of the shadow, of the rejected and vilified feminine. She is also Inanna's "dark twin," a part of Herself that Inanna needs to come face-to-face with. Indeed, it's only after Inanna goes through this ordeal that She is able to return to Her throne as Queen of Heaven, Earth, *and* the Underworld.

I have always been touched by the story of Inanna, comforted and inspired by eroticism and orgasm, the Divine Feminine, sacred chaos, and immanence. I think of Goddesses of Healing and Protection as the "heavens," Goddesses of Love and Goddesses of the Earth as "earth," and Dark Goddesses and Goddesses of Sex and the Shadow as the "underworld." I honor Inanna's mythos as a guide in finding Divine union within myself, through uniting my heaven (or light) and underworld (my shadow) through the earth, my body. This framework has inspired spells, rituals, and practices that support my expression of erotic magick. I hope it will help guide you into the Divine union of your personal heaven, earth, and underworld.

ONE GODDESS OR MANY?

Like the Goddess, your beliefs will evolve. You may believe something now and not believe it later, and that's okay, normal, and, in fact, encouraged. In my house, we adore growth and transformation. Let's lay out a couple of frameworks that will help you make sense of the rest of this book in a way that resonates *for you*.

On one hand, the Goddess is beyond comprehension, unknowable in Her entirety. In this camp, Her manifestations are personifications of the Numinous Great Goddess—Herself part of the Divine/Universe/All—because although the Goddess is unknowable, Her faces are not. These faces are deities and energies in their own right, yet they are still aspects of the whole. I call this "soft polytheism." My teacher Naha Armády of 22 Teachings School of Hermetic Sciences and Magical Arts describes the palm of the hand as the Divine and the fingers as the individual Gods and Goddesses—distinct, but attached and made from the same stuff. So, for example, Goddesses of Love like Venus, Aphrodite, Hathor, Isis, Inanna, Ishtar, Babalon, and Parvati make up the current of the Great Goddess in Her guardianship over love, romance, and the heart.

Or consider that the many faces of the Divine are their own entities, independent of any singular Goddess or God. The Goddesses are individual and shouldn't be lumped together or thought of as syncretized. Here, there is no one divinity but many individual Gods, Goddesses, and spirits. This is "hard polytheism."

There's also a middle ground, which is where I fall (and which I irreverently call "half-chub polytheism"). I believe that the Divine is bigger than anything I can comprehend. I believe in an all-encompassing Goddess. I also believe that Her manifestations are distinct and individual. It's like a mother with her children; the child comes from the mother, is made of the mother, but is a unique being. Goddesses deserve to be revered in their own right, yet I can't deny that they make up something greater than the sum of their parts. In this way, I honor Her various faces through specific acts of devotion and ritual while also recognizing that they are part of the Great Goddess. If I'm trying to ring up the Goddess, it's easier for me to reach my party when I know the extension.

FORMING A RELATIONSHIP WITH THE DIVINE FEMININE

I wish I could tell you that there's an easy, one-size-fits-all approach to working with the Goddess, but like witchcraft or magick, it's not cut and dry. Your relationship will be specific to you and the Goddess(es) you choose to work with. I use the word *relationship* intentionally because being devoted to and in reciprocity with the Goddess is more than just *work*. It's more than a transactional exchange.

How do you maintain a friendship? You find a balance of give and take. You spend time with them, learn about their interests, family, stories, and past. You respect their boundaries, needs, and time. You listen when you're meant to listen and talk when you're meant to talk. This is the same foundation your practice should be based on.

You bond with the Goddess through devotion, time, communion, and offerings. In return, you receive guidance, support, growth, and healing. You don't turn to the Divine Feminine because you *need* something, but because being in relationship with Her feeds, nourishes, and sustains you and gives your life deeper meaning (although, of course, there will be times when you need the Goddess as well). What each Goddess rules over will shape the container of your worship, but committing in this way will remind you that you're not praying to a lifeless icon, but a dynamic spirit with whom you have the joy of interacting.

Start with the following suggestions and the journal questions, affirmations, and meditation in this chapter to reach out to the Goddesses who are calling you.

+ *Open your heart to the Goddess.* Seek out art, media, books, and music that is immersed in Her energy. Flip to the bibliography (page 285), check out Spotify or YouTube, or go to your local library or metaphysical bookstore. Find where the Goddess already lives in your culture, your tradition, your soul by asking friends, family, and community. If you are called to a certain Goddess, research Her history, story, characteristics, and mythos. Record your findings in your Goddess Grimoire for future exploration.

* *Create an altar.* An altar (page 88) is an energetic home for your relationship and a place where the Goddess resides within your sacred space. Make it beautiful. Leave offerings or petitions (written prayers or pleas), light candles and incense, and spend time here in contemplation and reflection. Place flowers, crystals, icons and statues, jewelry, magickal tools, and devotional items here. This is also where you can perform spells and rituals for the Goddess.

* *Meet the Goddess through prayer.* Whatever your association with the word, prayer is simply a way of communicating with the Divine, a way of creating intimacy, a way of being vulnerable. You may read an Orphic or Homeric Hymn or a prayer that speaks to you. Don't overlook the power of a prayer from the heart either. Write your own prayer to say to the Goddess as a daily offering.

* *Meditate.* Meditation is another form of intimacy that can allow you to meet the Goddess heart-to-heart. Try a guided meditation in this book (for example, the one on page 37), or simply open yourself up and ask Her what she would like you to know. If you've never meditated, start with YouTube or an app like Insight Timer, which has many Goddess-themed guided options. Practicing for as little as five minutes a day can bring benefits. Try meditating on the following:

+ All the ways in which the beauty of the universe manifests within you
+ A specific Goddess, or on how Goddess energy feels in your heart
+ The resilience and strength of your heart, sending it love and gratitude and asking it what it needs
+ How you are a reflection of the Goddess in the flesh, and how seeing yourself as such will transform your life for the better
+ The way your evolution and path have led you to where you are right now, and how that's a blessing
+ The Goddess journey you're on and have been on, and how you're capable AF to face any shadowy demons and underworld journeys
+ Moments of joy and play, what they've inspired in your life, and how this has been a path toward understanding the Goddess
+ The overwhelming expansiveness of the Goddess and the ways in which She has made Herself present in your life
+ Those you love, how much you love them, and how this brings you to a place of ecstatic transcendence
+ The faces of the Goddess and how they show up to you in your day-to-day life
+ The gratitude you have for your life, for your magick, for the Divine, for yourself

+ *Spend time in contemplation.* Think about the ways the Goddess shows up for you. Use the journal questions throughout this book to guide you. Expand your mind with Goddess energy, noticing how you're already rooted in this.

- *Allow art and beauty to move you.* Beauty isn't frivolous; it is one of the virtues of the Goddess. This may mean adorning yourself or wearing something that links you to Her. It may mean going to a museum and noticing each face of the Divine Feminine you see. It may mean taking a hike and allowing the natural world to speak to you. When you feel a sense of awe, when you notice something that moves you, thank the Goddess, for these are Her gifts.

- *Bask in love and gratitude.* Love is the language of the Goddess, and expressing it through gratitude is one of Her virtues. Want to truly know Goddess frequency? Find love and gratitude in your life, and express it to the ones who bring it. It's really that simple. Receiving Her gifts and abundance with gratitude is a means of reciprocity; this way the Goddess knows you're able to receive what She is sharing. Spend time each day listing things you love and things you're grateful for, whether out loud or in your Goddess Grimoire, and don't forget to thank the Goddess as you do.

- *Don't be afraid to play.* Who decided that the fun stops when you reach adulthood? I hold firm to the idea that the key to not being a miserable adult is *play.* Play keeps you young, it nurtures your inner child, it helps you channel your creativity, and, oh yeah, it's fun! Play helps you bond with your loved ones, gives you a new perspective, helps you be present, and can remind you that you're nothing but a flesh-covered skeleton hanging out on a rock floating through space—in a good way. Sometimes it's best not to take things too seriously.

+ *Dance.* Dance has been used to raise energy, channel, and pray since the beginning of time. It's one of the ways in which you can *feel* the Goddess's presence. Dance is an expression of joy, gratitude, and prayer, although it also can be one of sadness or grief. Dance is the container for whatever expression you need. Whether you're sad or angry or happy or grateful, you can dance it out—as an offering or as a manifestation of your rage, it really doesn't matter. When you dance, and you get in touch with your flesh in this way, you're honoring yourself as the Goddess incarnate by allowing the life force of the universe to flow through you.

   A note: If you are physically disabled and can't dance, you may use your breath to dance, or to move whatever part of your body you have access to. You also can watch videos of people dancing, breathing into this as if you also were dancing, or simply sway your head, move your wheelchair, or allow yourself and your body to be expressed in whatever way you're able. You can practice dance in visualization and meditation if you like, closing your eyes and seeing yourself dancing, or what it would look like to you if you were dancing around your room.

+ *Hone your intuition.* Intuition is your gut feeling, your inner knowing. It will never lead you astray. Close your eyes and think about a time when you had an instinct about something or someone that you chose to ignore . . . and it ended up being true. The more you honor your intuition, the stronger this sixth sense will become. You can't think your way to the Goddess. She must be felt, and intuition is one of the ways She speaks.

   Note that intuition is distinct from anxiety, although they can feel similar, especially if listening to your intuition is new or if you live with anxiety. Your intuition is clear and never unsure. It is a message to tell you what's up, but it won't be catastrophizing in the same way anxiety can. Your intuition is supportive; it won't make you more anxious. To distinguish anxiety from intuition, notice what each feels like in your body. If you're someone who lives with anxiety, as I do, then the next time you feel it, close your eyes and take note of *where* it feels. How does your anxiety manifest physically? What are the emotions that come with this? The next time you feel your intuition, or get a gut sense, ask the same questions. How does your intuition manifest? What are the emotions that come with this?

In my life, anxiety manifests as a heaviness in my chest, like a rock has been placed near my heart. My intuition lives in my gut. It's clearer, and it doesn't have the same weight. These physical anchors help me distinguish the two. Remember that your intuition is a supportive force from the Goddess. It does not yell or make you feel less than. You always can ask yourself and the Goddess, "Is this intuition or anxiety? What is this feeling trying to tell me?" The more you do, the easier it will be to be guided by your intuition.

JOURNAL QUESTIONS

Each chapter includes journal questions meant to invite you into Goddess energy. In your Goddess Grimoire, you may doodle, free write, mind map, or answer these prompts in whatever way feels supportive and resonant. Allow your heart and the Goddess to lead you. Simply respond with honesty and without judgment. Turn answering these questions into a ritual if you like: make tea, light incense or candles, meditate with the Goddess, or set up an inspiring sacred space before journaling.

Begin here:

+ What does the word *Goddess* mean to me? When I close my eyes and breathe into this word, what do I feel?
+ What am I looking for in my relationship with the Goddess? What am I hoping to get out of this?
+ Are there Goddesses I'm drawn to? Any who have been calling to me?
+ Are there Goddesses in my religion or culture I'm aware of and can begin connecting to?
+ What inspires me? What am I passionate about? How is this a part of my magickal practice, if at all? How can this inspire my path with the Goddess?
+ What does the word *devotion* mean to me? *Worship? Prayer?* How can I define these words in a way that reflects what I believe in? How can I redefine them to release any negative associations?
+ How does the universe communicate with me? In what ways do I feel and foster this?
+ How can I work with the Goddess through this same language?
+ What are the virtues of the Goddess that I integrate into my own life?
+ What kind of relationship do I want to build with the Goddess? How can I incorporate my passions into this?

RITUALS AND PRACTICES

Two practices that are foundational for magick and especially for reaching out to the Divine Feminine are ritual and meditation. I define ritual as a repetitive action that marks something as sacred and beyond the scope of ordinary life. A ritual is something you return to often, consciously or unconsciously, and in this case, it's a sacred container you use for an intention, one that has the space to shift based on your desires and needs. Rituals can include practices like lighting a devotional candle on your altar or reciting a prayer—routines that, when imbued with intent, become rituals.

Meditation and visualization are also important tools for any witch, mystic, occultist, or devotee. Meditation helps you slow down your mind and return to the moment. The classic Zen style of meditation is a practice of releasing all thoughts and finding peace in the present, yet there are also mindfulness, walking, mantra, and guided meditations. It may look like drawing a picture, gardening, practicing tai chi, or doing breathwork. Meditation helps your mind stay on the task at hand while also becoming aware of your internal state.

The fact that meditation facilitates communication with the Goddess/es is itself a reason to meditate, and the more you meditate, the more you'll notice which psychic sense is the strongest for you. Maybe you hear the Goddess, as if She is whispering in your ear (clairaudience), maybe you see Her in your mind's eye (clairvoyance), perhaps you feel Her as if She were in the room (clairsentience), maybe you smell Her like She's draped in rose or jasmine (clairalience), or maybe you just know what She's trying to tell you (claircognizance). Like any muscle, you can strengthen your psychic senses, which will allow you to know the Goddess more intimately.

The following meditation is a good place to begin. If you already have a practice, you can expand it by speaking affirmations, pulling an oracle card, adding a visualization, or whatever else you like. Let your heart guide you.

My suggestion is to read it over first and then record yourself reading it for use as a guided meditation. *Before you begin, settle into an environment conducive to stillness and inner exploration*, setting up your space as you see fit.

A MEDITATION TO COMMUNE WITH THE GODDESS

Begin where you are, as you are. You're in the perfect place right here, right now. Allow this moment to exist in whatever way you need. Take a deep breath in through your nose and out through your mouth, exhaling with any sounds or growls or purrs you need to release. Do this again, inhaling through your nose, breathing into any tension or anxiety in your body, and out through your mouth as you release it. Take a moment to feel the space you opened in yourself, and melt into this inner sense of peace and expansion. As you feel ready, begin to visualize golden light pouring forth from the heavens, engulfing you in protective warmth. Allow this light to wash away any worry, fear, or anxiety you've been harboring, and let it bring you back to your magnificence.

As you feel calmed and centered by this healing light, visualize yourself in a space in nature, one where the Sun or Moon shines with no distractions. Bask in the holiness of the sanctuary of the earth. Feel the beauty of the natural world. Linger here as long as you'd like. As you find resonance within this scene, feel the spirit of nature come alive. It vibrates and shape-shifts, as if the golden light that poured into you is taking form. As you breathe in this light, you become aware of the fact you're in the presence of the Goddess. She is everywhere, within you, personified by the flora and fauna surrounding you. Allow Her to share Her knowledge in whatever shape or form She chooses. Be in Her presence, imbued with Her intuitive intelligence. What does She tell you? What do you smell? What do you feel? Linger in this sensory exploration as you feel blessed by the presence of the Goddess. *(If you're recording this, take a few minutes of silence here to commune or sit with the Goddess.)*

When you feel like you've received what you need to receive, thank the Goddess with a gesture or greeting. Before you leave, She hands you something—a gift that is totally personal to you. Feel gratitude swelling in your heart, and know that She receives it. Feel surrounded by the golden light from before, warm and soothing, protective and nourishing. Come back into your body, returning to the present and your breath. Take a few slow, deep breaths as you wiggle your fingers and toes, and open your eyes.

You may wish to write down in your Goddess Grimoire what you experienced, what the Goddess gave you, and any details you noticed. You may leave an offering on your altar—honey, flowers, wine, chocolate, or bread or make art, read a poem or prayer, or play music.

AFFIRMATIONS

An affirmation is a phrase you repeat to align with and manifest its energy. Because the Goddess is a vibration or frequency you can tune to, and because words themselves are vibrations, affirmations allow you to access the vitality of the Goddess, connect with the Goddess, and live as the Feminine Divine. Work with affirmations to remind you of your sovereignty and to invite the Goddess to make Herself known in your life.

One part of my morning practice is saying affirmations in the mirror, both ones that are unrelated to my work with the Goddess, and ones I wrote specifically for the Goddesses I worship. This daily ritual strengthens my relationship to the Goddesses I'm devoted to because I regularly feel and embody my commitment. Affirmations are a self-fulfilling prophecy—you say what you want to happen, and after a while you start believing it, which is when it really materializes. Like confidence, you have to fake it 'til you make it.

I include affirmations in each chapter of the book, and my suggestion is to say them daily, or as often as you'd like. Saying them at the same time every day becomes a ritual, or you can work with affirmations on an as-needed basis or as a part of your rituals or spells. As you practice, I suggest looking at your nondominant eye in the mirror. (If you're right-handed, look at your left eye, and vice versa.) Or close your eyes and feel spirit moving through your body as you repeat each affirmation. Or stand in front of your altar as you speak them. Try saying each affirmation at least three times, allowing yourself to really feel it, or write down your affirmation, at least five times, in your Goddess Grimoire.

Use the following affirmations for inspiration, or create your own. Jot them on a sticky note or piece of paper to stick on your mirror, make them your phone background, or repeat them as you wake up or fall asleep. Creativity is a virtue of the Goddess, so don't be afraid to be innovative.

+ I embody the Divine frequency of the Goddess.
+ I am inflamed with the love and lust of the Goddess.

- I live in Goddess energy.
- Everything I do is an expression of the Goddess.
- I embrace my own Divine essence.
- I receive all of the Goddess's messages with ease.
- I honor the Feminine Divine through everything I do.
- I trust the Goddess. I trust the universe. I trust in myself.
- I am a child of the Goddess.
- I am a Goddess.
- I align with the highest frequency available to me at this time.
- I shine in the light of love.
- I am an embodiment of the cosmos.
- The Goddess speaks to me on all planes and in all ways.

A TAROT SPREAD FOR MEETING GODDESS ENERGY

The tarot is a deck of seventy-eight cards that originated in Italy as playing cards, and today is used as an intricate system of divination. The tarot is made of two sections: the major arcana and the minor arcana (meaning "mysteries"). The major cards—for example, The Star or The Lovers—represent key milestones along the pilgrimage of human consciousness. The minor arcana cards are divided into four suits: pentacles, swords, cups, and wands, with an ace through ten and four court cards in each: classically page, knight, queen, and king. The minor arcana cards represent the daily trials and lessons we face, the ordinary challenges between the big hurdles, with the court cards representing the folks we know who can act as guides or the archetypal energies we need to call in. The tarot is an intuitive system you

use to uncover hidden truths and a map back to the moment, to the self. It doesn't show you a future set in stone, but a possibility that *could* manifest, influenced by your current ambitions.

This book includes tarot spreads to support the themes of each chapter. You also can use an oracle deck, which is a deck of cards for divination and self-inquiry with no specific structure that's created by an artist. Both tarot and oracle decks use symbols to convey meanings; they speak in the tongue of the Goddess, felt and understood through the heart.

On the next page, you'll find a tarot spread to experience your own Goddess energy. Use whatever deck you want—a classic like

Smith-Waite, the esoteric Thoth, or one specifically made for this purpose, like my *Goddess of Love Tarot*.

A note: Some people read the cards reversed, or upside down. A reversed card can indicate that its meaning hasn't manifested yet but will, or it can represent a reversal of the traditional meaning or an energy that's stuck. You don't have to read reversed if you don't want to.

Before you begin, cleanse and clear the cards of any energy by running them through sacred smoke, like that of mugwort, ethically sourced palo santo, lavender, or frankincense. You also may take and hold a deep breath and then forcefully exhale onto the deck. When your deck is cleansed, get clear about your intention and formulate a question, preferably one that requires more than a "yes" or "no" response. Ground and center using the instructions on page 12, and when you're ready, shuffle the cards as you focus on your intention. Take as long as you want, infusing the cards with your question.

Split the deck into two or three piles and then place a new pile on top. This is referred to as "cutting" or "splitting" the deck. Pull six cards, one for each question in the spread below. Before you research the "official" interpretation of the pulled cards, tune into your intuition and the Goddess. Feel into the messages of the cards, and when you're ready, look up the meanings and record the results in your Goddess Grimoire. And so it is!

Card 1: How am I being called to meet the Goddess?

Card 2: How can I embody Goddess energy?

Card 3: What does my heart want me to know?

Card 4: What fears and worries can I release?

Card 5: What guidance and support can I open myself to receive?

Card 6: How can I ground myself in Goddess consciousness?

The Goddess of the Earth

To know the Goddess is to step outside, into the wild, to surround yourself with Her flesh: the earth. Through the body of the Goddess, in Her sacred sites like mountains and deserts; hidden springs, waterfalls, and oceans; and megaliths and fairy mounds, you learn Her language. In *The Woman's Encyclopedia of Myths and Secrets*, Barbara Walker describes the Goddess as "the deity who infuses all creation with the vital blood of life." To know the Goddess is to know the life-giving and cyclical qualities of nature. Since the Paleolithic era, which began roughly 2.5 million years ago and ended around 10,000 BCE, the Goddess has been worshipped alongside the earth and Her creatures. The Great Mother is in the stars and the Moon, in the changing of the seasons, in the animals whose lives are sacrificed for sustenance.

It is through the body of the Goddess that you unravel Her age-old symbolism and understand the way that animals reflect Her infinite depths.

> ## The Goddess has always and will always be incarnate through the earth.

The earth itself isn't an inanimate entity made of rocks and water, but a living, breathing life-form that reacts to the way humans treat (and abuse) it. As Indigenous peoples, witches, and pagans have long known, the earth is alive; she's from where you come and to whom you will return. In Greek mythology, the earth is personified by the primordial Gaia, the first being to emerge from chaos.

Begin to form a relationship with the Goddess just by being in nature. Finding a place of natural beauty, away from the hustle and bustle of the city, and spending time there in communion is an invaluable place to start. Honoring the children of the earth by working with her living creatures is another access point. Animals and plants that hold a special reverence to the Goddess include birds, snakes, cows, fish, bees, lions, tigers, and other cats.

The Goddess is also in the untamed, feral aspect of nature that lives within us—the overgrown forest, the hurricanes, the mountains where no humans can survive. She rules the untamed expanses of the psyche, wild and mysterious, and in this way, the Goddess of the Earth—of life and fertility—and the Dark Goddess—of death and the decay—are two sides of the same coin.

Even if you can't escape into the wilderness to meet Her in Her natural habitat, you can nourish a relationship with the Goddess through her elements. Since writing my second book, *Bewitching the Elements*, and my guided journal, *Embody Your Magick*, I have continued to explore the elements—earth, fire, air, water, and spirit—as a framework for magick and ritual, each with its own energetic signature and correspondences. The elements are one of the most accessible ways to initiate a relationship with the Goddess because you already interact with them each time you feel the sunshine on your skin, wash your hands, drink a glass of water, take a deep breath, pull a tarot card, or pray. In the following pages, find four Goddesses who can lead you into the elemental magick of the earth.

THE GODDESS AS EARTH

One of the most unifying myths across cultures is the idea of the earth being the body of the Goddess. To the Incas She is called Pachamama, to the Greeks She is Gaia, to the Romans She is Terra, to the Celts She is Tara, to the Igbo people of Southern Nigeria She is Ala, and to Hindus She is Prithvi Mata. It is said that on the eve of the Buddha's enlightenment, to defeat the demon Mara and become an enlightened one, he had to touch the earth, known as Bhuma, another name for Prithvi Mata or Mother Earth, indicating that the Goddess acted as a sacred witness in his transformation of consciousness, and serving as a reminder that to be of this world means to be of the earth.

The Goddess religion may not be alive to as many of us as it was during the Paleolithic and Neolithic eras, but we still have the chance to draw on its ancient knowing. When there was no separation between humankind and the earth, we relied on hunting and foraging for sustenance and survival. We used soil from the earth to build homes and temples, often finding a beautiful natural spot, close to a water source, that faced east and west to witness the rising and setting Sun. Most of us live in a society that would be unrecognizable to our ancestors, yet we still can summon this reverence by communing with the earth.

Artemis

Every culture has deities who are associated with Earth, but the Greek Goddess Artemis (known as Diana to the Romans) encapsulates this element because She rules over the feral and forgotten places as well. As the Goddess of the Wilderness, Animals, the Moon, and the Hunt, Artemis reminds you of the piece of yourself that is free, ravishing, savage—your untamable aspects that are inseparable from the wild. Artemis is the forest, the caves and crevices that make up the primal face of the Goddess, the natural realm untampered by man. How can anyone own the earth? (Hint: they can't.) As a Virgin Goddess, Artemis exists outside of any marriage or social contract that binds Her to another.

Artemis embodies the totality of life because She is creator and protectress of animals—and also hunts them with Her trademark bow. She walks with a stag or doe by Her side and rides in a chariot pulled by two stags. Both the Huntress and the animals are facets of the Goddess, so killing them doesn't break the sacred contract or vow between living beings. The divine life cycle is still revered because death is only one stage of many.

Our society expects women to be easily digestible and to fit into a certain mold. Artemis cuts through that expectation without fear or guilt to remind you of the innate connection you have to the unknown. As the process of childbirth is the most ancient and intense of rituals, Artemis is also patron of people in labor. She reminds us that our animalistic parts are holy, and that like the Moon, cycles of growth, death, rebirth, and decay are inevitable. Artemis also demonstrates the power of harnessing fear, and festivals in the ancient past to celebrate Her often included animals as a blood sacrifice. There comes a time to offer up something to the forces of the unknown, and although blood sacrifices may have worked back in the day, you may choose to offer up your fear, or moments of darkness or pain, instead. Ask Artemis to make Herself known in the expanses of your inner wildness.

Connecting with Artemis as Earth

Go to a wooded area, a meadow, or a part of the beach or ocean shore where no one wanders, as untouched as possible. Bring an offering of red wine, meat, menstrual blood, honey, sweet cakes or baked goods, or herbs like mugwort. Or you can sing or dance as an offering, or pick up any trash you find. If you can go here at night, all the better. Wander (safely, keeping track of where you are) until you find a spot that calls to you, where you feel both the earth and the Goddess. Place your palms or the soles of your feet on the earth, and breathe as you call in Her intelligence. Remember a moment when you felt fierce and wild. Notice what you feel without judgment. Concentrate on this untamed aspect of yourself, and breathe into it, willing it to grow and grow. As you feel this freedom expanding throughout your body and soul, express it in whatever way you wish. Move, dance, howl, or shake. Feel Artemis's presence, asking you to fully feel into your undomesticated core. Keep raising this energy, and as you're ready, speak out loud something like the following:

My wild, feral self is called forth
An offering to Artemis from my heart
I cultivate this undomesticated part of myself
To learn the freedom and power within

Let Artemis know that this offering is for Her, sharing it now alongside anything else you want Her to know. Continue to sing, dance, howl, pray, or just take a moment to say thanks. Stay here as long as you like and then make your way back to your vehicle or home.

Journal Questions

+ How do I relate nature to the Divine Feminine?
+ What natural spot inspires me with Her mystery? How does going there help me connect to the Goddess?
+ How does Artemis inspire my bond with Mother Earth? What does She teach me?
+ What rituals link me with the earth? How can I deepen them into a practice to call in the wisdom of the Goddess?

THE GODDESS AS AIR

Air is holy, air is sacred, and your breath and mind represent your kinship with this element. Your breath is a wonder, cleansing your microcosm and releasing what you no longer need back to the macrocosm.

Air teaches of expansion because air is buoyant and transformative. When you think of the Goddesses of Air, think of the far-reaching corners of the sky, the wind on your cheek, the strength of a tornado or hurricane. The easiest way to know this element within yourself is through breathwork, known as pranayama in yoga, which is a ritual of following certain patterns with your breath, such as three-fold breaths (inhale-hold-exhale or inhale-exhale-hold) or four-fold breaths (inhale-hold-exhale-hold). Each has its own elemental association, but all are grounded in finding a sense of peace and presence. When we use the air in our lungs to claim something, and when we ritualize, we can transform our inner world—and eventually our outer world.

Air has to do with the mental body—the way you think, analyze, and communicate and the way you craft spells and declare your boundaries. Find inspiration in Goddesses like Isis, who learned the secret name of the God Ra, allowing Her to take his powers. To know something's name is to control it.

In its encumbered state, air can feel like rushing, speediness, impatience, and even envy when you perceive others moving in a direction you want to go, faster than you can go. Air also is linked to the sword's ability to protect and pierce through veils of illusions, exposing reality. It can cause pain or clarity, depending on how it's used, and it can take us to new heights.

The Goddess in Her form of the Fates is a potent example. The Fates remind us of the power of the mental body and the ability of the mind to forge, unravel, and weave together again. Above all, the Goddess as the Fates can lead you to become an active participant in finding your True Will.

The Fates

If you've ever had the pleasure of seeing the Disney classic *Hercules*, then you are familiar with the Greek Fates, known as the Moirai, represented as crones who share one all-seeing eye: Clotho the spinner, Lachesis the measurer, and Atropos the cutter. They are sassy and all-knowing, weaving, measuring, and cutting the strings of fate. The Fates spin a person's destiny into a tapestry that no one else is able to touch or question. Even Zeus is unable to reverse Their decisions. This trinity is also a lunar triad, connected to the waxing Moon, the full Moon, and the waning Moon, as well as the seasons of spring, summer, and winter, and They represent the life stages of the maiden, mother/queen, and crone. Iconography of the Fates has not always shown Them as old women, although that's often how we think of Them. Demetra George explains, "Earlier images described them as dwelling amidst celestial spheres where, clad in robes spangled with stars, and wearing crowns on their heads, they sat on thrones radiant with light." The Fates remind us of the alignment of heaven, earth, and underworld when it comes to your destiny. Like the Egyptian Goddess Nut, who cradles the sky on Her back, the Moirai remind us of the expansive magick of the air, of life.

Like the Great Goddess, fate is a universal concept. The Romans worshipped Fortuna, the Goddess of Prosperity and Fortune. The Anglo-Saxons called the Fates the Wyrd; the Celts, the Morrigan;

and the Scandinavians, the Norns, who tended the World Tree and controlled the living earth. In Hindu mythology, the spider is the spinner of fate known as Maya. It may seem like the existence of fate eliminates the possibility of free will. But if you remember that you are a fractal of the Great Goddess, that all Her power lives and resides within you, then it's easy to remember that *you are both the Fates and the fate She controls.*

As Demetra George so wisely states in *Mysteries of the Dark Moon*, we are both living out the fate the Fates control and also operating with free will. The Moirai are not outward forces controlling our lives, but rather are energies and archetypes that live within the "dark unconscious realm of the psyche." The more you work alongside the Fates, the more you become a self-fulfilling prophecy. If you believe they are only weaving misfortune, sadness, and pain, you may unconsciously choose situations that reflect this. If you believe in their sense of justice, love, and autonomy, then you may unconsciously choose to live in this way.

Because air has to do with the mental body and your beliefs and patterns, the Fates and free will are both echoed in this element. Work with the Fates to embrace the life you want to weave for yourself.

Connecting with the Fates as Air

You will need: A white ribbon, a black ribbon, and a red ribbon, cut to the same length, at least twelve inches long (white = the past/the maiden, red = the present/the mother/queen, and black = the future/the crone); honey or flowers.

In this version of a witch's ladder, you will experience the magick of the Fates by weaving a spell of free will: releasing something from the past, embracing something from the present, and setting an intention for the future.

Set up your space (page 12) and then meditate on your intention. *You are the weaver of your fate. What do you want to attune yourself toward? What do you want to release? To embrace?* Use the journal questions on page 54 to dive deeper. You will be performing this spell on your altar, and although you don't need anything besides the ribbons, you may work with crystals or candle magick if it's in your practice.

When you're clear on your intention, take a few deep breaths and ground and center, as on page 12, performing any other opening rituals in your practice. Honor and acknowledge the influence of the Fates, and in whatever words resonate, let Them know that this working is an offering to Them and to Their sovereignty within you. With the white ribbon in your hand, imagine whatever you want to release. This can be a traumatic event you have healed or are healing from, a mental or thought pattern you're ready to let go of, or an old wound.

Holding the white ribbon in your palm with your other palm floating above it, feel white light emanating from the cosmos and the Fates, clearing you and the white ribbon of negative energy or any energy that doesn't belong to you. Then you may say something like the following:

> *Through the blessing of the Fates, I release* [declare your intention for what you're releasing]. *As this is no longer serving me, I let it go with ease, so mote it be.*

Stay here as long as you'd like. Then put the white ribbon aside and grab the red ribbon. What do you want to embrace in the present moment? This could mean feeling in control of your actions; embracing your power as an embodiment of the Goddess; or cultivating healthy physical, emotional, and mental habits. Let your heart and spirit guide you. Hold the red ribbon in your palm with your other palm floating above it, sending it white, healing light from you and the Fates, clearing it of negative energy and any energy that isn't yours. Focus on your goal as you say something like the following:

> *Through the blessing of the Fates, in this moment I embrace* [declare your intention for the present moment]. *Through this I embody my power, through the potencies of the present moment. So mote it be.*

Stay here charging the red ribbon as long as you need and then pick up the black ribbon. This represents a wish for your future self, and it can be specific or general. Maybe it's to continue fostering a relationship with the Goddess, maybe it's to bring in a certain kind of relationship, or maybe it's to age with grace and softness. Hold the black ribbon in your palm with your other palm floating above it. Feel the white light infusing energy into the ribbon, releasing any energy that's negative and doesn't belong to you. Say something like the following:

> *Through the blessing of the Fates, I declare this for my future state,* [declare your intention for what you want in the future]. *Aligned in love and aligned in light, I make it so through this rite. So mote it be.*

With the white ribbon on the left, the red ribbon in the middle, and the black ribbon on the right, knot the three at one end. Beginning with the white ribbon, braid the ribbons, and as you do, feel into your connection to the Fates and to your free will. You may say something such as, "*Like the Fates, I weave my fate*," or "*I claim my fate with the strength of the Fates.*" Hold your vision and intention in your mind's eye until you finish the braid, and knot it at the end. Take a deep breath, visualizing the white light from the universe moving into your lungs and body. *Hold this breath*, and feel your intention grow and grow. When you can no longer hold it, breathe forcefully onto the braid, cleansing it with the breath of life. Then declare, "*This or something better for the highest good of all involved, so it is, this spell of Fate is done. So mote it be!*"

Leave an offering of honey and/or flowers on your altar next to the braid. Thank the Fates, and yourself, and clap your hands or stomp your feet to ground and come back to the physical realm. Close and ground, and perform any other rituals in your practice. And so it is!

Leave the braid on your altar, or keep it somewhere you can visit it regularly, like hanging on your wall or in a drawer.

Journal Questions

+ How do I relate to the element of air?
+ How does this reflect my relationship with the Goddess, if at all?
+ What does air teach me about my voice, my magick, and claiming my fate?
+ How do the Fates help me embrace my future? How do they remind me of free will, of the power I have in my life?

THE GODDESS AS FIRE

Radiant and untouchable, expansive and erotic, fire reigns with the intensity of a Goddess who does whatever the fuck She wants. To control fire is to dance a duet of painful potential, accepting a possible burn and attempting to tame something that is forever evolving. Fire is the inner spark. Fire sustains your personal ecosystem, your portal to rebirth. Like the earth, to know fire is to be in relationship with it, not to own it.

When you consider fire as an aspect of the Goddess, it reveals the immeasurable force and fierceness within each of us. The Goddess isn't all good or all bad. She is not easily castrated of the darker aspects that many spiritual seekers ignore. To know the flame is to know its shadow, and the Goddess's ability to feed and ravish and rage. To stand under the Sun, to gaze upon a bonfire, and to light a candle as a ritual are all aspects of magick rooted in Her duality.

The erotic self is also an aspect of fire. To the Goddess, sexuality, sensuality, and the erotic are expressions of creativity, pleasure, and joy. They are not something to be ashamed of or to ignore, but rather aspects of self to be cultivated and explored. Consider the Virgin Goddesses, who were wed to themselves and whose Priestesses would embody them in sexual rites with Her devotees. Fire is freedom.

Fire reflects your yearning to grow, to feed, to share; you can light one hundred matches without losing any spark of your own. Learn of fire through Goddesses like the Egyptian lion-headed Sekhmet or the Hindu Kali, who rules over destruction *and* creation. Lean into this elemental power by working with faces of the Goddesses who mirror it.

Sekhmet

Lion-headed Sekhmet is fierce, independent, and an embodiment of heat and passion. As the daughter of the Sun God Ra, Sekhmet's mythos is grounded in Her larger-than-life attitude—and Her ability to destroy. She is the Goddess of Bloodlust and Unbridled Sexuality after all! As a Goddess of War, Sekhmet reflects the aspect of fire that cannot be controlled.

One of Sekhmet's myths tells of how, after a couple thousand years of worshipping Ra, humans began to forget about him, which upset him deeply. To get revenge and a little more devotion, Ra sent Sekhmet down to Earth, where She ravaged and devoured all in sight. But soon Sekhmet became so bloodthirsty and filled with bloodlust that She spun out of control. Eventually, Ra drugged his daughter to sleep with an herbal concoction dyed to look like blood, and the carnage ended.

In astrology, each of the twelve zodiac signs is assigned a modality, which explains how its elemental vibration is manifested: cardinal (the sign that begins a season), fixed (the sign in the middle of a season), or mutable (the sign that ends the season). Cardinal is initiatory and activating, fixed is grounded and stable, and mutable is adaptable and flexible.

We can think of Sekhmet's story, and the element of fire, through this lens. Cardinal fire (Aries) is the strike of a match and the flame that leaps to burn things down. Fixed fire (Leo) is fire in its most stable state, able to be controlled and used for light and heat. Mutable fire (Sagittarius) adapts to the situation at hand. Sekhmet has that cardinal ability to attack and expand, but She also is associated with the stability of the Sun. Sekhmet in Her mutable form takes on a role of Divine healer, offering Her courageous heart to those who need the ferocity of fire to heal their wounds. Within the inner sanctuary at the Temple of Edfu in Egypt hung an image of Sekhmet, in which the Goddess took the form of a lion-headed cobra. As serpents are one of the oldest manifestations of the Goddess, representing the life force within all of us, Sekhmet displays this regenerative power.

Sekhmet also teaches us about the truth of fire, anger, and rage. Living in these emotions for prolonged periods of time is counterproductive, yet they serve a critical purpose, telling you that something is off, or that someone crossed a boundary that was put there for a reason. Anger calls for action, but you also need wisdom to discern the correct course. To work with Sekhmet as a portal of elemental fire means commitment to shadow work, to doing the uncomfortable self-inquiry necessary to identify the rejected or "unlikable" aspects of yourself. Sekhmet knows that devotion to honoring the *entire* self, shadow and all, is everything; that fury can be holy; and that anger can be a sacrament. Incorporate this message by creating a rage or anger practice.

Connecting with Sekhmet as Fire

An anger or rage practice is a ritual that helps you release those emotions in a safe way, without trying to suppress them. Instead of casting them aside as "low vibration" or "negative," this practice gives you the space you need to channel them into something else, like peace, or action, or just relief. As the ever wise and fabulous Deanna Troi of *Star Trek: The Next Generation* says, "Feelings aren't positive or negative. They simply exist. It's what we do with those feelings that becomes good or bad." (This why I don't believe in "black" or "white" magick. Energy is just energy, babe!)

There are many ways to channel your anger, and my suggestion is to try a few different approaches. Allow this to be an exploration.

Ground and center as laid out on page 12 and then meditate with or call upon Sekhmet and let Her know this is in dedication to Her. You may light a red or gold candle and gaze at its flame first. Then pick an action (or two or three), using the examples below as a jumping-off point to perform in a safe space like your bedroom. If you really just need to get out your rage and don't have time for the whole ritual, that's okay; a few deep breaths and a small acknowledgment that this is a bridge to Sekhmet and for Her is plenty. When you're ready, pick an activity and let it out:

+ Screaming into a pillow.
+ Hitting the bed with your pillow, a rolled-up towel, a crop, or a paddle, and making noises or screaming.
+ Jumping and shaking your hands, shoulders, and body as you make noises and scream and growl.
+ Writing a letter filled with all your inner turmoil, and burning it up in a cauldron or fireproof bowl or over a pot of water.
+ Punching, kicking, or shadowboxing (safely).
+ Dancing ecstatically by moving your body intuitively, breathing through any discomfort, and making sounds like moaning or growling or sighs.
+ Punching a pillow (safely and carefully).

When you're done, take a few deep breaths and meditate or journal about your experience. Thank Sekhmet, and remind Her this was in dedication to Her. Notice how you feel, if this has helped you generate space and a sense of peace. If not, it's okay. Try again whenever you need to, and adjust accordingly. The point is to witness your inner fire as something that should be exalted and channeled, even if it feels dark or unworthy of attention. Allowing Sekhmet to lead you into your body's insight by creating space for that which society often deems as too intense is a holy practice of honoring your entire self. May Sekhmet remind you that even your temper is worth celebrating.

Journal Questions

+ How do I relate to the element of fire? What does this feel like?
+ How does this reflect my relationship with the Goddess, if at all?
+ How does fire inspire me to honor my rage and anger?
+ How does Sekhmet help me channel and transmute this intensity, if at all? How can She help me accept my fullest expression?

THE GODDESS AS WATER

Perhaps with more than any other element, you can learn of the Goddess through water. This element is both tangible and ineffable in its ability to shape-shift depending on whatever holds it, evasive and effervescent in its ability to remind you of the esoteric. Like the tarot's High Priestess, whose dress turns into waves and who sits before the veil that hides the unknown, water reflects the ability of the cosmos to transform, to support, to sink. As the ebb and flow of the ocean is determined by the cycles of Lady Luna, the Goddess who is reborn on each full Moon, and whose darkness overcomes Her on each new Moon, water reminds us of the endless possibilities of death and rebirth.

On the Tree of Life, a living glyph (or egregor) brought forth by ancient rabbis who studied Kabbalah, the Jewish sect of Mysticism, the Goddess resides in the third sphere of Binah, which means "understanding." The Divine Mother is depicted there in Her Saturnian aspect of giver of life and bringer of death, and She also is called the Great Sea, for She came before all else. There's a sense of sacred understanding that comes with dwelling in and feeling it in your heart. This is what water can teach you. Water is intuitive and psychic, and many ancient temples and churches were built at sacred springs, where the Goddess energy is most potent.

Picture the ocean. She can be calm and loving, holding you as you play in her waters. But she also can be terrifying and chaotic as a hurricane or tsunami. Even the Goddess of Love—*especially* the Goddess of Love—can bring pain. To work with water and to know it through the Goddess is to realize that your feelings are sacred, that your heart is sacred, that love is the truth, and that no one can take this away. Goddesses of Love associated with water and the ocean include Aphrodite, born from the seafoam; the Virgin Mary, whose name comes from the Latin *mara*, or "sea"; Hathor, known as the "watery abyss of Heaven"; and Isis, patron of the sea. But to truly understand the spirit of water, the heart and love, let's turn to the Hindu Lakshmi, born of an ocean of milk, stirred up from the depths of the sea alongside the nectar of immortality, amrita.

Lakshmi

Lakshmi is a Goddess of Love, Abundance, Wealth, Beauty, Sweetness, and Joy. She sits on a lotus petal, a symbol of transmutation and blooming even in the muddiest of waters, hands dripping gold, and two elephants (that symbolize abundance) behind Her, pouring water from their trunks.

Lakshmi rules over four kinds of wealth: kama (pleasure and enjoyment), artha (physical wealth and prosperity), dharma (cordial and peaceful relationships), and moksha (spiritual sovereignty). Just as there is water enough for everyone on the planet, so is Lakshmi's abundance unyielding. She reminds you that material wealth is just one aspect of true prosperity. This is the realm of water: joy, love, depth, and connection to your intuition and your purpose. Lakshmi teaches that to dwell in abundance externally means to live in vibrance internally. Lean into Her powers by loving and caring for yourself, by bathing in light and rituals of self-devotion. In recognizing the gifts of physical, emotional, spiritual, and mental wealth, you are able to live in gratitude and prosperity. When you're unbalanced or fixated on one of Lakshmi's four gifts, though, you may attract something less auspicious—a storm rather than a cool breeze. Instead of the beauty-bestowing Lakshmi, you may attract Alakshmi, Her shadow form who personifies poverty, ill repute, and unbalanced relationships.

Luckily, Lakshmi and Alakshmi can never dwell in the same place, and the sound of chanting and the sweet smell of incense are enough to keep Alakshmi away. Acts of devotion, of love, and of the heart will be your protection. Swim in the crevices of your soul with reverence and honesty. This is shadow work—checking in with yourself to see where your desires come from and transmuting the challenges into wisdom. Obsession and overindulgence may satiate in the short term, but they're not going to lead to a life filled with love and reverence. Like holding a hose too tight, clinging onto your expectations of what prosperity looks like is only going to stop the water from flowing. To work with Lakshmi is to surrender and bask in the waters of abundance, purpose, and love.

Connecting with Lakshmi as Water

One of the ways to embrace this Goddess is by speaking Her mantra. A mantra is a string of classically Sanskrit words used for concentration and meditation, repeated 108 times, a sacred number in Hinduism, Buddhism, and yogic traditions. (Mala strands, used in these devotional practices, have 108 beads.)

For this ritual, you will be working with an affirmation or mantra to welcome in pleasure, prosperity, fulfilling relationships, and spiritual empowerment—all of which will hopefully coalesce into love. Consider the following and pick whichever one resonates, or write your own. Check out the affirmations at the end of this chapter for more inspiration.

+ I am a vision of Divine Love.
+ I am a vessel of true abundance.
+ I am guided toward my heart.
+ I open my heart on all planes and all ways.
+ I trust in my intuition to guide me to an abundance of love and pleasure.

If it is in your practice, after you sit down to meditate, you also may begin speaking Lakshmi's mantra, *"Om Shrim Maha Lakshmiyei Swah"* (*ohm shreem mah-ha laksh-me-yay swa-ha*), which means "My salutations or adoration to the great Lakshmi."

Find a quiet space where you can meditate in peace. If you have mala beads, grab them, as well as anything else that inspires—citrine for prosperity, for example, or a rose quartz or rhodochrosite for love. If you have incense, light it. Rose, lavender, amber, sandalwood, or a blend for love or abundance would be a great fit.

Settle in and locate your sense of inner peace, tapping into your heart center and breathing a glowing pink light into your being. Let this loving pink warmth surround you, and surrender more to this vibration with each breath. As you feel ready, say the mantra or affirmation *of your choice* 108 times, using your fingers or mala beads to keep count. Allow your heart to fill with love, and wash away any expectations of what the process will be like.

When you're done, dwell in this space of peace, noticing what feels different. Take a moment to thank the Goddess or Lakshmi for the gifts She's granting, and invite Her into all areas of your life. Bow in gratitude, bring your hands to prayer position above your heart, or lower your head in reverence. Thank yourself for creating this sacred space.

Open your eyes and declare, *"By the Power of Goddess it is so."* Then leave an offering on your altar or a spot in your home where you would like to invite abundance, whether it's in your bedroom for love, or in your office for financial prosperity. Leave flowers, chocolate, honey, red wine, sweet breads, or fruit; burn incense; or play music as an offering. Record insights, feelings, visions, or downloads in your Goddess Grimoire for further contemplation.

Journal Questions

+ How do I relate to the element of water?
+ What does water teach me about myself, my emotional nature, love, and the Goddess?
+ What does Lakshmi teach me about abundance, beauty, peace, and joy?
+ Where in my life am I connected to pleasure and enjoyment? Physical wealth? Peaceful relationships? Spiritual sovereignty?

The elements will be your muse and inspiration as you live with the Divine Feminine, and you also can work with the Divine union and powers of the Sun and the Moon to draw in Goddess energy.

THE SACRED MARRIAGE

The Sacred Marriage is a story and ritual dating back to ancient Sumer that also can be thought of as the union of the higher and lower self, or the conscious and the unconscious, as represented by Sol and Luna, respectively. It is one of the longest-lasting myths of the Goddess, which can even be seen in the sacrifice, death, and resurrection of Christ. Tales of similar rituals and the sacrifice or death of a God were widespread from the Neolithic period through the emergence of Abrahamic monotheism five thousand years later, including in the Akkadian Ishtar and Tamuzz, the Sumerian Inanna and Dumuzi, the Egyptian Isis and Osiris, and the Greek Aphrodite and Adonis.

The ritual was enacted through an act of sacred sex between the Priestess of the Goddess, who represented Her living embodiment, and the king of the land, who played the part of the dying and resurrected son/lover, in an offering of fertility to the crops. There is evidence that this High Priestess not only held high accord for her association with the Goddess, but was often the queen. Some of the first writing in history has been found at ancient sacred sites in ledgers of ownership or property of the temple that were kept by the High Priestess/queen. What this tells us, alongside biological evidence of queenship passing through the mother's bloodline, is that matrilineal descent, not patrilineal, was honored. Power and property were passed down through women, and religious sites were often run by women.

THE FEMININE DIVINE AND THE LUNAR CYCLES

The ancients also noticed how crops were affected by the lunar cycle. It allowed them to track their periods and pregnancies, and they later built megalithic structures to monitor lunar eclipses. Folks who menstruate are naturally linked to the Moon's cycles: the number of periods in a year, for example, is the same as the number of full Moons—thirteen. This is also the holy number of the Goddess.

The mysteries of the Sacred Marriage are a key to the way humans connect the natural world to the all-encompassing powers of the Goddess, an example being in the powers of Lady Luna. The Moon

is 4.5 billion years old. Everyone who has ever existed has gazed at that same rock in the sky. In this way, it is both a physical thing as well as an egregore, or a nonphysical entity or spirit that takes on a life of its own by being worshipped. Working with the Moon's phases is a central aspect of witchcraft and neo-paganism, and you can adapt it specifically to honor the Goddess in both Her light and shadow aspects. As astrologer Demetra George says, "The Goddess is essentially a personification of the Moon's lunar energies." These cycles give you space to honor your own cyclical nature, your totality, and the Divinity in your multitudes.

To align yourself to the Moon is to align yourself with the Goddess. The Goddess is not static, staying in a fixed state for eternity, contained in the imagination of Her ancient devotees. No, like the Moon, She is dynamic, ever changing, ever evolving. The Goddess is as vital and alive as you can get.

The New Moon

The Moon's trek begins when it is inky black, with no light from the Sun spotlighting its surface. A portal to the unconscious with no external stimulus illuminating the conscious mind, the new Moon is the birth of the Goddess and the beginning of Her journey. It is a time that is fertile with possibility, the proverbial dark night of the soul. This is a time of stillness and silence, when the Goddess whispers to you even more reverently than usual and when the Moon retreats into total darkness for three days and nights. This is the time of planting seeds, of rituals of devotion for the month ahead, of coming home to yourself.

As the new Moon is also the beginning of the Moon's twenty-eight-day course, it is when you can set intentions for the month ahead, aligning with the Goddess to do so.

> *Goddesses of the new Moon:* Artemis, Diana, Athena, Nyx, Nut, Selene, and Luna
>
> *Focus on:* Embracing the shadow/rejected aspects of the self, setting goals for the month ahead, clearing and cleansing your space, beginning a new cycle, and reflecting on how you can turn poison into medicine in your ritual practice

JOURNAL QUESTIONS

+ What seeds am I planting?
+ How can I tend to myself through this darkness?
+ What is the darkness teaching me?
+ What am I looking to call in?
+ What aspect of myself is longing for transformation and rebirth?

The Waxing Moon—the Maiden

The new Moon is when the Goddess is pregnant with potential, a time of conception when the unknowns are pervasive, hanging in the air like smoke. The waxing Moon, then, is when something begins to form as the light of the Moon grows. In the state of the Triple Goddess, you can think of the waxing Moon as the maiden: adventurous, daring, and bold, continuously coming into her sexuality, pushing against the barriers of what others think of her. This is the time of committing to the self and to the intentions you set during the new Moon. This is when you can breathe life into the darkness and watch your vision take shape as Goddess energy vibrates within.

Goddess of the waxing Moon: Persephone

THE WAXING CRESCENT MOON

The waxing crescent emerges in the days following the new Moon's three nights of darkness. This is the smallest curve of light along the Moon on her right side. It's the very beginnings of waxing, when you're still under the Dark Moon but able to expand your psychic abilities and tend to the seeds you planted during the new Moon.

THE FIRST QUARTER MOON

The first quarter Moon happens a week into the cycle of the waxing Moon, halfway between the new and full Moons. Shadow and light are both accessible, granting entry into the conscious and subconscious with ease. A perfect time to realign with your desires for the Moon, the quarter Moon can teach you how to relate to the Goddess as maiden, experiencing the wonders of love and life. Revisit the story of Persephone, who spends half the year as Hades's consort as the Goddess of the Underworld and the other half alongside her mother, Demeter, as Queen of Spring. Persephone represents the power inherent in both shadow and light.

THE WAXING GIBBOUS MOON

The gibbous Moon is the Goddess's last trimester, when Persephone has one foot out of the underworld days before the moon is full. This is your chance to do last-minute work on your goal and to reflect on what the darkness and light continue to teach. It's a time to tie up loose ends and honor the remaining gestation period.

> *Focus on:* Realigning with your intention; growth; committing
> to caring for your creative, spiritual, or energetic children
> before birth; artistic exploration; and finding balance
> between yourself and your shadow

JOURNAL QUESTIONS

+ How did I work with the waxing Moon to set my new Moon intention into action?
+ What does the waxing Moon mean to me? How does this balance of light and dark relate to my personal mythos and narrative?
+ What differences did I feel in the waxing crescent, quarter, and gibbous Moons?
+ How do I relate to the maiden? In what areas of my life can I bring in more curiosity and awe?

The Full Moon—the Mother/Queen

The full Moon is the peak of the Moon's cycle and a moment of intense dualities: birth is a beginning for the child and an ending for the mother. The full Moon is when the subconscious surfaces and your emotional currents are strongest, reflecting those relationships with the tides. It is the time of nurturing and fecundity and the ability to care for what you have manifested.

This is the Goddess as mother and queen, basking in the light of love and balanced in body, head, and heart. It's birth; it's entering a new chapter; it's welcoming something into the world, whether that's a literal child, a magical or creative child, or simply the intention you brought along for this lunar cycle. Because the full Moon represents the height of the Moon's influence, this is also a wonderful time to perform ritual, divination, or spellwork (although save banishing for the waning Moon), especially by using sexual energy.

Goddesses of the full Moon: Isis, Aphrodite, Tara, Kwan Yin, Mother Mary, Chang-O, and Ixchel

Focus on: Caring for your goals; nurturing that which you have shared with the world; standing in your power; owning your erotic self; fostering a relationship with the Goddess and source; redefining motherhood, self-care, self-love, and self-lust; stepping into your queendom; birthing something new; ritual; divination; magick; and owning what you've created

JOURNAL QUESTIONS

+ What has come to completion since the new Moon?
+ What am I nurturing right now?
+ What still needs to be nurtured before the completion of this lunar cycle?
+ What does my relationship with the archetype of mother mean to me? With that of queen?
+ How can the full Moon and the Goddess teach me to honor my fullest expression?

The Waning Moon—the Crone

The most misunderstood aspect of the Goddess is easily the crone, she who is full of experience and inner knowing. The waning Moon is when the Moon begins to lose light, when you are drawn back to letting go of what you no longer need. A time of surrender, the waning Moon is a chance to meet your shadow, work with it, and release what is no longer aligned with your intention.

Baba Yaga is a Goddess from Slavic folklore who appears as an old woman and lives in a hut on mobile chicken legs. Baba Yaga lives on Her own, deciding not to conform to social contracts, and the waning Moon likewise represents the importance of retreating, of celebrating the shadow, and of turning into the self.

Goddess of the waning Moon: Baba Yaga, Hekate, Ereshkigal, Kali, Medusa, Lilith, and Nephthys

THE WANING GIBBOUS MOON

During the waning gibbous Moon, Lady Luna continues to lose light, shedding the last of her life blood. It's a time when you can loosen your grip on anything that is keeping you from growth. To align with the Moon means to align with ebb and flow, active and receptive, inner and outer. The waning gibbous Moon is the beginning of the death process, when there's still plenty of light to work with, but the veil starts to thin.

THE THIRD QUARTER MOON

The third quarter Moon greets you at the halfway point between the full and new Moons. It is time once again to find balance between shadow and light, to honor Persephone, to make your way down into the shadows, using the last of the Moon's light as guidance. If Persephone is the Goddess of Spring during the first quarter Moon, at the third quarter, she is stationed in the underworld as queen. Witness the ways dark and light, structure and flow, and yin and yang have woven themselves throughout your life.

THE WANING CRESCENT MOON

The last glimmer of light hangs in the air like a kiss from the Bright Mother before the Dark Mother's underworld trek begins. This is the crone's final breath, the beginning of the end, the last moment of light before the death and renewal process begins. Know that death isn't an ending, but one aspect of a singular cycle. This is a time to ritualize stillness, to commit to excavating your darkness, and to work with the guidance of the crone.

THE DARK MOON

The Dark Moon is the very end of the lunar cycle, the true depths. This is when you have access to the Dark Goddess, the Dark Mother, and your shadow. (For more on Dark Goddesses, see chapter 5.) This phase acts as an initiation into the death process that transfigures and transmutes. Fear and shame may bubble up as hallowed mirrors of your truth when you are asked to face your demons. This is when sacred rituals of the Goddess take place, including the kinds of erotic witchcraft that can lead you into sexual sovereignty. This is when the silence offers up insight you have missed, ignored, or rejected. It's a time to return to the scrying mirror of your soul.

Focus on: Cultivating a relationship to the shadow; tending to your inner world; banishing what is no longer aligned;

nurturing the intuitive and psychic self; embodying your erotic essence; acclimating to, contemplating, and spending time in the darkness; releasing fear of aging and change; finding strength in the unknown; and cultivating a relationship with the Dark Goddess

JOURNAL QUESTIONS

+ What am I releasing in the waxing cycle?
+ What has this part of the lunar cycle taught me?
+ What am I scared of? What have I rejected in myself?
+ What have the darkness and the Goddess taught me about myself?
+ How can I work on embracing this shadow self?

THE GODDESS AS THE SUN

Many people think of the Moon as feminine and the Sun as masculine, thanks to the modern neo-pagan perspective that says as much, yet this isn't the case. These luminaries are complements and can be worked together as such. The Sun is the illumination of the Goddess, seen in Her ecstatic brilliance. In the Japanese Shinto religion, the Goddess of the Sun is Amaterasu, and in the New Testament's book of Revelation, the Whore of Babylon is contrasted with Mary, who is "clothed with the sun." The Celts' Sun Goddess was Sulis, which means "eye" and "Sun." She was Sunna to the Germans, and Sol to the Norwegians. The Romans saw Her as a face of the Goddess Minerva, with the title of Sulis Minerva.

The Sun is the Goddess at Her most fiery, passionate, and angry, able to warm even the coldest heart or ravage through a forest like a wildfire. Like the Moon, She also can cloak, protect, and hide with brilliant light instead of darkness. The solar light of the Goddess is Her healing, Her warmth, Her ability to bring forth mystery into consciousness. She is a kiss of sunshine on a tough day, the power of fire to transform food into sustenance, the ability to cauterize a wound.

You may witness the cycles of the Moon more easily than those of the Sun, but the seasons—as marked by the equinoxes, solstices, and cross-quarter days falling in between them—represent the cycles of the Goddess in Her solar phase. You may wish to work with the witches' Sabbats, or solar holidays, as a means of honoring this face of the Divine Feminine.

Journal Questions

+ How does the Goddess speak to me in Her solar phase?
+ How can I honor Her through the potencies of light, fire, and sunshine?
+ How can I work with the witches' Sabbats to honor the Goddess in Her solar guise?
+ What does the light of the Goddess illuminate within me?

MORE GODDESSES OF THE EARTH

It's impossible to quantify the Goddesses who belong to the earth, and who are represented by its seasonal cycles, but the mythologies of Demeter and Isis are a fitting place to start. Both are Goddesses of the Earth and its prosperity. Both go through an immense loss, one that They must grieve, one that transforms Them. These Goddesses typify our own worldly struggles of loss, pain, and death, and They sing of the long-lasting domain of the Divine Feminine. Both were widely worshipped for millennia—Isis for 3,500 years and Demeter for 2,000. Their myths continue to reflect the lives of modern-day people, and you can tap into Them through learning Their sacred stories.

Demeter—Greek Goddess of Grain and Fertility

The Greek Goddess Demeter (known as Ceres to the Romans) represents fertility, abundance, and nourishing and caring for others.

Unlike Her great-grandmother Gaia, Demeter isn't the Goddess of the Earth itself, but of the ability to sustain life through the bounty of the harvest. Demeter oversees the cultivated earth and all her fruits, and She is best known in relation—to the earth through food, and to Her daughter Persephone.

Like nearly every other deity, Demeter's origin story is a bit dramatic. As a pre-Olympian Goddess whose mythos was most likely adopted from Crete, Demeter is the daughter of Cronus (Saturn to the Romans) and Rhea, and the sister of Zeus (Jupiter), Poseidon (Neptune), Hades (Pluto), Hestia (Vesta), and Hera (Juno). Demeter has a daughter named Persephone (Kore) with Zeus, and Their relationship demonstrates the Divine dance between heaven, earth, and underworld.

The love between Persephone and Her mother runs deep. No matter the advances of the Gods, Persephone rebukes them all to rule over heaven on earth alongside Demeter as Goddess of both springtime and the fecundity of the earth—the corn maiden. Persephone embodies the potential for all living things to bloom and the youthful glow of innocence and play. Demeter is the ear of corn or stalk of wheat that grows aboveground, and Persephone is the seed, the embryonic bounty that rests in darkness below the surface.

One day, as Persephone plays in the fields, She notices an especially beautiful narcissus flower, which has been enchanted by Hades, the King of the Underworld. As She bends over to smell it, Hades rises from a split in the earth and snatches Persephone to be his consort. Demeter becomes frenzied as She tries to find Her daughter. After nine days, the Crone Goddess Hekate suggests that Demeter talk to Sol, the God of the Sun, who was the only one who saw what happened.

Demeter disguises Herself as a mortal woman and roams the cities of ancient Greece, becoming a nursemaid to the son of King

Celeus of Eleusis. Secretly, She begins the work of making Her charge immortal by holding him over a divine fire, day after day. But one day, as Demeter is going through the alchemical working, the child's mother walks in and screams at the sight of her son in flames. Demeter reveals Herself to be a Goddess, declaring that a temple should be built in Her honor in that very spot. This is where and how the Greater and Lesser Mysteries of Eleusis came into being.

Demeter continues to seek Persephone. She declares that the year ahead will be the cruelest and most grueling yet, and that if She has to suffer, so does all of humanity. Zeus realizes that if all the humans starve to death, they won't be able to worship the Gods and asks Hermes to demand that Hades return Persephone to Her mother.

Hades agrees . . . but has a final trick up his sleeve. He offers Persephone some pomegranate seeds, which She accepts, not knowing that this makes Her a prisoner to the underworld. Zeus devises a compromise: Persephone will spend part of every year as Queen of the Underworld and part as Queen of Spring, back on Earth with Her mother. Some myths say that Persephone ate four pomegranate seeds and thus must spend four months of the year in the underworld. In some tellings, it is six. I like the neatness of the latter: from the spring equinox in March until the fall equinox in September, Persephone rules on Earth as Queen of Spring, and from the fall equinox to the spring equinox, she is Queen of the Underworld.

Persephone returns to the underworld year after year, ensuring that Her mother will nourish the earth. Death is an integral piece of the puzzle. Likewise, by recognizing that Her daughter must separate from Her—reflecting the psychological process that every child goes through of individuating from the mother—Demeter is like any human mother facing the pain that comes when their children grow up and seek independence.

My favorite aspect of this story isn't one I have seen discussed often: Demeter and Persephone aren't separate Goddesses but two aspects of the same deity. Peering through the lens of the underworld and the earth, life and death, what we are seeing is the remnants of the Great Goddess brought into the Hellenistic period of the ancient Greeks. Demeter is the Bright Mother and the light of the full Moon, and Persephone is the Dark Mother, the crone, the darkness of the new and Dark Moon. Persephone is the root, and Demeter the fruit. In this way, They embrace wholeness.

Isis—Egyptian Mother Goddess of Healing, Magick, and Love

The ancient Egyptian Goddess Isis (the Greek spelling of Aset) is one of the most venerated Goddesses in history, worshipped widely for more than two thousand years. *Isis* means "throne," which was Her hieroglyph, and the crown She is depicted wearing distinguishes Her from other deities, including Her sister, Nephthys. Isis is a many-faced Goddess, much like Demeter, ruling over love, magick, the home, fertility, the earth, necromancy, and the underworld.

This Goddess of Ten Thousand Names is relatable—human, even—in a way that many other Goddesses are not. Like Demeter, She experienced loss and an underworld passage. Like Demeter, She was offered the first yield of the harvest. Like Demeter, She loved and lost and mourned and resurrected. There is a power in encountering a face of the Divine who not only understands but empathizes with your experience.

Through Isis's story, which has been shared for millennia, you can feel Her vastness and understand Her immense spirit. Isis is the daughter of Geb, the God of the Earth, and Nut, the Goddess of the

Skies and Heaven. She was born alongside a sister, Nephthys, and brothers Osiris, Set, and, according to some sources, Horus the Elder. In the womb, Isis and Osiris fell in love, a bond that only strengthened after incarnation and birth. They eventually ruled Egypt together. Osiris was the first King of Egypt, beloved for bringing peace and prosperity. When he traveled, Isis was in charge and was a hallowed leader in Her own right.

While Osiris and Isis fall deeper and deeper in love, their sibling Set, God of Chaos and the Desert, who is married to Nephthys, stews with jealousy and decides to trick Osiris out of his reign. He brings a coffin to a party and says that whoever fits inside will win a prize. It is made to Osiris's measurements, and, sure enough, he fits. Set and seventy-two coconspirators close the lid and throw the coffin into the Nile, where it floats onto an embankment and grows into a tree.

Isis is inconsolable. Like Demeter, She disguises Herself as a mortal and wanders around Egypt, eventually learning of Osiris's transformation. At Byblos in Phoenicia, Isis discovers the coffin, which has grown into a tree outside the home of Queen Astarte. The queen is entranced by Isis and welcomes Her into her home, eventually hiring Her as the nurse for her baby son. Also like Demeter, Isis holds the baby over the fire each night in hopes of making him immortal, and also like Demeter, she ultimately reveals Her Divine nature and demands that the coffin-tree be cut down.

Isis travels back home with Her entombed husband. The Goddess then takes Her form as a kite—the bird being one of Her most ancient symbols—and, wings beating with magick, circles His coffin (some versions of the myth say She lies on him) and conceives their son Horus, either through the sexual act or through Her wings beating sacred breath into Her husband's lungs.

When Isis leaves Osiris to take care of Horus, Set takes his revenge once again. The God of Chaos finds the coffin and splits Osiris's body into fourteen pieces, scattering them across the Nile. This time, Isis is aided by Thoth, Mercurial God of Communication and Magick, and Anubis, the jackal-headed God of the Dead and Embalming, alongside Nepthys, Her sister. Together they set out in search for Osiris's missing pieces and find them all except for one: Osiris's phallus, which is said to have been eaten by fish in the Nile. Isis makes Osiris a new phallus (possibly out of gold), consecrates it, and pieces together all the parts of Her husband, creating the first mummy.

Isis once again brings Her beloved back to life by fanning the mummy with Her kite wings. From then on, Osiris is King of the Underworld while Horus rules alongside Isis on Earth, marking a new eon for Egypt.

The myth of Isis holds so much, including the Sacred Marriage of feminine and masculine, the kiss of Sun and Moon, day and night, conscious and subconscious. Like Demeter and Persephone, Isis and Osiris play the roles—the beloved nourishing the seeds of the underworld, the Goddess aboveground, searching and rescuing. Their Divine union results in something new—Horus—the fresh crop, the rebirth, who takes his station as ruler of Egypt as Osiris becomes King of the Underworld.

Isis is a lunar Goddess, but She encompasses these dualities as the active figure here. She goes to the underworld, She rescues Osiris, and She performs magick in his name. In this way, She represents the solar influence on Her midnight Sun of a husband, rooted underground. Just as Persephone descends, so She returns. Just as Osiris is killed, so he must be reborn. Isis's searching can remind us of the temporary darkness that predicts the light of rebirth.

───────)) ● ● ● ((───────

THE GODDESS JOURNEY

One of the themes of the Goddess is Her journey to the underworld. While Joseph Campbell popularized the idea of the hero's journey, the Goddess's is less talked about, yet it's there, dwelling, hiding, waiting to be excavated. In myths of the Goddess spanning from ancient Sumer to Greece to Egypt and beyond, you witness the Goddess cross thresholds, surrender to the domain of the shadow, and travel into the underworld or darkness to retrieve something She loves, something important to Her. When She returns from the chthonic realms, She is not the same. She is transformed. This framework is something we all experience in our lives, whether it's grieving a death, moving through a breakup, or suffering an intense injury. But the story of the Goddess can remind us that this moment of death and decay, of sadness and pain, of wandering far and wide in search of the self or love is vital, ancient, and necessary. Through this mythos, you can remember that even the Goddess experiences this. And through this, She can act as a system of love and support for you as you retrieve an integral part of your soul and being along the journey of darkness.

We also can learn more of the Goddess from Her associations with animals, who are reflected in Her mythos.

──────────────

THE ANIMALS OF THE GODDESS

Animals are guardians and gateways to Goddess energy. We modern humans tend to think of ourselves as above animals, as separate from them; factory farming and the inhumane meat industry are testaments to that mindset. But as Anton LaVey points out, what are humans but human animals? Ancient people knew that we are part of the earth, and her creatures aren't separate and distinct. Instead, all animals are direct reflections of the Goddess, an embodiment and aspect of Her power. Animals are sacred teachers, too.

That said, some animals have been associated specifically with the Goddess across time and culture. A few are listed in the following pages. Watch videos of these animals, learn about them, spend time creating art about them, or visit them in real life to feel the Goddess energy they can stir in all of us.

The Serpent

The serpent is a symbol of renewal and revitalization. As the serpent sheds its skin, it reflects the cyclical nature of the Goddess. As it curves and curls, so does it reflect Her spiral path.

Many of the ancient Egyptian deities are therianthropic, or humans with the heads of animals, not because they're half animal, but because they have the qualities of the animals they are merged with. The serpent is embodied as the cobra Goddess Wadjet, the Goddess of the Nile Delta and Lower Egypt. Certain pharaohs and deities also are shown with the uraeus, or a cobra emerging from their forehead—a personification of Wadjet that represents Divine authority and acts as a talisman of protection.

In the Neolithic period, the serpent is seen in the Minoan Snake Goddess, often portrayed with a serpent in each hand, representing the duality of life and death, and Her breasts out. Living the dream!

Hindu mythology features the snake Goddess Kadru, who gives birth to cobra people known as Nagas. In Hinduism and yogic thought, the life energy—and sexual energy—of the universe is personified as a snake known as Kundalini, which lies dormant at the base of the spine, coiled up at the pelvis. Enlightenment may be attained when this serpent stretches up through the spine and chakras to the crown of the head, unfurling as a thousand-petaled lotus that results in union with the Divine.

Later, of course, the serpent in the Garden of Eden offers knowledge, wisdom, and understanding to Adam and Eve. It says a lot about our culture that many folks consider that the beginning of the end. Learning about the far-reaching associations between snakes and the Divine reminds us that, like so much else we take for granted, it doesn't have to be that way.

Serpent medicine can be worked with to experience and transmute sexual energy, and to intimately connect with this current within the body as a path to gnosis and knowledge.

The Fish

Another ancient symbol of the Goddess, which dates to the Paleolithic era, is the fish, with the pointed oval known as the vesica piscis coming to represent Her as well. This form, or the "vessel of the fish," is depicted as one circle overlapping another, in which the resulting image looks like a vulva.

This sacred symbol reemerges in the imagery of Christ, but the sacredness of the fish dates to well before the CE. In Greek, the word *delphos* means both "fish" and "wound," and it was the oracle of Delphi who was originally thought to be incarnated as a great fish, whale, or dolphin. In Roman mythos, dolphins are associated with Venus, the Goddess of Love, because of their penchant for riding on the waves of the ocean, from which She was born. When Aphrodite, Venus's Greek counterpart, appeared as a dolphin, She was called

Aphrodite Salacia, which meant "fish teeming with womb." In this form, Aphrodite is said to bring "orgiastic fish-eating" on Her sacred day of Friday (*dies veneris* in Latin)—perhaps where the concept of seafood as an aphrodisiac began.

The fish can be worked with as a guide into the waters of the heart and as a spiritual mentor for the surrender that takes place when you fearlessly dive into the profundity of your being on the spiritual path.

Birds

Able to move between the earth and the heavens and back again, birds go where humans cannot. Bird motifs are found in shamanistic practices in the South Pacific, Indonesia, Central Asia, and Siberia, in which becoming a bird in an altered state of consciousness was seen as an initiation or doorway to transformation, just as the soul may leave the body through meditation or astral travel and return reconfigured. The bird links dimensions and is a sacred messenger of the Feminine Divine.

The Egyptian Goddesses Isis and Nephthys are both able to take the form of kites, and swallows are sacred symbols and beings to Isis and Inanna. The dove, an emblem and emissary of Aphrodite and Venus, was later adopted by Christianity as the symbol of Mary and the Holy Spirit. Owls are also linked to the Goddess, and in particular to Athena, as both an omen of death and a friend to those who are grieving. The Sumerian Goddess Inanna, like the Dark Goddess Lilith, has talons for feet, and occasionally She's also pictured with wings, perhaps signifying Her ability to fly to the highest high and lowest below.

The bird can be honored as a tutor in what it means to experience the purity and love of the heavens in your being, as an emblem of expansion, and as a mirror to the Divine union of the heavens and the earth within the self.

The Cow

Cows are special creatures. They're emotional animals who have the ability to make friends and who feel distress when they are separated from those friends. In the Vedas—the oldest of Hindu scriptures—the cow is a sacred symbol of life, representing the Goddess Aditi, the mother of all the Gods. In Germanic paganism, Nerthus, a Goddess of Prosperity and Peace, has Her cart pulled by heifers.

Egyptian cosmology features Hathor, the cow-headed Love Goddess whose udders produced the Milky Way. The Egyptian Goddesses are, in fact, often rendered as suckling the Pharaohs, nourishing them with milk. Hathor, Isis (who came later and adopted many of Hathor's qualities), and the Greek Hera are frequently shown wearing the lunar crescent, which also looks like bull horns. Think of these headdresses as absorbing lunar or Goddess energy.

The cow can be revered as a teacher of fierce loyalty and sensitivity as a map back into loving connection with the self, the Goddess, and community.

The Bee

Bees reveal the microcosmic aspect of the Goddess. Where their queen goes, the worker bees follow, and in their mutual devotion, they produce honey. Never forget the communal aspect of the Divine Feminine that is so central to Her worship.

Moreover, bees give us the gift of honey, of course, and they remind us of the duality of the world: they can share sweetness or inflict stinging pain. The Priestesses of Demeter were called Melissae (which means "bee" in Greek), and the ancient Minoans were beekeepers. In Crete, honey was used to preserve the bodies of the dead, and for their New Year rites, which coincided with the rising of the star Sirius, they drank fermented honey—mead.

The bee invites you into revering the Goddess as a central figure in your life and passions, and it reflects the power of sacrifice when necessary.

Lions, Leopards, and Jaguars

Across cultures and lore, we see big cats standing aside the Goddess or underneath Her. Jaguars, lions, and leopards are strong, fluid, and formidable hunters—especially the lionesses, who hunt for their pride, inverting our twenty-first-century stereotype of the "masculine" provider. Jaguars were central to the Mesoamerican culture of the Maya, reflected in many deities, including the Goddess Ixchel. Ixchel, or Lady Rainbow, is often portrayed as a crone with jaguar ears and seen with a serpent and a water jug. She rules over the arts, transformation, and the Moon.

In ancient Sumer, Inanna, the Great Goddess of Love and War, is associated with lions and leopards, and Cybele of Anatolia and Rome is idolized in the same way. Sekhmet, the solar lion-headed Goddess of ancient Egypt, is a Goddess of War, Sexuality, and Rage. The Hindu Goddess Durga is depicted astride a lion or leopard, and the Buddhist Goddess Tara sits on a lion throne, surrounded by animals.

Big cats can be called on to awaken power and ferocity as medicine, as a path to honoring your fierce sensuality, and as a means of protecting what is important to you.

CREATING AN ALTAR TO THE EARTH GODDESS

Altars are portals to the Goddess, and creating one should be a priority in building a relationship with Her. An altar is the energetic focal point of a room and a physical representation of an intention. Yours can be dedicated to whatever you want (although in this case it will be to the Earth Goddess). It is where you perform spells and rituals, and where you can cultivate a relationship with the Goddess and the Goddess within yourself. An altar transforms a room into a sacred space.

To honor the value of something, you make room for it. Whether this is a trophy or award you place on your mantle or a new crystal that lives on your nightstand, carving out space—physical or energetic—for what you care about is a reflection of your devotion. So when you're beginning the wondrous journey of working with the Goddess, erecting an altar—a physical manifestation of that devotion—is an easy way to start.

What you put on your altar, and where you place it, are up to you. You can make an altar on a nightstand, dresser, windowsill, desk, or hearth; in a kitchen; or wherever feels right. If you're not able to be open with your practice, or if you travel frequently, you can create a portable altar that you can tuck away in a shoe, plastic, or wooden box, or you can make one in an Altoids box, arts and crafts style.

What you place on your altar likewise is personal. Think crystals, candles, talismans like jewelry, ritual tools like a cauldron and chalice, offerings to the Goddess, oils and incense, tarot or oracle cards, flowers, plants, dirt or sand from sacred places, statues of deities or animal guides, photos or art, a crystal ball, and whatever else helps you cultivate magick and connection to your desired aim.

In this case, you will be creating an altar to the earth, or to Gaia, Demeter, or Isis; the serpent, cow, bee, or bird; or whatever land, animal, or earth spirit you want to conjure a bond to.

First, consider your purpose. *Is it to align more fully to the earth? To the Goddess of the Earth? To the animals and flowers that are the children of the Goddess? To a specific Goddess?* There's no right or wrong answer, and remember that like anything else in your practice and relationship to the Goddess, your responses will evolve—and that's a beautiful thing!—so stay curious. Let your altar be a testament to that evolution.

You will need: Herbs like mugwort (ruled by the Moon; elevates intuitive and psychic abilities), lavender (ruled by Mercury; heals and relaxes), roses (ruled by Venus; draws in love of all kinds), or sweetgrass (welcomes in positive spirits and vibes) and anything you want to include on your altar, like green candles, a plant, crystals, any pentacle tarot cards or The Empress (connected to the element of earth), any icons or images of Goddesses, oracle cards, . . . etc.

Step 1: Gather your supplies
When you're ready, figure out where you will be setting up your altar and then gather your supplies, which may include herbs for burning. Or you can substitute rose water, holy water, or Moon water instead.

Step 2: Ground and center, and cleanse the space
When you have your space set and your supplies gathered, ground and center (page 12). Then, cleanse the area for the altar, either by passing sacred smoke over it or by wiping it down with the water. As you do, say something like the following:

Great Goddess of the Earth, in your name I do this work. May you cleanse this space's energy, so I can erect this altar in honor of Thee.

You may hold your palms over the area, visualizing white, healing light moving from the heavens, through the crown of your head, through your arms and body, and out from your hands, infusing Divine energy into this space.

Step 3: Create the altar
When you're ready, place your objects. Allow this experience to be fun—put on music, light incense, and allow the Goddess to flow through you as you conjure this sacred space. Keep your intention in

your mind's eye. Play around until you find a configuration that's beautiful to look at and that helps you experience the beauty of the Divine.

Step 4: Charge the altar

Dip your fingers in a bowl of water (either regular water or one of the kinds listed on the previous page) and lightly sprinkle it on your altar, or wet your fingers and touch each corner of the altar and then the center. Run the sacred smoke around and above the items you placed on your altar. As you feel ready, take a moment to reconnect with your intention. You may wish to state it out loud to the Goddess, adapting the following or saying something you wrote to remember your objective:

> *In the name of Goddess, in honor of the earth, I cleanse, consecrate,*
> *and charge this altar in honor of my highest good.*
> *In honor of the Feminine Divine, in honor of my highest self, I*
> *dedicate this altar as a temple for the Goddess to rest.*
> *And so it is!*

After you've declared your altar a magical space, hold your palms above it again, feeling the white, healing light move through you, out from your palms, and onto the altar. With this declaration and act of devotion, you have transformed your altar into a living temple and portal of magick.

Step 5: Leave an offering, ground, and close

When your altar is set up and fully charged, leave an offering (page 17), and ground and close.

Step 6: Return to it again and again

Your altar is a living temple to the Goddess and the Goddess energy within yourself. Be sure to keep it clean—you don't want dust collecting—and cleanse it with smoke or blessed water regularly. Come back here to pray, to perform spellwork, to share offerings, and to talk to the Goddess. If you keep a plant or flowers here, tend to them. Come here to nourish the spirit of the earth, the land you live on, and the Goddess. Allow it to evolve alongside you.

I will be referring to your altar throughout this book, so you will have many chances to sustain your relationship with this sacred space.

JOURNAL QUESTIONS

Grab your Goddess Grimoire, and use these journal questions to guide you deeper into seeing the earth as an expression and manifestation of the Goddess. Allow them to show you how you can ground into the Divine Feminine and connect to the earth as Her body. Use the steps on page 15 to make this into a ritual to return to any time you need.

+ What is my relationship to the earth like? How do I care for and nurture this relationship?
+ How is my reverence for nature reflective of my reverence for the Goddess?
+ To what Goddesses of the Earth am I magnetized? How does the earth represent the Goddess to me?
+ What element do I feel the strongest draw to? The weakest?

+ How can working with the elements be a part of my relationship with the Goddess?
+ What rituals do I practice or want to practice to engage with Mother Earth and the Goddess?
+ What animals am I drawn to (whether or not they were listed in this chapter)? What are their qualities?
+ How can working with the animals of the Goddess facilitate my connection to Her?
+ How does honoring the Goddess help me honor the earth?

AFFIRMATIONS

I hope this chapter has helped you see the world in a new way. In an embodied way. In a way that helps you notice the Goddess through every sacred spring, every tree, every serpent, every flower, every field. Getting out into nature and feeling the Goddess as the earth is a powerful way to incorporate Her messages. You also can use affirmations to bring Her to you on the days you're not able to get outside. Use the steps on page 38 to help make this practice everything it can be to support you.

+ I am grounded in my magick, in my power, in my heart.
+ I am one with the earth, I am a child of the Goddess of the Earth.
+ I surrender to the abundance of the Goddess, and I receive with ease.
+ I am a child of the Goddess.
+ I surrender to the feral, potent powers of the Goddess.

- I call on the serpent to release and renew with ease.
- I call on the flexibility of the feline to tap into my magick, no matter the situation.
- I call on the freedom of the bird to change my perspective and see new paths before me.
- I honor the sacredness of all life.
- I honor the cycles of the earth as a reflection of my inner world.
- I honor the earth and all her children as manifestations of the Goddess.

A TAROT SPREAD FOR GROUNDING INTO THE POWERS OF THE GODDESS

Another way to approach the Goddess is through this simple three-card spread. Sometimes you need a quick reading to summon Goddess energy for a given situation and find strength in your cycles. Allow it to remind you of the nourishing, healing, and grounding capabilities of the Goddess.

I suggest doing this outside or near an open window. Turn it into as much of a ritual as you wish, using the steps on page 42 to read your cards before recording the spread in your Goddess Grimoire.

Card 1: How can I ground into the powers of the Goddess?

Card 2: How can the beauty of nature help me do so?

Card 3: What am I meant to remember about my cycles of death and rebirth?

The Goddess of
Protection and Healing

L iving as a human on Earth means facing hardships, pain, trials, and tribulations, but no matter how much is out of your control, connecting to the Goddess is not. You don't need anything except your mind and heart to call on Her in these times. She is there when you need Her the most.

The Goddess is a lifeline to the Divine, to your highest self, to that which is beyond words and understanding. And when it comes to protection, forming a relationship with the Goddess is a big step in self-sovereignty and responsibility. To rely on Her during tough times means honoring your vulnerability as strength. It doesn't mean weakness or failure, but radically accepting wherever you are and claiming your needs. It's not a replacement for asking for help in the real world, which is a true form of magick, but it is a key spiritual supplement.

> **When you are in reciprocity**
> **with the Goddess, when you are in a**
> **relationship with the Goddess, you can**
> **lean on Her whenever you need help,**
> **and *especially when you need help.***

You can reach out in many ways: in ritual, in meditation, with affirmations, through art and writing. Your request can be initiated by creating a talisman or words of power; carried with you in your bag, heart, or car; and pulled out or recited whenever you feel the need.

Having comforted millions during eons of existence, the Goddess isn't just an invisible energy in the ether, but a palpable power embodied in the fierce archetypal expressions of deities like Tara, Guanyin, Bastet, and the Virgin Mary. In moments of pain, horror, or fear, you can choose to turn your heart to the Goddess. Confide in Her when you're walking to your car alone at night, when you're feeling anxious, when you're healing from trauma, or when you need a cosmic mother to hold you after a fight with your partner.

The Goddess has been there for me through the death of family members, through my dad's heart attack, through my sister's cancer diagnosis and recovery, through a worldwide pandemic, and through saying goodbye to my family dog of nearly seventeen years. She's been there for me through heartbreak and medical issues and sadness and pain. She is always there, no matter what. Yet I have found that there are specific attunements of the Goddess I can call upon most reliably.

In my practice, when I need support, healing, and protection, I call upon Isis. I ask Her to wrap Her golden wings around me, to help me in Her expression as protectress. I visualize myself held by Her, Her ankh shining bright at the crown of my head. As I breathe into this, I feel comforted. I know She is there.

I will be sharing specific Goddesses of Protection and Healing in this chapter, but you do not need to call on a certain face of the Goddess when you are in trouble. Calling an aspect of the Goddess is like dialing a phone number with a direct extension, but you can still buzz the general hotline and get through. If you already have a relationship with a Goddess of Protection and Healing, by all means, call on Her in moments of crisis. But I believe that even a Goddess of Love or of Death and Necromancy is available whenever you need Her, if that feels like the right move.

And you don't have to wait for a particularly low moment to initiate this relationship. If you're feeling pain and heartache, or sadness or exhaustion from being a human, reach out to the Goddess through the portal of your heart. Ask for Her love, guidance, healing, and protection. Pray to Her as you move through your day, or bring offerings for when things feel especially tough and you need extra support.

WAYS TO CONNECT TO THE GODDESS OF PROTECTION AND HEALING

Whether you already have a relationship to a Goddess of Healing, want to establish one, or are looking to experience the Great Goddess in Her role as healer and protectress, start here:

+ *Notice the people in your life who feel the most healing, supportive, and nourishing.* Notice what it is about them that makes them a safe space. Use this as fodder and information, allowing it to guide you into Goddess energy. Write about this in your Goddess Grimoire.

+ *Take note of the ways you've been a haven for healing for yourself and for others.* Reflect on how you've been your own Goddess of Protection and Healing.

+ *Keep tabs on whatever healing techniques you practice or you're drawn to,* whether this is herbal healing, Chinese medicine, reiki or other forms of energy work, acupuncture, breathwork, or massage. Look into classes or courses, take trainings, receive bodywork, or begin studies to be certified in the techniques that inspire you. As you're exploring your own ability as a healer, and your ability to receive healing, *I invite you to dedicate this to the Goddess* or to think of Her as you're doing this work, allowing this exploration of healing to be done in Her name. In this same way, if you are comfortable within a Western medical paradigm but have had negative experiences, it's worth the time to find doctors who listen to you and support your healing (easier said than done, I know). In this same way, you may wish to dedicate your healing journey to the Goddess.

✦ *In moments when you need peace, healing, inspiration, or protection, call upon the Goddess.* Pray and ask for Her guidance, for Her to fill your heart with Her love and protection. Don't worry about saying the right thing, or being in the right space to do so, or seeking out the "right" face of the Goddess for the situation; simply be present and speak your need.

✦ *Make a sigil for protection or healing, working with a specific Goddess to do so.*

----------------------------------)) ● ● ● ((----------------------------------

MAKING A SIGIL

Choose a phrase or affirmation that embodies what you're looking for (e.g., *I am held, healed, and protected by the Goddess against all illness and maladies on all planes and in all ways*), write it in your Goddess Grimoire, and then cross out the repeating letters and, if you wish, any vowels. Form the remaining letters into a symbol that doesn't look like the phrase or anything recognizable, overlapping and rearranging the letters as you see fit. There's no wrong way to do make your sigil. Charge this symbol through chanting, dancing, movement, or sex magick (page 155)—anything that generates a lot of heat and gets your heart pumping. As you get to the peak of the energy raising, look at the sigil and send it the energy. You can then destroy the sigil by burning it, throwing it away, or burying it, or you can carry it with you as an amulet of blessings and protection.

✦ *Create an altar,* allowing the Goddess to inspire you in its construction (adapting the instructions on page 88). Bring in colors like white and blue if you want to feel the Moon's healing energies, or go the solar route with yellows and golds. Place items that represent your healing here—talismans or heirlooms; medicine bottles; images or icons of the Goddess or Her emissaries like Archangels (especially Raphael for healing); candles, herbs, or oils of eucalyptus, lavender, or mugwort; symbols of healing like the ankh; symbols of protection like the evil eye; and crystals like black tourmaline, amethyst, or clear quartz.

✦ *Work with the ankh.* One of my favorite ways to align with Isis—the Goddess I call upon in my practice for protection and healing—is through Her sacred symbol of the ankh. The ancient Egyptian symbol represents long life, eternity, and health. I like to trace it above my crown chakra (the top of my head) as I pray to Isis to wrap Her golden wings of healing and protection around me and then I visualize light moving through me in the shape of an ankh. I breathe energy from the base of my spine up to the crown of my head, where I visualize it looping like the top of an ankh, moving down to my heart, and spreading out left and right from my heart before returning to my heart and moving down my spine. I breathe through this in meditation for five or ten minutes until I feel complete and then thank Isis and close the practice.

✦ *Turn to guides of healing in your life,* whether they're in the astral, on the other side, or hidden in the natural world. Think of the Goddesses, saints, animal spirits, ancestors, flower and tree spirits, and angels who feel empowering, and read about their healing powers and medicine. Use practices of divination and self-inquiry—like meditation, tarot or oracle cards, or free writing—to unravel the spiritual systems of support you have available, remembering you always can ask the Goddess to show Herself to you in this way.

GODDESSES OF PROTECTION AND HEALING

These Goddesses of Protection and Healing will stoke the fires of your heart and assist you when you need it most. These are your guardian angels, working through the current of the Divine Feminine, in whom you can find reprieve even during the chaos of life. Allow the following Goddesses to inspire your own research and relationship.

Tara—Tibetan Buddhist and Hindu Goddess of Compassion

In Tibetan Buddhism, Tara is a Goddess who transcends Her context, whose heart is open to all beings, regardless of initiation or religion. She even transcends Her role as a Goddess because She encompasses all things, all beings, all time, and all space. She is the mother of compassion, a protectress with twenty-one faces who can be called upon by anyone in need. Tara is also the great liberator of fears. She is known for Her responsiveness and accessibility, and Her mantra, "*Om Tare Tuttare Ture Swaha*" (*ohm tara tu-tara too-ray svah-ha*), which means "Om [the seed sound of the universe] and salutations to She [Tara], who is the source of all blessings," is a Divine doorbell to Her power. Asking for Her Divine intervention is enough to bring the miracle you need down into the material plane.

With Her twenty-one faces, Tara displays many manifestations of the totality of the Goddess, although you most commonly see White Tara and Green Tara in the art and icons of Tibetan Buddhism. White Tara sits on a white lotus, granting blessings of healing and longevity. Green Tara sits on a lotus with her right leg extended, holding a blue lotus in her hand, and offering protection, especially around fear. Tara also has special place among women working with the Goddess. Before Tara became a buddha, She was told that She wouldn't reach enlightenment in a woman's body and that She should reincarnate in a man's body to do so. Tara refused, saying She would continue incarnating exclusively in a woman's body, offering Her female followers the same opportunity for enlightenment.

As a Hindu Goddess, Tara is more severe and emancipating, seen holding a knife and skull in Her right hand, and a sword and a blue lotus in Her left. She has three red eyes and is draped in serpents and tiger skin. This is a Goddess of the Left Hand Path (or the path of using the transgressive as a means of finding the Divine in everything and thus becoming Divine), and Her worship is inspired by the forbidden and out of reach, a way of transmuting the taboo into "spiritually transformative instruments." Tara exists on the liminal edge of realities, alchemizing the prohibited into gnosis. She is independent, not reliant on other Gods, and linked to the destructive and transformational potential of fire. She holds an excess of power and heat that has the potential to burn *or* protect with its brilliant illumination.

To connect with Tara: If you are drawn to one of the faces of Tara, honor Her as a guide in your journey of continued healing and wholeness. A potent way to do so is by repeating Tara's mantra over and over, preferably 108 times, using mala beads, while sitting comfortably in meditation: "*Om Tare Tuttare Ture Swaha*" (*ohm tara tu-tara too-ray svah-ha*). Spend time meditating with this Goddess, allowing Her different faces to come to you. Feel Her warmth, Her support. Or if you choose, allow Her more ferocious aspect to lead you toward a darker compassion, one that includes the subversive and taboo. Request Her knowledge of nondiscrimination and compensation to guide you in supporting and caring for all beings, and for all aspects of yourself. Volunteering or donating money to protect those in need can be an offering in Her honor.

Shekinah—Hebrew Goddess of Dwelling in the Heart

One of the milestones I encountered during my journey into Goddess energy was recognizing the faces of the Divine Feminine in Judaism, the tradition I grew up in. Judaism doesn't personify God as male—and instead sees God as a Divine androgyne—yet in biblical Hebrew, words are gendered, including the words used to describe God. Thus, the Hebrew God takes on a masculine countenance while using masculine pronouns.

But the Hebrew-speaking people who lived in the lands of ancient Israel were influenced by their neighbors, who worshipped Goddesses like Astarte and Asherah. They adopted some of these Goddesses of the Earth and Love and reconceptualized an aspect of their God to serve the purpose of the Goddess, a "divine, compassionate, feminine presence." This presence was known as the Shekinah, who represented their longing to worship a divinity on Earth. Although She is not mentioned in the Old Testament, She is seen in the holy readings of the Midrash and the Talmud, where She is said to comfort the sick and help those in need. Good deeds, or mitzvahs, attract Her.

Shekinah means "indwelling," and I like to think of this indwelling as the powers of the Goddess filling the temple in Jerusalem, like smoke used to clear the energy of a sacred space. Shekinah is a face of God that can be perceived by the senses, that can be felt, that can bring the Goddess of the past back to the people who worship Her. Shekinah also expressed an equilibrating and "punitive power," descending to the earth to defend the Jewish people when they were in need, like when they escaped from Egypt.

We all need to feel the Divine in our hearts, something that can be called on to fill the space of the soul in moments of pain, sadness, or fear. Shekinah celebrates the Jewish people and their survival during millennia of persecution and also the depth of the Hebrew Goddess, seen through her countenances of Asherah, Anath, Astarte, Lilith, and Matronit. She reminds us that even thousands of years of monotheism cannot contain Goddess energy.

To connect with Shekinah: To honor Shekinah, take note when you feel the Goddess dwelling in your heart, whether during sacred or mundane moments. Breathe into this, inviting Shekinah to expand into this space. You may dedicate an altar to Shekinah, inviting Her into your shrine, praying and meditating with Her when you need Her protection. You also can invite Her in on Shabbat, lighting candles and calling Her into your space and heart if celebrating Shabbos is in your practice. Because Shekinah lives in the temple, cultivating a space of the sacred numinous within your heart and home is a way to honor Her.

Guanyin—Chinese and Buddhist Goddess and Bodhisattva Compassion

Guanyin, also spelled Kwan-Yin, Kuan Yin, and Guan Yin, is a Buddhist Goddess of Mercy, Compassion, Women, and Children whose name derives from Guan-shi-yin, which means the "one who listens to the cries of the world." Known as a bodhisattva, Guanyin is technically not a Goddess, but one who has chosen to continue incarnating until all sentient beings reach enlightenment. In this way, She is still a container and emblem of Goddess energy. Holding them in loving consciousness, Guanyin guides Her devotees toward incorporating, incarnating, and personifying Her Divine Love in aligned action and an aligned heart.

The origins of Guanyin represent the merging of two different beings. By the fifteenth century BCE, the Indigenous shamanic religion of China recognized a Queen Mother or Great Goddess, and when Buddhism was later introduced about two thousand years ago, a bodhisattva named Avalokiteśvara (a masculine figure known as the embodiment of compassion) was paired with this Queen Mother, resulting in an independent Goddess: Guanyin.

Every prayer uttered for support, for protection, or for liberation from fear is said to fall on this Goddess. Her boundless compassion is there for anyone who needs Her. Guanyin's maternal love and devotion are a source of strength and resilience, especially when your human allies aren't able to protect you in the way you need. Her mantra, "*Om Mani Padme Hum*" (*ohm mahn-ee pawd-me hum*), which means "praise to the jewel in the lotus," is also a Buddhist mantra used to invoke Chenrezig, the Buddha of compassion, and it is a hotline to emotional protection and compassion within the self to awaken Guanyin's energies.

To connect with Guanyin: Spend time in gratitude for all you have, either speaking it out loud or writing down a list of what is overflowing within your heart. Prayers are a potent way of appealing to this Goddess, and because Her domain is protection and healing, She is particularly empathic to these requests. Meditation on this face of the Feminine Divine also will lead you to personify Her stillness, to receive Her medicine, and to rouse Her qualities within you. You may volunteer at a women's shelter in the name of this Goddess, or donate to a cause that helps relieve suffering in Her name. You can work with one of Her mantras, "*Om Mani Padme Hum*" (*ohm mahn-ee pawd-me hum*), saying it 108 times, with the assistance of mala beads if you like. Any act of compassion carried out for the sake of it—and not for what you expect in return—is an offering to Guanyin.

The Virgin Mary—Catholic Goddess/ Mother of God

The Goddess is alive in the Western world's day-to-day; She's just been hidden in plain sight as Mary, the Christian non-Goddess Goddess and mother of Christ. The Church may have renounced all other deities long ago, but the Goddess's devotees weren't ready to give Her up, and many adopted and acclimated Her many faces into Mother Mary, turning Her into the "unrecognized Mother Goddess of the Christian tradition." We know Her as "just" the mother of Jesus, yet Mary is the many faces of the Goddess before Her. She is still Cybele, Isis, Aphrodite, Demeter, Astarte, Hathor, and Inanna.

In the new era of Christianity, Mary became the veiled home for the current of the Goddess. The classic iconography of Mary holding a young Jesus is nearly identical to earlier depictions of Isis holding Horus. Mary is in the New Testament's book of Revelation, too, described as clothed with the Sun, with the Moon under her feet and the twelve stars of the zodiac surrounding her like a crown, linking her to Goddesses such as Inanna and Ishtar, who also wear a coronet of stars. Many temples to Goddesses like Isis and Athena were rededicated to Mary, and Her cult continued until around 400 to 600 CE, cloaked in the safety of Christianity.

Mary's compassion and mercy is omnipotent to those who honor Her, and even sometimes to those who don't. During the last thousand years, there have been 21,000 visions of the Virgin Mary, with many churches constructed on locations of these sightings. Catholic women who want to have a child pray to Mary, and like Guanyin, She is called upon for protection in birth. She also may be called on during moments of hardship through her most famous prayer, the Hail

Mary. Even this not-quite-Goddess Goddess is there for those who need Her, offering peace and protection to anyone who asks.

It is in Her role as the Black Madonna, or Black Virgin, that Mary's love shines forth like the Dark Moon, rebirthing light into being, especially in moments of pain and darkness. Evidence of the Black Virgin has been found in France, Spain, Switzerland, and Poland and is thought to be connected to the gnostic Sophia, or the ancient Christian Goddess of Wisdom. The Black Madonna is Mary in Her role as a Dark Goddess, or Goddess of the Shadow.

Mary also expresses Herself with inspiration, specifically through Her face, as Our Lady of Guadalupe, or La Virgen de Guadalupe. In 1531, the Virgin Mary showed herself to a man named Juan Diego just outside Mexico City as he was traveling to find a priest to help his sick uncle. Speaking Nahuatl and disguised as an Indigenous woman, She told the recent convert to build Her a shrine right where She had apparated to him in Tepeyac Hill. When Diego finally reached his bishop to tell him what he'd seen, the holy man wasn't convinced. But La Virgen had said She would give Diego a sign, and when he released the roses he had been clutching to his chest, a gift from the Goddess— Her image—was imprinted on his cloak. This image can be seen at the Basilica of Guadalupe, near my mom's home in Mexico City.

La Virgen de Guadalupe represents a return to the feminine in a Christianized culture that reveres the masculine and whose religion does the same. This Virgin Mary watches over the marginalized, disenfranchised, and othered. Those who worship Her find a face that survived colonization and still retains the knowledge, healing, and magick of the Indigenous people of Mexico.

To connect with a face of the Virgin Mary: To honor the Virgin Mary, you may wish to visit a church or basilica specifically dedicated to Her, or spend time looking at them in books or online. You also may wish to go to a museum to view art made in honor of the Virgin Mary (or use Google Arts & Culture) because Her art represents the thousands of years of Goddess worship before Her. Honor Mary by praying with a rosary, saying the Hail Mary if it's familiar to and resonates with you. Set up an altar for Her or La Virgen de Guadalupe with roses and holy water, and use frankincense and myrrh to cleanse your sacred space in Her honor. Pray to Her when you need it, and charge a piece of jewelry with the intention of connecting with Her to form a talisman; anything with Her image on it would be appropriate.

Bastet, Sekhmet, and Isis: Egyptian Goddesses of Protection, War, Healing, and Magick

We've already met Sekhmet and Isis, but I wanted to share how these ancient Egyptian Goddesses—along with the cat-headed Bastet—act as omens of protection, guarding their devotees with fierce love and devotion.

Isis's nature may be described as loving before protective, but you can't truly separate the two. Isis's loyalty and love manifest as unyielding commitment to what She values. This face of the Goddess smites Her enemies, protects and leads Her people during war, and is unapologetically loyal to Her worshippers. When you want to invoke this powerful manifestation of the Goddess, use Her epithets (or the names and associations of the Goddess given to Her by ancient devotees) of Isis the Flame, Isis the Fiery One, and Isis the Powerful. Isis is also a Divine healer (She revived Osiris from the dead) and a supportive ally whenever you need some mending. As a Mistress of Magick, Isis has the tools available, both physical and spiritual, to conjure miracles.

Bastet, or Bast, is the Goddess of Cats, the most sacred animal to the ancient Egyptians, and much like Guanyin, she is also the patroness of mothers and children. Although Bastet and the lion-headed Sekhmet are understood as different Goddesses, one theory suggests that Bastet came after the domestication of cats and represents the tamed version of Sekhmet. That is, They are two aspects of the same Goddess, wild *and* gentle. Bastet, like Sekhmet, is the daughter of Ra, the Sun God. In ancient Egypt, "nearly every household that had children had a wall niche devoted to Bast," where offerings such as fresh flowers and milk were placed to remind the Goddess of Her worshippers' commitment. She is the protectress of the home, ready to pounce when necessary, all her vigilance and care coming from a place of love.

You already know about Sekhmet, but if you need a refresher, flip back to page 56. Call on Her when you need a lioness's strength to care for what matters most. Sekhmet, after all, is a Goddess of War, heeding the righteous call of action to protect what you love. Sekhmet's compassion may not always be Her guiding force, yet Her passion for whatever it is She is fighting for is undeniable. If you need to protect something with the fierceness of a thousand blazing Suns, then Sekhmet may be just the Goddess to invoke.

To connect to Bastet: If you want to connect to Bastet, make an altar for Her in your home and place offerings of milk and flowers there. Donate money to or volunteer at a women and children's shelter or animal shelter (or better yet, a cat rescue), or give clothing to those who need it. Spend time with cats, adopt a cat, and tend to your human and animal friends.

To connect to Sekhmet: To connect to Sekhmet, adopt a big cat (like through the World Wildlife Fund), donate to or volunteer at a large cat rescue, or watch videos of lions—specifically how lionesses hunt and care for their cubs. Scry with fire, and ask Sekhmet to guide you in your worship of Her. Spend time in your body, roaring, moving, and absorbing Her fierce essence. Offer blood or red wine, placing it on an altar dedicated to the Goddess.

To connect to Isis: To form a bridge to Isis, especially as a protectress, pray to Her through Her epithets of Isis the Flame, Isis the Fiery One, or Isis the Powerful as you gaze at a candle. If you are in need of healing, call on Isis in Her role as a Divine healer, working with the ankh and prayer to ask for Her Divine help, feeling both your body filling with golden light and Her golden wings wrapped around you. You also may wish to dedicate a piece of ankh jewelry to Isis.

Mercury/Hermes/Thoth/Odin: Protector of the Shape-Shifters

Once you get to know Her, the Goddess regularly destroys your perception of who She is by showing you faces you never expected. The many manifestations of the Goddess that don't fit into a box include the Mercurial Gods: the Greek Hermes, the Roman Mercury, the Egyptian Thoth, and the Norse Odin. These Gods are shape-shifters and can be considered different facets of the same energy across pantheons. These are queer Gods, too, and through them, we can see the Divine androgyne that is the God/dess.

Hermes/Mercury is the Greco-Roman God of Magick, Travel, Communication, and Knowledge, who also happens to be a divine gender bender who can dance through the underworld. He is the guardian of time and, in this way, thresholds. Hermes has an inner sense of what could be considered feminine logic and is intuitive, expansive, and attuned to the vibrations of different realms. The word *mercurial* comes from Mercury, naturally, and means lighthearted, sprightly, volatile, changeable, and quick, which is how this God rules (and these qualities also apply to the planet he rules over). It is

Mercury's ability to transform that marks him as a God of the liminal and a protector of the in-between.

In Hermes' role as Hermaphroditus, the child of Hermes and Aphrodite known as the Divine androgyne, we see another example of how he exceeds many of our expectations and earthly limitations. The priests who presided over Aphrodite's Cyprian temple wore "artificial breasts and female garments . . . in the guise of the God Hermaphroditus," and in the time of the Gnostics, Hermes came to represent the Divine within the self, and his bisexuality was translated as self-love for all aspects of the self. It's even said that Hermes invented masturbation as a gift for his son, Pan.

Hermes and Mercury may not seem like classic deities of protection, but let's take into account what they rule over. LGBTQIA+ identities still need protection, more in some parts of the world than others. As the patron God of Travelers, Thieves, and Tricksters, Hermes/Mercury is a defender of the transgressive, champion of that which goes against the grain. And as a God who exists between dualities, I argue that Hermes/Mercury is also an aspect of the Feminine Divine.

In the Middle Ages, Hermes once again took on a new role, this time as Hermes Trismegistus, Hermes the Thrice Great, adopting and merging traits from Hermes, Mercury, and the Egyptian Thoth. Thoth is the ancient Egyptian God of Words and Writing, and it is through his consort (either the Goddess Seshat or Ma'at) that Thoth received his magick. In the Norse pantheon, the God Odin, known as the All Father, takes on this similar role. While hanging on the World Tree for nine days and nine nights, Odin received the teachings of the runes, including the feminine mysteries, like sacred poetry and words of power, from the Goddess Freya.

These Gods aren't the only ones who embrace the expansiveness and queerness of the Goddess. Ancient priests of the Anatolian and Roman

Goddess Cybele would cross-dress and, while in ecstatic trance, castrate themselves to embody their worship of the Goddess, blurring the lines between pleasure and pain. Dionysus, the Greek God of Wine, Theater, Ritual Madness, and Ecstasy, is the patron deity of intersex and transgender people. The Norse trickster God Loki also disguises himself as a woman, and in the Aztec pantheon, Tlazolteotl (Goddess of Vice and Filth) and Xochiquetzal (Goddess of Fertility, Sexuality, Weaving, and the Moon) were served by transgender and lesbian priestesses.

If you are intersex, queer, trans, or nonbinary, I want to remind you that you have every right to walk the Goddess path. You are valid and special and beautiful, and it's not your fault the world hasn't caught up to understanding the multitudes of gender that exist. You walk an ancient path, and I hope no one is able to rob you of your innate magick. The Goddess welcomes you with open arms.

To connect with Mercury/Hermes/Thoth/Odin: Set aside time on Wednesday (ruled by Mercury) to write and study magick in this God/ess's honor. Read myths about these deities, and work with the planet Mercury and the sphere of Mercury—Hod, or "splendor"—on the Tree of Life. Any form of knowledge, magick, and travel can be dedicated to this God, and reading the *Corpus Hermeticum* is one way to understand them.

If you are trans and transitioning, call upon Mercury, Hermaphroditus, Hermes, Thoth, or Odin to protect you in this liminal space, or work with Them as a guide and mentor, dedicating your sacred exploration and transformation to this deity. If you want to connect to Odin, study runes, a medium of divination using symbols drawn on squares of stone or clay that can be cast and read. If you feel drawn to Dionysus, leave wine on your altar for Them and spend time dancing, having sex, or working with plant medicine to reach an altered state of consciousness.

CREATING ENERGY SIGNATURES FOR PROTECTION AND HEALING

As you build a relationship with the Goddess and Her specific faces, you will gather symbols, words, and actions that reflect this bond. This may be unintentional (like starting to notice repeating numbers or Her sacred animals) or intentional (saying a specific prayer for Her). And although both ways hold magick, let's begin with creating an energy signature for protection that you can work as a through line to the Goddess when you need Her.

This energetic symbol is something that you will repeatedly imbue with Goddess energy so that it eventually becomes a shorthand way for you to call it in at a moment's notice—which I call an "energy signature." Instead of a sigil that you use once and then throw away, your energy signature is something you can weave into your practice and daily life.

Ideally, it will be a simple gesture, something you can trace in the air to conjure the Goddess's power. Here are some of the ways I use my energy signature: I visualize tracing it in light when I'm sending out reiki, I trace it over my tarot cards, I use it to charge my magickal tools and any items I work with in ritual, I carve it into my candles, I trace it in the air when I want to call on the Goddess quickly, I trace it over my water and food to give thanks, I use it in art and collages, and I write it in my journal. But *my favorite* way to work with my signature is to trace it over an energy center in my body with my finger or a crystal while in meditation.

An energy signature that you can trace with your fingers or visualize will be a key instrument in your mystical toolbox. Keep in mind that you can craft different versions for different intentions, like one for your work with Hermes Trismegestus, one with Tara, and then another with a Goddess of Love like Venus. I have one for every Goddess I'm devoted to. In this same vein, you also may have an energy signature you use for love, one for protection, one for healing, and so on. Right now, let's focus on protection and healing, but keep the possibilities in mind as you move through this book and feel called to invent different energy signatures for different intentions.

Step 1: Set up the space, ground, and center
Following the steps on page 12, set up your space and gather your supplies. When you're ready, ground and center.

Step 2: Craft an intention
Before you create and charge your energetic signature, get clear on your intention.

Then, consider your intention. Do you want to feel safe and protected from any negative influences through the love and power of the Goddess? Do you have a chronic illness with which you always could use some healing support? How can the Goddess help you feel empowered in this situation? *You are welcome to create new energy signatures depending on what changes in your life. But keep in mind, the longer and more deeply you work with them, the stronger the magick will be.*

Write out a few intentions in present or past tense, whichever feels better for you, avoiding future tense, which will trap this protection and healing in the future. Your intention may end up being your affirmation, so don't skip this step! Here are some examples:

+ I am healthy, feeling good in my body, and supported in my journey.
+ I am held in the Divine light of the Goddess.
+ I am healed from _____ on all planes and in all ways.
+ I am totally and completely protected from outside influences and veiled in the love of the Goddess.
+ I am safe, healthy, healed, and protected by the Goddess.
+ I am held, healed, and protected by the Goddess, on all planes and in all ways.
+ I am safe; I am healthy; I am protected; I am thriving.
+ I am healthy and protected as I move through _____ treatment with the Goddess supporting me.

+ I am free of all illness and am the healthiest I have ever been in my life.
+ I always feel safe, protected, and healthy and call on this energy whenever I need.

Your intention may have multiple parts (like to be safe *and* healthy), and your energy signature, and any related affirmations or prayers, will reflect this.

Step 3: Create a representative energetic symbol

Now that your intention is set, pick a symbol to represent it. Don't worry about making it too complicated—in fact, the simpler the better. This is something you'll want to be able to bust out whenever— in a waiting room, in traffic, in line. You don't have to make it up either. Sacred symbols such as the pentagram, ankh, evil eye, or hexagram are already infused with the energy of everyone who's ever worked with them, so if you're repurposing one for your own use, then you're also tapping into this energetic current. This can be really powerful!

Take time to consider any symbols you're naturally drawn to and what they mean to you. I would suggest picking one to start with, but if you wish to pick two or three to try together, you most certainly can do so.

Examples of protective and healing symbols include the ankh, the banishing pentagram, the hexagram, lightning, a heart, the seven-pointed star, a peace sign, a flower like a lily, an equal arm cross, an alchemical symbol, and the evil eye. If you already have a relationship with a Goddess of Protection and Healing, consider Her symbols and how you may be able to use these as your own energetic signatures. Spend time in research if you need to, remembering that this, too, is an offering and act of devotion.

Of course, you may wish to summon your own symbol, or overlay multiple symbols to create a personal energy signature. The most important thing is that you feel inspired and enthralled with the results. It may take a bit of experimenting to see what feels right, but repeat the following steps as many times as you need to until you find something that works.

Step 4: Write an affirmation or prayer (or both!)

Now that you have your intention and symbol, write an affirmation and/or a prayer to go with it. Your affirmation is a sentence or two you can use to connect with the Goddess for protection and healing whenever you need. You can say it under your breath or in the mirror or write it in your phone notes. It's the Cliffs Notes version of a prayer—user-friendly.

A prayer is longer and more substantial than an affirmation, something you can say each morning in your practice, each night at your altar, or whenever you have the time. You may choose to write one or another, but I suggest you write both: an affirmation so you have it for when you're in a hurry, and a prayer for when you have time for something longer like meditation or ritual and want to honor the Goddess more thoroughly.

Use the following to inspire you, or write your own using your intention from step 1.

Examples of affirmations:

- I am safe, supported, and protected by the Goddess.
- I am protected by the Goddess always in all ways.
- I am healed and protected by the Feminine Divine.
- The Goddess holds, heals, and protects me.
- I am healed from _____ and protected from all disease and illness.

+ I trust in the Goddess to continue to protect me and heal me.
+ I am as vibrant and healthy as possible.
+ I am supported and protected by the Goddess in all planes in all ways.

If you wish, expand this further into a prayer of healing and protection. For example:

> *Great Goddess of the Heavens, Earth, and Underworld, I call upon You in Your fullest form to ask for Your protection and healing. I ask for safety and for protection from any negative influences, from any illness, from anything that doesn't serve my highest good, and from anything that does not vibrate in 100 percent Divine light. Goddess, may I be surrounded and embraced by Your healing and protective light, and may I carry it with me, wherever I go, whenever I need. May I feel Your support and love no matter where I am. May You continue healing me of _____ and protecting me from _____. May I tap into Your celestial love whenever I feel called, and may I have the clarity of mind, body, and heart to see this is always around me.*
> *This or something better for the highest good of all involved, by the blessing of the Goddess, so it is done.*

Step 5: Activate the symbol

When you have your symbol, affirmation, and/or prayer, you will activate the symbol. To do this, draw it on a page in your grimoire. You may add the date and astrological correspondences for future reference.

Breathe and come back to your heart. Feel the Goddess surrounding you. As you feel ready, ask the Goddess for Her blessing and protection of this symbol, taking the time to let Her know your intention. Then pull in Her energy through the crown of your head, through your body, out your palms. As you're ready, *read your affirmation out loud as you trace your energy symbol in the air three times.* (Three is one of the numbers of the Goddess.) *If you're activating your prayer, also read this out loud as you trace your symbol three more times.*

Then say the following, rewriting it if you feel called:

> *On this day and at this hour, I activate this energetic symbol of*
> *Divine protection and power. I am held, healed, and protected*
> *through the Goddess's light. And I turn to this symbol whenever*
> *I need, on all planes, both in and out of sight.*
> *I activate this energetic signature now, at this hour, by my voice and*
> *through my power. So it is, and it is done.*

Step 6: Charge through sex magick (optional)

If you are comfortable with it, you may send more energy to your energetic signature by performing sex magick. Allow yourself to feel present in the pleasure and sensations you experience as you masturbate, and at the peak of energy raising (at orgasm or as close as possible), open your eyes and direct your intention and energy into this symbol. Stay in the afterglow, feeling held by the Goddess.

Step 7: Close the working

To close the ritual, close and ground (page 13). When you're done sending the energy back to the celestial and terrestrial realms, stay in meditation as long as you need. When you're ready, say something like the following to thank the Goddess:

Goddess, thank You for this blessing of healing and protection.
Thank You for the support in this magical working. I come in
perfect love and trust, and leave with a connection to all that
is, will be, and was. The ritual is done, the magick has begun,
and I thank You with my whole heart.
And so it is!

Use your energy signature, affirmation, and prayer to bring a little
more magic into your day-to-day. Draw it on the tags of your clothing
or on the bottom of your shoes; trace it in oil on your body; or use it
in meditation, art, and healing. Repeat with other Goddesses or intentions, and remember that these energy signatures get charged with
use. And so it is.

JOURNAL QUESTIONS

These questions will help you reflect on the times when the Divine
Feminine was there to hold and care for you. They also should remind
you of how far you've come with your healing, and how you are supported in so many ways, no matter what you're going through. Allow
them to inspire you in writing and contemplation, using the steps on
page 34 to make the most of them.

+ What God/desses of Protection and Healing am I drawn to?
  How have They made Their presence known in my life?
+ How does calling upon the Goddess in times of need feel to me?
  How does Goddess energy feel in my body?

+ What area of my life could use healing? How can my work with the Goddess help support this?
+ In what ways am I already committed to my healing? To my protection? To the Goddess?
+ In what moments of my life have I felt divinely protected? Divinely healed?
+ Who are the guides in my life who have supported me in moments of healing? Who have protected me?
+ What rituals of protection do I have in my life? What practices or superstitions did I grow up with surrounding this? Which do I want to keep?
+ What offerings can I leave at my altar to the Goddesses of Protection and Healing? What represents this in my own world?

AFFIRMATIONS

I am passionate about affirmations because they are practical, and they work. With something as important as protection and healing, it's vital that you have as many tools as possible to keep safe on every level: spiritually, physically, mentally, and emotionally. And although affirmations and magick can never replace modern medicine and protective measures like locking your door, getting a restraining order, or taking the medicine you need, they act as an energetic supplement. Use them whenever you need, paired with a simple visualization of a sphere of protective light surrounding you. Know that anything that doesn't align with your highest good and vibrate in 100 percent Divine energy cannot move through this protective barrier.

+ I am divinely held, divinely protected, and in perfect health.
+ I am supported and protected by the Goddess.
+ I trust in the Goddess; I trust in myself; I trust in my body; I trust in my health.
+ I am veiled by the white light of protection. I am protected by the Divine Feminine.
+ I move through the shadows with ease, and I am as protected as can be.
+ I am held, healed, and protected by the Goddess on all planes and in all ways.
+ Only that which serves my highest good and vibrates in Divine light has access to my energy.
+ I release any energy that does not belong to me and call back all my energy and power from wherever it may be.
+ The Goddess guides me, supports me, protects me, and heals me.

A TAROT SPREAD TO RECEIVE HEALING FROM THE GODDESS

Working with the tarot, or an oracle deck, is one of my favorite ways to commune with the Goddess. In times of pain and healing, in times of suffering or sadness, I know I can whip out my cards. If you need healing, or want to receive love and guidance from the Goddess or a specific face of the Goddess, work with the following spread. Follow the steps laid out on page 42 to aid you in your reading.

Card 1: How the Goddess is healing your mind.
Card 2: How the Goddess is healing your body.
Card 3: How the Goddess is healing your heart.
Card 4: How the Goddess is healing your soul.

The Goddess of Love

L
ove is not just a virtue of the Goddess; it's Her most potent force and form. Defining love is difficult because it is both elusive and temporary, permanent, and fleeting. Love always exists, but the way you experience and cultivate it changes based on your circumstances, your relationship to yourself, and the "other" of your affection. My definition will differ from yours, but like magick, to feel love is to know love. For our purposes here, I define love as union with something greater than yourself, whether it's the Divine, a partner, or the higher self or soul. Love is greater than the sum of its parts.

One of the unsurpassed lessons I've learned from working with the Goddesses of Love, and being devoted to Them, is that love isn't something external you strive for. It's not something you conjure up. It's a way of being.

You ARE love. And when you commit to
working with the Goddess in this way,
you become a vessel, a channel,
a conduit for love. You become
the Goddess of Love incarnate.

You become a sacred chalice filled with Her love, and in turn, this flows back to that from which you came: the Goddess Herself.

The Goddess also can expand your idea of love. There's a weird belief in our society that the only sort of connection that matters is romantic—that you're only half a person until you fall in love, and that falling in love and being in a romantic relationship is the pinnacle. Well, guess what witches, that is simply untrue! Just as the Goddess loves Her animal children, the earth, and humans alike, so, too, is the array of love in your life sacred in all its forms. Platonic love between friends, love in a family, sexual and erotic love, self-love, the love for the earth and cosmos and Divine—these are all valid expressions of love. My hope is that, alongside cultivating a relationship with the Goddess and the Goddesses of Love, this chapter reminds you of all the love you already have.

The Goddess of Love also can help release shame around your sexuality and erotic expression. Living in a largely Christian society (at least here in the United States) comes with plenty of beliefs and conditioning that love and sex are heterosexual and monogamous, and that sex without love is dirty. It's my goal to assist you in releasing this pattern, because it's a lifelong process of undoing, and to remember that the Goddess sees sexuality, sensuality, and eros as sacred conduits for spirit, power, magick, and, of course, love. The Goddess of Love is the Goddess of Lust, after all.

The way you share your sexuality with yourself, with the Goddess, and with others is a gift. If it's between two consenting adults, then go for it. Sexuality is worthy of exploration if you feel called to explore it, and when you bring an awareness of your own innate divinity, then this becomes a sacrament to the Feminine Divine. I have said it before, I'll say it again, and I'll write it on my gravestone if I need to: it is your decision to make your sexuality sacred that makes it such. No one else can do this for you, and there's no one way for your sexuality to look for it to be worthy of this reclamation. As soon as you claim your sexuality as nothing short of divine, it is.

My ethos and my work with the Goddess of Love, and with sacred sexuality in general, is rooted in self-love and self-lust, all in devotion to the Goddess. Self-love is the act of giving yourself the love you long for, supporting yourself with integrity and compassion so you can then share it with others. It means turning the gaze of love upon yourself, as much as it does caring for yourself.

Self-lust is likewise the act of finding lust for the self, through self-love and self-seduction, and of more than anything, fulfilling your own desires with passion and commitment. Both self-love and self-lust require self-inquiry, knowing when to deny or indulge your desires, acknowledging what is in alignment for your highest good, and taking the time to understand what you like in the first place. Sometimes this means hedonistic instant gratification, sometimes it's epicurean, and sometimes it means saying "no" to short-term pleasure for long-term pleasure. But as you remember that you *are* an expression and a fractal of the Goddess, having self-love and self-lust becomes an act and commitment not only to yourself, but also to the

Goddess. *By the end of this chapter, you will see lust and love as offerings to the Feminine Divine that you can share with Her, yourself, and others.*

This chapter may bring up insecurities, worries, fears, and feelings of discomfort. Both sex and love tend to do that, and there is absolutely nothing wrong with you if they do so. Whatever you're feeling or experiencing is normal. If you're ace, or on the asexual or aromantic spectrum, there probably will be aspects of this chapter that don't vibe with you. Skip ahead and let them go. You don't need to be a sexual person to be a devotee of the Goddess. You don't need to work with sexual energy to work with the Goddess or Goddesses of Love. If you've never practiced sex magick, if you've never been in love, if you don't even really know what love means to you, there's nothing wrong with you. Part of the process of working with the Goddess is surrendering, opening yourself up to discovering what resonates, and releasing your feelings of judgment and shame.

In fact, releasing shame is a huge part of the work of being a love and sex witch devoted to the Goddess, something I share in my book *Sacred Sex.* Giving space to your feelings of discomfort without feeling like you've done anything wrong and just allowing them to be there, no matter how awkward or weird, is part of the work. I believe in you, and so does the Goddess.

CULTIVATING A RELATIONSHIP WITH THE GODDESS OF LOVE

Let's start with some ritual and non-ritual ways to begin to foster a relationship to your heart, to love, to lust, to your body, and to pleasure, all to and through the Goddess.

* *In your Goddess Grimoire, make a list of your personal definition of love, lust, sex, desire, pleasure, and sensuality.* Take the time to get clear about what these mean to you and then journal on how they relate to the Goddess. If any fear, anxiety, or worry comes up, take note of it and breathe into it. Reframing these definitions as sacred expressions of Goddess energy hopefully will begin the process of reprogramming your subconscious to see them as beneficial and worthy of your attention, not something to reject or feel shame for.

✦ *In your Goddess Grimoire, make a list of all the things that link you to your heart and to your ever-expanding definition of love.* This will be an ongoing list, one that you can add to and expand on whenever you want. The goal here is to have a list of activities, feelings, and associations to return to when you need to feel love. Examples include songs, scents, activities, people, books, and memories that remind you of the experience of being loved and giving love. You may make different lists for familial or platonic love, romantic love, sexual love, and self-love.

✦ *Work with rose medicine.* Roses are an incredibly sacred plant, with the highest frequency of any plant, at 320 megahertz. Their cultivation goes back five thousand years, to Babylon and Assyria, where Venus's predecessors of Inanna, Ishtar, and Astarte lived. Roses are intimately tied to Goddesses of Love (including Babalon, Mary Magdalen, Isis, Inanna, Ishtar, Venus, and Aphrodite), and the planet Venus's orbit in the sky mimics that of a rose. Offering roses on an altar, spraying rose perfume on yourself and in your space, growing roses in your garden, or buying roses for your bedroom are all ways to invite the Goddess of Love into your life. Allow the rose to be your muse, noticing the way it protects itself with thorns so it can bloom fully, and honor your boundaries as paths for your beauty and radiance to flower in safety.

✦ *Work with color magick and crystals.* There's a reason that Valentine's Day's colors are red and pink; these colors carry the vibration of desire, romance, love, passion, sensuality, and pleasure. Red confronts you with action, passion, sexuality, and lust, and pink invites compassion, romance, and love. These colors can act as a bridge to the Goddess when you decorate your space, adorn yourself, and create art with them. Red or pink crystals hold this same correspondence, and the rose quartz is one of the most beloved crystals for any work around the heart. Place rose quartz, rhodochrosite, pink moonstone, or rhodonite on your altar; wear it as jewelry; carry it with you; tuck it into your pillow; or hold it as you meditate on your heart.

+ *Dream up an environment that taps into your inner Goddess of Love.* If you don't know where to start, start with your bedroom. Even if you can't give your space a physical or energetic makeover, try creating an altar to love and the Goddess of Love (page 88). Get some red or pink sheets (even better if they're satin); hang up red or pink art; burn rose incense or spray rose water; place a statue of a Goddess like Venus; or get a smart lightbulb that can change to soft pink, red, or a warm golden glow. Think of the senses; what can you touch, taste, feel, see, and hear that leads you to the Goddess of Love? Use this as fodder for turning your room into a shrine for the Divine Feminine.

+ *Meditate with your heart.* It can be harder than you think to break through the barriers and really listen to your heart. Our hearts are the portals to the wisdom of the Goddess, so it is a worthy process to begin healing and reconciling your kinship to your heart.

In a quiet space where you can have a moment to yourself (at least five or ten minutes), find a comfortable position seated or lying down. Take a few deep breaths. As you feel centered, drop into your heart. There's no one way to do this, so allow your instincts to guide you. All I ask is that you become aware of your heart, of the energy at the center of your chest, and feel yourself descending into this space. Breathe into this. Notice what comes up. Ask her what she needs, and see what images, sensations, feelings, and colors surface. Do you notice any blocks? Do you notice any resistance? This is a litmus test to see how in touch with this part of yourself you are. Stay here as long as you need, and when you feel ready, record your findings in your grimoire.

+ *Adorn yourself like the Goddess of Love.* What makes you feel beautiful, sensual, majestic, ravishing? See your body as a sacred space for the Goddess to reside, and adorn it as such. This process will be uniquely yours. Enjoying the ritual of glamour, of honoring the Goddess through the flesh, and then connecting to Her through beauty is both ancient and sacred.

+ *Watch rom-coms; read romance novels, erotica, and love poems; surround yourself with love; and make art inspired by love.* Sympathetic magick is magick that imitates its desired outcome as a way to manifest it. An example is lunar magick: focusing on what you want to attract and manifest as the light from the Moon grows, and focusing on what you want to release and let go of as the light from the Moon shrinks. If you want to conjure up more love or eros in your life, tap into the energetic current of love through film, books, poetry, and art. Maybe you watch a favorite rom-com, read a smut novel, or explore Rumi or other love poems. The idea is to get you into the hands of love, feeling love, remembering love. Allow this to be sacred research, and take note of what helps you feel it, recording it in your Goddess Grimoire so you can come back to it as you need.

* *Be a vessel for love.* The easiest way to call in the Goddess of Love is to become love. Allow love to guide you. Check in with your heart regularly. Allow Goddess to permeate your day-to-day life, and share moments of love and joy with Her and in Her honor. Commune with loved ones with heart-centered attention, and remember that every person is a reflection of your Divine essence. Allow eye contact with strangers to be a moment of love, and let a smile transport you deeper into the Divine. See everything and everyone you touch as a manifestation for love, and it will beckon you deeper into its mysteries.

GODDESSES OF LOVE

These Goddesses of Love form an ancient current that can help you live from and express your heart in new ways. This is a means of infusing Goddess energy into your being; it's an act of unyielding opening to Her truth. May They help you find new avenues into this, and may They inspire your creativity, sensuality, and self-expression.

Venus and Aphrodite—Roman and Greek Goddess of Love, Sexuality, Desire, Victory, and Beauty

Writing this book has been the biggest blessing of my life. Devoting myself to the Goddess through this work is something I never take for granted, and sharing it with you, beloved, is the biggest gift of all. One of topics I am most excited to write about is the Goddesses I am pledged and devoted to—the Goddesses with whom I have personal experience, who shine through in my art, magick, and writing. This is especially true with Venus, the Roman Goddess of Love, Sexuality, Desire, Beauty, Glamour, and Victory.

Venus is my Matron Goddess, the Goddess I am in sacred service to, who stands as the anchor in my heart and practice with the Divine Feminine. I also am dedicated to Isis and Babalon, and consider Them Matron Goddesses, but first I was devoted to Venus, and She has a significant place in my life and practice. I pledged myself to Venus in December 2016, and my love for Her has only grown, deepened, and evolved since then. It is around the time I began working with Venus that I started to see the power in my sexuality and in my body. I built a shrine for Her in my room, and I began offering up my orgasms and exploring my erotic self with reverence. I began to see myself and my body as a living temple to Venus, and I began treating myself as such. This not only helped my self-esteem and confidence, but also helped me release comparison to and envy of others; my self-expression is special and sacred, and, quite frankly, it's between Venus and myself and no one else.

Over time, my exploration of kink and BDSM became part of my magickal practice as well. I started incorporating wax play (dripping body-safe candle wax on skin) and erotic rope bondage into my rituals. I found a sacred rhythm in impact play and incorporated conscious submission as a tool in my devotion. I saw Venus not only as a protector and guardian of my heart, but also as my muse. She became a patron of my sexual explorations, my sex magick, and my exploration of kink and submission.

Over the years, Venus has held me. She has helped me see myself as an embodiment of love and lust. She has whispered in my ear when things are falling apart, when my heart is broken, and when I feel lonely and sad. She has brought me back to myself by reminding me that the greatest magick you can offer yourself is becoming a vessel for love.

Venus is a Goddess of Love and an alchemical Goddess, who sees love as the ultimate act of magick. She is the Roman face of the Greek Aphrodite, who hails from the Mediterranean island of Cyprus, where She was likely revered as a local nature Goddess. The Cypriots worshipped a local priestess and queen known as Wanassa, which translated into the Middle Eastern Goddesses of Love: Sumerian Inanna, Mesopotamian Ishtar, and Semitic Astarte. This trinity presided over love and war, lust and rage, the sacred and the profane, and as They merged with the local Cyprus deity, They were adopted by the Greeks in the form of Aphrodite and later by the Romans as Venus. Aphrodite is a shape-shifter, transforming with those who worship Her, and through this merging of cultures, She found Her own special form.

In Greek mythos, Aphrodite is born from blood and cum, from the foam of the ocean, from violence and regeneration. The key players in this myth are Cronos, the God of Time, Boundaries, and Death—known as Saturn to the Romans—and his father, Uranus (Caelus), the God of Risk, Upheaval, and Transformation. When Cronos decides he is tired of coming in second to his father, he decides to castrate him. After ambushing him with the help of Uranus's wife, Gaia, Goddess of the Earth, Cronos does the deed using a sickle (one of Saturn's symbols) and then tosses his father's penis and the sickle into the ocean. From this cosmic orgasm, Aphrodite/Venus, the Goddess of Love and Sex, is born, and the world was never the same.

Aphrodite has been worshipped as Aphrodite Ourania, or heavenly Aphrodite, who presided over Divine Love, passion for ideas, and the soul. She is known as the "morning and evening star," reflecting Her association with the planet Venus. She also is venerated as Aphrodite Pandemos, or Aphrodite of the people, the Goddess of Nature who unites humanity through sexual love and the body. Aphrodite also was called Ephistrophia, the deceiver; Melanis, She of the dark night; and Androphonos, the killer of men, showing Her darker aspects and the potential of love to destroy. The Roman Venus likewise was considered a Goddess of War and Victory—the shadow aspect of this face of the Divine Feminine.

Venus, meanwhile, was Venus Genetrix, or Venus the mother; Venus Obsequens, or obedient Venus; Venus Veticordia, or Venus the changer of hearts; and Venus Victrix, or Venus of victory. Like Aphrodite, Venus is known as the morning star and evening star—the first to rise, the brightest in the morning, and the brightest star in the evening. (If you want to excavate further, look into Her Hermetic Qabalistic association with victory and the sphere of Netzach.) The many names of these Goddesses can spotlight Their traits and the hidden facets of what They rule over, and They can be used in devotion, ritual, and prayer to call upon certain qualities.

In the modern zeitgeist, Aphrodite/Venus is known for Her affiliation with love and desire, but She definitely has a bite. This is a Goddess who is a patron of sex workers and rough sex, war, and victory, and She loves to be draped in gold and fine garments. She can teach us how to think with the heart, and how, in excess, this can cause chaos—like when Aphrodite is caught sleeping with the God of War Ares (Mars) by Her then-husband, the God of Smithcraft, Hephaistos, who traps them in a golden net while they are having sex.

Aphrodite/Venus is a Goddess of Love who is transformative. She loves effortlessly, fluidly, completely, and not just in one way. To know Her is to know not only love but also lust. Aphrodite/Venus is not a virgin Goddess in the typical sense; even though She has many lovers, She remains independent, which resonates with the maiden's way. She is a Goddess of Beauty, Desire, and Adornment, and—before She became the Goddess we are familiar with, nude in all Her glory— She was typically seen wearing sensual fabrics and luxurious regalia. She reminds us of the alchemical qualities of glamour, surrender, love, pleasure, and desire; of allowing the sexual and erotic instinct to guide you toward ecstasy and initiation into the mysteries (or the cult and secret teachings of the Goddess).

To connect to Venus and Aphrodite: To connect with Venus and Aphrodite, turn yourself and your life into a living altar to and ritual of love. Dedicate an altar to Her, your heart, self-lust, and self-love. Take salt baths with rose petals, and place red roses on Her altar.

Allow roses to be your muse; ask them what they want to teach you. Have sex, make self-love, go on a date to an art museum, or take yourself on a date to honor the Venusian within. Adorn yourself in copper (Venus and Aphrodite's metal) or gold (She loves bling), and wear red lipstick and something that makes you feel beautiful. Write a love letter to yourself that you read out loud on Friday, Venus's day. Go to the ocean, breathe through its ebbs and flows, and call out to the Goddess and ask Her to bless your heart and life with love. Check your birth chart for what houses Taurus and Libra are in, as well as planets, nodes, or asteroids here and what's aspecting this, if at all. Allow this to help you form a map for exploring Venusian energies in your life.

Mary Magdalene—Christian and Gnostic Goddess of Divine Union and Love

Although the Virgin Mary exists as the mother of Christ himself, it's through Mary Magdalene that you can view the face of the Goddess not as separate from the teachings of Jesus and his disciples, but as central to them—and as a channel for the very message of Jesus himself.

In the gnostic texts, specifically the Nag Hammadi library, which are early Christian and gnostic writings discovered outside the Egyptian town of Nag Hammadi in 1945, the veil is lifted from Jesus's actual teachings. These texts contain books like the Gospel of Mary and the Gospel of Philip, which were removed from the Christian canon by the Roman Catholic Church. These texts reveal the truth of who Mary Magdalene is: the most loved of all of Jesus's apostles, his wife, and perhaps even the mother of his child.

A Goddess of Love and Wisdom, Mary Magdalene is a facet of the Divine that emphasizes "inner preparation, introspection, and inner transformation." She was called the "apostle of apostles"; She discovered Jesus's empty tomb after his death, was told by an angel that Jesus's tomb was empty because he was resurrected, and was given the responsibility of sharing his teachings.

The way through the "world of corruption" around us isn't by denial of the flesh, but *through* the flesh. Mary's MO is gnosis, or *personal and direct experience with the Divine.* Unlike the later Church, Magdalene (how I will refer to Mary Magdalene in this chapter to avoid confusion with the Virgin Mary) wasn't preaching that Jesus and his message could be understood only through outside teachers, but that the kingdom of heaven was within the self. She teaches the power of love, devotion, and inner knowing to lead the way to immanence and to finding enlightenment in the present, in the body, and in the flesh. Magdalene exemplifies the Feminine Divine in gnostic teachings, also known as Sophia or wisdom.

Magdalene is also a symbol of the union of the Divine Feminine and Divine Masculine, the chalice that receives the blade, as exemplified when Jesus says, "When you make the two into one, and when you make the inner as the outer, and the upper as the lower, and when you make male and female into a single one, so that the male shall not be male, and the female shall not be female: . . . then you will enter [the kingdom]." This reflects the saying of the Emerald Tablet of Hermes Trismegistus: "That which is above is like to that which is below, and that which is below is like to that which is above."

Magdalene is a Goddess of Illumination, of the Heart, of the Alchemy of Embodied Understanding. Magdalene also pulls through the ancient story of the sacred marriage of the Goddesses of Love before Her. She is intricately connected to the sea (or *mare* in Latin), the Moon, and caves. Her symbol is the chalice, linking Her to the waters and womb of the Feminine Divine and the lunar cycles.

After Jesus's death, Magdalene went to France with their daughter,

Sara, where She is said to have converted pagan sites of worship to Christian ones. It's said that Magdalene grew so horny for Her deceased beloved that She moved to a cave, where She lived and fasted for thirty years, Her only sustenance from the angels who brought Her nourishment from the heavens. The cave is an ancient, ancient symbol for the life-giving potential of the Goddess, the womb of the earth, where sages and mystics have been meditating and praying for centuries. For Magdalene to honor the Divine Masculine in a place so hallowed for the Divine Feminine is another example of the alchemy that She and Jesus speak of in the gnostic texts.

To connect with Mary Magdalene: If you want to understand the story of Magdalene and be led through an alchemical initiation of Divine Love, start with *The Magdalen Manuscript* by Judi Sion and Tom Kenyon. Her correspondences include the month of May, doves, and rose medicine. Spend time in prayer and ritual sauntering through the rose, visualizing yourself moving through a labyrinth of petals until you reach the secret doorway of your heart. Pray to Magdalene with a rosary, write a mantra that invites Her into your heart, ask for Her presence and Divine Love, or state that you have received it. Allow the mysteries of love to inspire your rituals, and read the Gospel of Mary Magdalene. Put a photo or icon of Her on your altar, and spend time with Her presence. Ask Her what it is She can teach you, and dedicate the time to unraveling this.

Xochiquetzal—Aztec Goddess of Love, Sex, Art, and Magick

Often depicted covered in roses and decadent fabrics, Xochiquetzal oversees love, sexuality, weaving, art, and magick in the Aztec pantheon. Like many Goddesses of Love, including Venus, Xochiquetzal reflects the dualities of the heart. She also embodies the archetype of the maiden (Ichpochtli) in Her connection to fertility and sexuality and in Her expression as the blossoming of nature. Like the Moon, Her love and magick lead you to transform, to grow, to become. Xochiquetzal is always evolving, too.

The Goddesses of Love teach us that everything comes down to a divine and sacred paradox, including the ability to both cause pain and heal it. The Aztec Gods were givers and curers of disease (in Xochiquetzal's case, specifically venereal diseases). Like other Goddesses of Love, She's also a Goddess of War and patron to sex workers.

Her name comes from the Nahuatl words *xochitul*, which means "flower," and *quetzalli*, which can refer either to the quetzal bird or its prized feather, and thus She is associated with both flowers and birds. Her spirit is said to have taken the form of a dove and flown down to Earth to give humanity the gift of speech—the weaving of words—while flowers were considered sacred and their fragrance thought to hold Divine energy.

Xochiquetzal reminds us of the polarity that exists through love, romantic and otherwise. She reminds us of the power of desire. Although She is not a Goddess to be worked with lightly, I think it's important to highlight the Goddesses who go against the easier-to-digest ideas of the love deities we may be more familiar with. For the Aztecs, flowers were associated with the vulva, and in this way, Xochiquetzal bridges the sacred and profane, inviting you to release your expectations of what the holy looks like so you may embody the love of the Goddess no matter what you do or who you are.

To connect with Xochiquetzal: Explore the Aztec pantheon and the traditions of the Mexica, who were the rulers of the Aztec empire. Take stock of what flowers are blooming in your life, your heart, your magick, and your practice. Then notice what sickness or pain is in your life. Spend time in ritual, journaling around and breathing into it all. Find radical acceptance for it. Ask yourself what cures you have at your disposal. Ask Xochiquetzal for Her help and love in resolving this. Leave flowers for Her at your altar, and create art in Her honor, especially weaving, fiber art, metal crafts, or anything else charged with your intention. Study the quetzal bird, and delve into the art that has been made in honor of Xochiquetzal. Allow room for all experiences in love in honor of this Goddess.

Frigg and Freya—Norse Goddesses of Marital and Sexual Love

The Norse pantheon represents many polarities on the same divine spectrum. Frigg and Freya are two Goddesses of Love who testify to the variety of expressions of love and devotion that are already available to you and how to invite them into your life.

Frigg, who is part of the Aesir, or primary Norse pantheon, rules the spheres of devoted love; of marriage; and of the family, home, commitment, and relationships. She is wife to Odin, the Allfather and principal deity. She embodies what it means to be a multifaceted mother—loving, supportive, and mighty. There is power in leading alongside a loved one; She is the only deity other than Odin permitted to sit in his throne. She speaks of the revolutionary ability of the dedicated feminine and lights up the world of those She loves with her unfailing ability to show up.

Frigg also is associated with weaving, both literal and metaphorical, and can be petitioned to help deal with the intricacies of modern life, like having a happy marriage and raising a family. As a patron of marriage, and a Goddess concerned with the order of contracts, Frigg also can be called upon during rites of passage, such as getting hitched, having children, or getting a divorce, and to aid new or expecting mothers adjust to life with a baby. Look for Her when making sacred commitments that alter your destiny and in times of transition and rebirth.

Anything that is done with love and devotion—whether to yourself or others—is Frigg's domain. See the commitments you've made to friends and loved ones who you're not related to as expressions and offerings, because Her brand of committed love extends to chosen family, too. Cook in Her honor, if you choose to infuse love, support, health, and joy into the food as you make it, or simply hold your hands over a meal and charge it with Her love, as both an offering and a gift of nourishment. This is a potent spell and devotional act when shared with family or loved ones.

At the other end of the spectrum is Freya, the wild and lustful embodiment of the Goddess of Love. She is one of the main Goddesses in the Vanir pantheon, and She is married to the God Odur, which may be the old Norse name for Odin. Whereas Frigg is the Goddess of Maternal and Familial Love, Freya rules sexual love and lust and the thrilling abandon of the erotic. Like many Goddesses of Love, Freya is also a Goddess of War, proving that love is a force that can move worlds. She sees the future with a form of prophetic magick called seidr and is able to weave new futures into existence.

Freya reminds us that enjoying beauty, enjoying life, and enjoying delectable possessions isn't a bad thing. Like anything else, it's the balance that's important. Both overindulging and fetishizing asceticism are equally unhealthy. In one story, the Goddess is taking a walk when She sees dwarves making a necklace called the Brisingamen. She convinces them to sell it to Her, but only after She spends one night with each of them in return. These four dwarves were associated with the elements and cardinal directions, and Freya learned about elemental power this way. But after the trickster God Loki exposed the Goddess's indiscretions to Odur, Freya's punishment is to wear this necklace always and forever search for Odur, who had left Her.

There are discrepancies about whether Freya and Frigg are the same Goddess. This is up to you, dear reader, to decide. I treasure how the lesson teaches us that familial and sexual love are complementary—even if you're a woman, a mother, or have a devoted partner and family. The intensity of love and lust, working in tandem and given equal respect, shouldn't be overlooked.

Frigg and Freya remind us that love is all-encompassing, and it's a dynamic and nuanced force. To experience love in its totality, you most likely will need to seek out the sort of devotion that Frigg rules over *and* the carnal lust that Freya sings of. When you're working with either, think of them as separate poles of the same energy, compromising the whole of Divine Love.

How to work with Frigg: Think of all you are devoted to. Think of all those in your life who you love, care for, feed, and nurture. Cook in honor of this Goddess, sending healing into the ingredients and preparation. Leave food for Her on your altar and then feed yourself and family and friends the same meal. Pray to this Goddess, and leave offerings on your altar, especially if you are calling in a partnership, commitment, and/or a family or want to strengthen one of these bonds. This Goddess can shed light on your destiny as it involves committed relationships. If you are becoming a parent, or already are one, you may honor Her as a guide and force in this expression of yourself, perhaps blessing a talisman for yourself or your children and spending time in meditation and prayer with Her.

How to work with Freya: Think about what lust, sex, and the erotic mean to you. Explore this through journaling, divination, meditation, and visualization. Create an altar to this Goddess, or make space for Her in your shrine, and spend time here. Cleanse and consecrate a necklace by anointing it with water or sacred oil and running it through sacred smoke, or anointing it with sexual secretions if you wish to practice sex magick to charge it. Meditate on it, and send energy into the jewelry, dedicating it to Freya and asking for Her love and protection. Leave it on your altar overnight with offerings for the Goddess such as honey, wine, or mead. Allow this to be a bridge to Her.

Dedicate a Friday to both Freya and Frigg—Their sacred day, which is named after Them. Spend time in prayer and ritual, in devotion to love of all forms, to integrate Them more thoroughly into your life.

Hathor—Egyptian Goddess of Love and Fertility

Love connects us all, and all you have to do to remind yourself of this is to peer into the past and observe the ways people worshipped the Goddess. The Egyptian Hathor has been worshipped for more than six thousand years, and She is the most frequently seen deity in temples near the Nile. This cow-headed Goddess of Love is depicted wearing bull horns with a solar disk in the center. Remember, cows are an ancient symbol of the Goddess, partly because they are so loving and loyal, and also because of the nourishment they provide. As a Goddess of the Sky, Heavens, and Cosmos, Hathor birthed the world: the Milky Way is Her body, made of Her cosmic milk, and each star is a soul on its way to reincarnate or return to Her in the afterlife.

As a Goddess of Music, She is also a creatrix of harmony and beauty. Dancing and music were two forms of worship the ancients offered to Hathor. The way to embodiment and union with Her is through feeling and experience.

Sometimes referred to as the Golden One, Hathor can be considered the solar aspect to the lunar Isis, who was also often shown wearing a solar disk and horns and was at times referred to as Hathor's daughter. As with Freya, there is a transcendently sexual side to this Goddess. She is fertile with the possibility of life, and through Her relationship with the solar God Horus—specifically in the temple of Edfu—She embodies the role of Divine wife and consort. I consider it particularly special that Hathor is a sexually independent Goddess, even as a wife and even as a mother to all.

As a Goddess associated with the dead, Hathor became central to the Egyptian writings known as the coffin texts (written between 2181 and 2040 BCE), which teach the common people how to reach eternal life—magick and wisdom previously reserved for Pharaohs. Hathor's love is both sexual and divine, cosmic and earthly, of the heavens and underworld, like the sycamore tree, one of Her correspondences, whose branches are in the realm of the living and whose roots extend into the dead. Again: dualities. Hathor illuminates the wonders of love to ignite a sense of closeness and appreciation for all you have. May She guide you into the mysteries of beauty, harmony, and love, nourishing you with the sweet milk of Her affection so you may dance with all life has to offer.

To connect with Hathor: Honor what nourishes and sustains you. Make a list of what replenishes you, and update it often. Allow sexual energy and exploration of sensual love to be a part of this, however you are comfortable. Beauty, ritual, music, and love are your guides and inspiration. Leave an offering of milk on your altar, and pray to the Goddess for sustenance for your mind, body, and soul. Sing songs of love, and look up photos of Her temple complex in Dendera. See if you can hang out with a cow on a nearby farm, or attune to their vibration by watching videos of them. Another way to honor Hathor is by giving up beef or dairy, either for a set amount of time or permanently.

)) ● ● ● ((

CRAFTING PRAYERS
TO THE GODDESS OF LOVE

Prayer is an integral part of the human experience. To be human is to know love and heartache, to know ecstasy and pain, and prayer naturally follows many of these intense moments. So it makes sense to craft your own prayers to the Goddess around love, or to the Goddess of Love.

Prayer is a conversation. It can be as fancy or as simple as you make it. Sometimes, reading someone else's words is easier, especially if they capture the essence of your devotion in a way you may not be able to. But there is something special about fashioning your own words of power, of forming your own words of adoration and praise to the Goddess. Sometimes you want something formal, sometimes you want something simple, and sometimes you need something spontaneous and earnest. All are powerful. All are special. All are sacred. But one of the features of writing your own prayer is exactly that—*it's yours.* You get to say exactly what you want, how you want it, forged by your own heart and magick.

This outline for writing a prayer can be worked with for any Goddess, or in devotion to the Great Goddess. Adopt the framework for a prayer to a Goddess of the Earth, a Goddess of Protection and Healing, a Dark Goddess, or, of course, a Goddess of Love.

Step 1: Research, read, daydream, and journal

Let this be a joyous process, one in which you get to spend time reading prayers written to whomever you're dedicating yours to. This is when you consider the energy of the prayer you're writing.

If you are working with Greek or Roman Goddesses of Love, read a translation of the Homeric or Orphic Hymns. The Homeric Hymns were written by different authors in dactylic hexameter—like the *Iliad* and *Odyssey*—most likely in the seventh century BCE. The Orphic Hymns are a collection inspired by the (perhaps) mythological hero Orpheus and the mystery religions in the third century BCE. Both books speak of trials and tribulations of the Gods and Goddesses and include epithets and mythos that may motivate you.

Look up pagan authors' interpretations of prayers, such as *A Book of Pagan Prayer* by Ceisiwr Serith; books such as the *Book of Coming Forth by Day*, better known as the *Egyptian Book of the Dead*; and stories and myths related to the Goddess to gain a clearer understanding of who She is. Take note of prayers you like—how they make you feel, how they inspire you, how they marry you to the Divine. You can emulate this in your own prayer.

While writing your own prayer, contemplate the following:

+ What are this Goddess's attributes? What is She pictured with? What are Her strengths? Her weaknesses?
+ What does She rule?
+ What are Her correspondences? Colors? Sacred associations like trees and flowers? What other Gods or Goddesses are in Her story, and how does this enrich Her mythos?
+ What does She look like? What physical attributes, if any, are mentioned? How does this correlate with your own vision of Her?
+ What is Her energy like? What does She feel like when you read Her hymns, meditate with Her, or look at art of Her?

- What aspect of your own psyche, heart, soul, and shadow resonate with this Goddess?
- What does She tell you of love? Of devotion? Of desire?
- What kind of love does She speak of? Is it familial, like Frigg? Or is it sexual, like Aphrodite/Venus?
- What does this Goddess inspire in your heart? What does She make you feel? How does She sound? What tastes and scents remind you of Her?

Step 2: Write it out

When you've gotten clarity on how the Goddess speaks to you and what She rules over, compose your prayer. Remember that this can be a work in progress; after saying your prayer, you may feel that it needs to be tinkered with.

- Open by saying the name of the Goddess.
- Share Her attributes, that with which She is identified.
- Let Her know what you love and admire about Her, what you are in awe of.
- Remind Her of your devotion, of your curiosity, or of your hope to cultivate a relationship with Her.
- Ask Her what you need from Her, what you want to call forth into yourself.
- Let Her know how you will embody this and share it with the world.
- Close with gratitude and love.

Here is an example of a prayer I wrote as part of my devotion to Venus. In it, I share my love for Her, what I hope to learn through Her, and how I plan on sharing this with the world. I haven't shared this before, but Venus always appreciates more public adoration. Feel free to use this in your own prayer to Venus, or to adapt and write it in your own way.

A PRAYER TO VENUS

Venus
Goddess of love and desire, of beauty and pleasure
I bow to You with a humble heart
So You may fill my chalice with Your Divine nectar
I come to You, golden Goddess, with adoration and praise
With gratitude for the sensual magick You infuse into the world
    and my life
O Venus
Goddess of the sea, born from ecstasy
I pray to know Your pleasure
I pray to feel Your eros coursing through my veins
Your conch shell singing my praises in Your ear
And Your doves carrying my love for You to the heavens
May I be a channel for your Divine lust
May my body be fertile with Your desires
May I be infatuated with life in Your honor
And may Your alchemical love guide me through life
So I may be a vessel for You and Your love and erotic essence in
    all I do
And so it is

CONNECTING TO
YOUR INNER LOVE GODDESS
WITH SEX MAGICK

The frequency of the Goddess is one of pure transformation, and pleasure places you in this same vibration. Anything in excess can be dangerous, whether it's alcohol, drugs, chocolate, working out, or meditation. The same is true of pleasure; too much and there comes a dissatisfaction with anything less than pleasure fueled. But as the Goddess teaches us, the cyclical nature of this existence is rooted in birth *and* death. To each beginning there's an ending, and to live in only one part of the spectrum of all human emotions means missing the magnificent depths that this incarnation makes available.

Just because you want to experience pleasure doesn't mean you'll suddenly stop experiencing pain. The universe, like you, contains an infinite number of contradictions and multitudes. *Intentionally tapping into pleasure is life changing because it reminds you of what's possible when you revere your desires, your heart, and yourself.* To know pleasure is to crave pleasure, but it also can mean shedding new light on your preconceptions, on what you've been told is right or wrong. Whether this is coming to the realization that you're gay while in a heterosexual marriage, taking a hit of cannabis for the first time and liking it, or practicing sex magick and recognizing that you deserve pleasure is irrelevant. Pleasure is a gift, and it's one the Goddess shares with you.

Cultivating love and pleasure in honor of something larger than yourself, in this case through sex magick, is both subversive (because this is usually practiced through masturbation, which our culture considers taboo) and Divine. Sexual ecstasy, lust, and love aren't seen as holy sacraments in the religious institutions you probably grew up with, but through the lens of the Goddess, they are sacred offerings. In Her religion, love and pleasure are rituals of great importance.

A note: You do not have to practice sex magick if you don't want to. If you're ace (or asexual), have a low libido, or are just not into it, skip this section and I will see you in just a bit! I would like you to keep in mind, however, that sometimes the things that are your biggest "no"s, or that produce a strong and negative reaction, are the things that you are meant to explore. Those forceful reactions mean something, and if you feel safe digging into this, you may find some of the most boundary-breaking magick and pleasure on the other side. Even if you don't think you'll like sex magick, or feel immediately shut down to the mere suggestion, you can honor that reaction while staying open. Allow it to simmer. Don't rush it. Your "no" might never change . . . but it might. When the time is right, you will know. You can always come back to this section when you're ready.

SEX MAGICK 101

Sex magick is working with sexual energy and orgasms as a way to fuel your spells and rituals, and using them to charge and manifest a desired outcome. However, although orgasms are undeniably powerful, you don't need to orgasm—or even need to be able to—to practice sex magick. It's more critical that you raise energy than fixate on orgasming and lose the connection to your sexuality, your body, and your intention.

Sex magick isn't one set of practices but a technique that can be combined with myriad other forms of magick. For example, if you are doing a candle spell to attract a community of like-hearted witches, you might anoint your candle, light it, and practice sex magick to raise energy and charge the working. Or if you are invoking the Goddess of Love, you could call Her into you and then masturbate as a way to experience this through the Goddess and to let Her experience pleasure in the flesh. You could produce an amulet for banishing negative influences in your work and charge it through masturbation, or practice sex magick with your partner to manifest the home of your dreams. In this way, masturbation or conscious sex can be its own ritual or part of another ritual. Sex magick is also a way to get in touch with your sexuality, to experience Goddess energy more profoundly, and to understand how your eroticism relates to the Goddess of Love.

Sex magick can be performed solo or partnered, but I encourage you to practice solo when you're just starting out. Not only will this get you in touch with the sensations and energies within, but it also will assist you in engaging, directing, and controlling this energy, without the distraction of a partner. Solo work also can awaken you to your own sexuality in a profound, empowering, and clarifying way. If you do want to work with a partner, I encourage you to bring in only someone you completely trust and love; someone who cares for you. When you practice sex magick, you are merging energetic bodies—literally sharing sacred space in the most intimate way possible. This fosters a connection, and things can get, ahem, sticky if there isn't a sense of mutual trust, care, and respect. Remember, there's no rush. You even can use solo sex magick to attract a partner, so it isn't worth it to settle. There's nothing wrong with working on your own for as long as you need to be comfortable.

Let's start with the basics. Keep in mind that these steps aren't the only way to practice; you may find different techniques that feel better for your purposes. Play around and figure out what works for you. Record your efforts in your Goddess Grimoire so you can track how things like pleasure and orgasm change and transform with practice. (If you find yourself wanting even more sex magick, check out my book *Sacred Sex* for a deeper dive.)

1. *Set up your space.* You want to feel yourself all around. Set your shrine; place toys, lube, or a vibrator nearby; and be sure you feel as comfortable in your skin as possible. Put on something that makes you feel sexy as fuck, like red lipstick and lingerie or silk boxers and leather. Put on a hip-swaying playlist (just be sure it's not too distracting) or solfeggio frequencies—whatever sets your mood. Follow the steps on page 12 for setting up your space. Drink an aphrodisiac tea like rose, blue lotus, damiana, or ginger, and light candles or sandalwood, jasmine, or cinnamon incense. Get the vibe right! You also may wish to include massage oils; kinky sex toys like a feather, a paddle, or rope; or a rose to caress your skin with. Perhaps you want to incorporate foods like chocolate or fruit as well. Allow sensual pleasure and decadence to guide you.

2. *Get clear on your intention.* The space is set, but what are you practicing sex magick *for*? Are you trying to summon a partner who

will love you the way you deserve? Are you trying to banish sickness from a loved one? Are you simply trying to get in touch with the love and sex Goddess within you? Use these questions to guide you and then ground and center (page 12).

3. *Call the Goddess and raise the energy.* You may wish to call in a Goddess of Love like Aphrodite, Venus, Frigg, Freya, Hathor, or Xochiquetzal. Pray, or tell Her that you are practicing sex magick in Her honor. Tell Her your intention. Tell Her the why. In other words, *tell Her what's on your heart.* Take a moment to receive any of Her teachings, be present, and breathe. You may also read the prayer you wrote for the Goddess of Love at this time. When you're ready, begin to raise energy in one of these ways:

+ Focus on your intention as you masturbate or have sex and raise energy.
+ Focus on your intention only at the peak of the energy raising and afterward.

In my practice, I choose to be present to the pleasure and energy I'm raising and then focus on my intention as I orgasm. I find that this helps me experience the sensations and energies with more ease because focusing on my intention during the entire process often can get me too in my head, out of the moment, and out of my body. My suggestion is to try both at different times and see which works better for you. If you keep your intention in mind, the aim is to do. so the entire ritual. Otherwise, focus on your intention only when you feel your energy peak. In both cases, feel into your intention, visualizing it as reality, through the afterglow. Take notes in your Goddess Grimoire, and know there's no wrong answer.

Begin by masturbating and practicing self-love in this way. Revel in the pleasure, in your skin, in your touch. Make it sensual, and remember the divinity inherent within every cell of your body. When you feel the energy peaking, meaning you're going to orgasm or get as close as you can, focus on your intention (if you haven't already) and reach out to the Goddess as you feel it emerging from you into the cosmos. Visualize the sexual energy moving from your genitals, up your spine in a beam of light, through the crown of your head, and into the universe, and see the Goddess receiving it. Or simply focus on your intention and feel the energy charging and fueling your desires, spreading through your body like wildfire before it bursts through the crown of your head, into the cosmos. Hang out in the afterglow, visualizing what it feels like to have your intention realized, feeling held by the Goddess in Her Divine ecstasy. This is when you manifest, holding space for your intention as if it's already happened. Stay here for as long as you need.

4. *Close the ritual, record, and leave an offering.* If you invited in a Goddess, thank Her and let Her know the ritual is closed. Tell Her that it was in honor of Her and that you are thankful for Her support—something like, *"This working is complete, thank You so much for guiding me and supporting me Goddess, blessed be."* Close and ground (page 13), and record your experience in your Goddess Grimoire.

Leave the Goddess an offering of food or drink, sharing and indulging in it with Her. And so it is!

AN APHRODITE/VENUS GLAMOUR SPELL
TO ATTRACT LOVE, LUST, AND DESIRE

Like Her foremother Inanna/Ishtar, Aphrodite/Venus is said to have an enchanted girdle that bestows Her with the affection, attention, and lust of others. This girdle, in other words, was cast with a *glamour*, affecting those who are in Her space with feelings of desire and adoration. A glamour is something like makeup, lingerie, or perfume that veils what lies beneath it, and it can be used with intention to shape the way in which you move through the world. Casting a glamour on a piece of clothing can alter the way you're seen, or at the very least, the way you *feel*, which is enough to transform how you act and are perceived.

This spell is written with a garter in mind, to keep with the mythos of this Goddess of Love, but *you can use any item of clothing or lingerie you wish*: a leather jacket, a T-shirt, a nightie, a teddy, a bra, or a pair of underwear. You even can bless an entire outfit, repeating the blessing over each piece of clothing, or a piece of jewelry, especially if it's copper or gold (both associated with this Goddess).

This spell invokes Aphrodite/Venus to bless your piece of clothing or jewelry with Her attraction, alchemical love, and lust so you feel like the Goddess you are whenever you put it on.

Cast this spell on a Friday—Her day—or at the Venus planetary hour (each hour of the day is ruled by a classical planet; use an app like Time Nomad to help), especially during a new, waxing, or full Moon.

Before you begin, get clear on your intention. What kind of love and desire do you want to attract? Do you want a romantic relationship? Sex? Lust? True love? Do you want to feel beautiful, adored, and cared for? Do you want deep, loving friendships? Spend time journaling around this and deciding on your intention, and write it out in detail so you can read it to the Goddess. Write it in present or past tense.

You will need: Your garter or chosen piece of clothing/jewelry/lingerie; a red or pink candle and a holder; honey; a glove or paper towel or something to wipe your hands with; a lighter or matches; a cup or chalice of water; incense or sacred smoke from myrrh, sandalwood, roses, ethically sourced palo santo, lavender, or mugwort; and a coal to light (and container) if you are using resin.

Optional: Crystals like rose quartz, peach moonstone, pink calcite, carnelian, or clear quartz and sex toys or lube.

Step 1: Get in the mood

Set up your altar, shrine, and yourself. Aphrodite/Venus is a Goddess of Glamour, Decadence, Pleasure, and Beauty. If there's a time to put on your favorite red lipstick, some perfume, and enticing lingerie, it's now. Adorn your space with fresh roses, decorative candles, colored lights, and sensual textures. I also highly recommend pregaming with a salt bath, especially with red rose petals or candles, or an aphrodisiac tea. You may dance, move your body, stretch, play music, or do whatever else you need to so you can dwell in your heart. Play a sexy playlist, send a flirty or sexy text, or eye-gaze in the mirror. This ritual can begin far before the actual spell does. Then set up your space following the directions on page 12.

Step 2: Ground and center

When you feel ready, ground and center (page 12).

Step 3: Invoke or pray to Aphrodite and/or Venus

Use the following invocation that I wrote and use in my own practice, or call on the Goddess through the Orphic or Homeric Hymns, adding "*I invoke Thee, Aphrodite/Venus*." If you don't feel comfortable invoking the Goddess, pray to Her, using the prayer earlier in this chapter or one of the hymns, asking Her for her blessing in this glamour and spell. Follow the steps on page 233 for invocation if you need more guidance.

Invocation to Aphrodite/Venus

The alchemical Goddess
She who glows pearlescent
Who's immortalized in song and exalted in love
Shining Aphrodite, the most sacred of the sea
Born by sea foam to bless the flesh,
To bless the heart and lips and breast
I invoke Thee
Golden Goddess
Venus
A delicious shadow of heart-centered expansion
Teach me to go deeply through all love has to offer
Venus, guardian of the sexual mysteries
Come to me in the morning dew
In red roses, amber honey, and skies perfectly blue
I transform pain to love through You
Lead me through the path of eros
That of lust and an offering of devotion evolving
Guide me in falling in love with myself
O Aphrodite/Venus
She of the subversive mysteries
I am devoted to my heart and humbled by Thy power
And welcome You into my flesh so I may know Your expansive
*   presence*
I invoke Thee
I invoke Thee
I invoke Thee
O Aphrodite/Venus
So mote it be

Now close your eyes. Experience whatever comes up, but try not to analyze it. Let the sensations, messages, sounds, tastes, and feelings expand. Visualize yourself dissolving into space, and reemerging as Aphrodite/Venus. You may be called to move, dance, laugh, or smile; allow the Goddess to move through you in whatever way She asks to. Remember, you *are* Aphrodite/Venus. You are the Goddess of Love and Desire, of Beauty and Pleasure. This is a cosmic gift.

Step 4: Anoint and light, cleanse and consecrate

Before you anoint the candle, taste a little bit of the honey, savoring its sweetness and letting the Goddess know that this honey is safe, that it's an offering. Then rub the honey all over the candle, from each end in, to draw in your intention, and place it in its holder. Light it.

Hold your palm over the chalice as you send it Goddess energy, infusing it with the essence of love and lust. Dip your fingers in the water, and sprinkle it over the garter, jewelry, or lingerie you are charging. As you do so, say the following or write your own declaration:

> *I cleanse this* [state the name of the piece of lingerie/jewelry/clothing] *in the name of Aphrodite/Venus. In the name of love and desire, of beauty and pleasure, I cleanse this of any energy that doesn't work in my heart's highest favor, of anything stopping me from embodying the vibration of love. So I may be as a Goddess of Love.*

Light your herbs of choice using the candle. After the flame builds a little bit, blow it out so it's smoking. Pass your garter, jewelry, or lingerie through this smoke, and say the following or write your own declaration:

I consecrate this [state the name of the piece of lingerie/jewelry/ clothing] *in the name of Aphrodite/Venus. In the name of love and desire, of beauty and pleasure, I consecrate this in the name of the Goddess of Love, in honor of my heart's highest favor, to attract all the love, lust, beauty, and pleasure I desire.*

Step 5: Infuse and cast the glamour

Now that your item has been cleansed and consecrated in the name of the Goddess of Love, it's time to cast your glamour. Pass your item above the flame, feeling Venus and Aphrodite imbuing it with the fire of Their power. Set it down, and hold both palms over it. *Be sure you have your statement of intention nearby.* Say the following, or write your own declaration:

In the name of Aphrodite/Venus, I cast this glamour of love upon this [name your item of clothing/lingerie/jewelry]. *Just as the Goddess of Love has Her own enchanted garter, so I have my own. I declare that this piece brings me everything I desire, that it* [read your intention out loud], *and that it helps me open my heart to the vast possibilities of love this universe has to offer. This or something better for the highest good of all involved, the glamour is cast, and the spell is done. So mote it be!*

Step 6: Sex magick

Wear the item of clothing, lingerie, or jewelry as you practice sex magick. Feel the love and pride of Aphrodite and Venus coursing through you. Your item is being infused with your intention and energy. Know that your desire is taken care of. This experience of pleasure and energy raising is a devotional act of commitment to the Goddess and an affirming of your path, your magick, and your heart. As you orgasm or near climax, pass this energy up your spine, down your arms, and through your palms into the item. In the afterglow, hover your palms over your item and continue sending energy as you visualize what it will feel like to have this intention manifested and met. Stay here as long as you like.

Step 7: Thank and dismiss the Goddess
Dismiss the Goddess by letting Her know the ritual is closed. Do this in your own words, or you may use the following:

> *Goddess of Love*
> *Aphrodite/Venus*
> *I have felt You coursing through me, Your Divine heart expanding*
> *   my own*
> *I thank You for trusting me with Your alchemical truth and erotic*
> *   glow*
> *I thank You for blessing this ritual of glamour and love*
> *In honor of my sacred heart and Divine lust*
> *This working is done, this ritual is complete, and You are free to*
> *   leave*
> *I dismiss Thee*
> *I dismiss Thee*
> *I dismiss Thee*
> *O Aphrodite/Venus*
> *I thank You with a humble heart, Goddess of Love*
> *So it is, and so mote it be*

Step 8: Close and ground
Visualize yourself as Aphrodite/Venus once again, and then allow this to dissolve into nothingness, and from this visualize yourself reforming.

Use the instructions on page 13 to close and ground.

Let your candle burn all the way down, placing it in your sink if you need to leave it safely. If you have excess wax from the candle, dispose of it in a garbage can at a three- or four-way intersection. Place your item on your altar with crystals on top of or near it, and let it charge overnight. Wear it whenever you need a boost, or wear it regularly to get in touch with Aphrodite/Venus and your heart. You also may leave an offering on your altar for the Goddess, whether that's honey, chocolate, red wine, roses, art, poetry, or whatever else feels right.

JOURNAL QUESTIONS

Love is the ultimate muse, but to know love within yourself is ever-evolving work. One way to honor this is to spend time untangling the messaging around love, sex, and desire you've been fed and to instead come to your own conclusions. Love is an intense experience no matter what, and it can be helpful to let off steam and process what you're feeling in a space that's completely your own, free from interfering eyes. That's where journaling comes in.

As always, these prompts are a jumping-off point. Follow the directions on page 34 to make the most of this experience.

- How do I define love? What does this mean to me? How has this shifted since I began to work with the Goddess of Love?
- How can I actively expand my definition of love?
- What do I feel in my body when I think of the Goddess of Love? What does She mean to me?

+ How do I relate to love, pleasure, and desire? How can I invite more of all three into my life?

+ How can I see love, pleasure, desire, and beauty as sacred offerings to the Goddess and to my heart?

+ How can I honor sexuality and eros as a path to my Divine essence? How can I walk this as a spiritual path? As an act of devotion?

+ With which Goddess of Love do I most connect and identify? How can I work with love to be of service to Her? How can I work with love to know Her more intimately?

+ How can beauty bring me more deeply to love? How can pleasure?

+ What have I learned about myself from love? From heartache? What has my resilience taught me?

+ How can I incorporate sex magick and love magick into my devotional practice with the Goddess?

AFFIRMATIONS

So many of us resist receiving or sharing the love we desire. We are told that love is shallow, or useless, or only in fairy tales. But as the Goddess of Love teaches, this couldn't be further from the truth. When you are feeling down, or lonely, or simply like you want to re-member your Goddess-given right to *love*, work with these affirmations. As they vibrate through you, claim your power and breathe love into the world you're creating.

Use the steps on page 38 to melt into the unfolding of your heart and into the ever-evolving essence of love.

- I receive the deep love I desire with ease.
- My heart is a portal to the mysteries of the cosmos.
- I receive all the love meant for me with ease.
- I am a Goddess of Love. I am a Goddess of Lust.
- I am Divine Love.
- I embrace the fluidity and tenderness of an open heart.
- I embrace the yearning of my heart and honor its needs.
- I honor the Goddess of Love by honoring the love within myself.
- I surrender to the awe-inspiring, numinous, and overwhelming power of love.
- Love is a gift with an unyielding supply, and I share it with ease and gratitude.
- The Goddess of Love guides me deeper into the mystic transformation of the heart.

A TAROT SPREAD FOR INVOKING YOUR INNER LOVE GODDESS

Sometimes you just need a little guidance to remember how to tap into your loving, sensual, and erotic power. Sometimes you just need some validation that you not only honor the Goddess of Love and Lust, but *are* a Goddess of Love and Lust. Use the following tarot spread to tap into your heart and to hear the Goddess calling whenever you need Her.

Use the steps on page 42 to prepare yourself. You may call upon the Goddess of Love or a specific Goddess of Love as a muse. Don't forget that your heart is your north star.

Card 1: How can I connect to the Goddess of Love in this
    moment?

Card 2: What does She want me to know?

Card 3: How can I embody and invoke Her power?

Card 4: How can I begin doing this through magick and ritual?

Card 5: How can I continue opening my heart to love and the
    Goddess?

5

The Dark Goddess

The Dark Goddess is known through sex and subversion, through fear and anger, through rage and death, and through places abandoned in nature. She is less of a kiss or hug and more of a feral howl, a guttural groan, a heart-wrenching scream, or a moan of ecstasy. The Dark Goddess is the aspect—and the faces—of the Goddess that many of us choose to ignore because it's often easier to do so than face what She represents. She is the demonized feminine, the part of your psyche that has been subconsciously, or consciously, rejected, often as a way to move through the world with safety and protection from the parts of yourself you fear or don't understand.

This is part of the witch wound that often goes unsaid. The witch wound is the fear of claiming, living, and publicly sharing a life rooted in magick because of the implications of being hunted, outed, exiled, or killed that this can lead to, and has led to in the past. The Dark Goddess wound is slightly different and even less forgiving. It is the witch wound plus the wound of the deviant feminine, which can become dangerous when rejected. The Dark Goddess wound, when not healed or healing, can become an energy vampire, hiding, sucking, and taking from the healthy part of our psyche because we do not take the time to feed it what it needs—namely self-compassion, self-acceptance, and the transmutation of our shadow selves from something to be feared into something that should be loved, accepted, and integrated in our psyche and magickal practice.

But still, who is She? Who is the Dark Goddess? She is the Goddess of the Shadow. She is the sexual, the conniving, the angry, the wrathful, the death bringing, the ecstatic, the subversive. She is Inanna/Ishtar and Her sister Ereshkigal, Kali, Morrigan, Babalon, Nephthys, and Hekate. She is a Goddess of that which humanity prefers to keep in a box, separate from the socially acceptable, hidden away for us to find only in our misfortune. The Dark Goddess is the Goddess of Sex, Necromancy, the Underworld, War, Anger, and Rage. She is the transgressive power of the witch.

She is everything the patriarchy tries so hard to suppress. She shines Her light of love on the taboo, on the subversive. What the Dark Goddess can teach you—if you embrace Her lessons—is how important, powerful, and magickal all your shadowy bits are, no matter how "unacceptable." The Dark Goddess reminds us that all aspects of self are sacred and worth uncovering and exploring.

After years of research, exploration, and personal gnosis, I have also come to realize that *every Goddess has the potential to be a Dark Goddess.* Every Goddess has her shadow because every Goddess is a fractal of the Great Goddess of Life, Death, and Rebirth. And what a damn relief this is! Because when you see your darkest moments, your most difficult experiences, your bitchiest attitudes, and your most unforgiving thoughts reflected in the deity you work with and honor, then it's like you're being granted cosmic permission to exist in your fullest state without shame.

Through the worship, veneration,
and embodiment of the Dark Goddess,
you get to own all aspects of your heart and
soul and see every aspect of self as holy.

Getting to know the Dark Goddess can be scary. But a bit (or a lot) of fear and awe is okay. *The Dark Goddess requires sacrifice and underworld initiation.* Worshipping Her isn't to be taken lightly. This truth has shown itself to me time and time again—and each time, I forget. I think this sacred amnesia serves a purpose; if I were to remember all the pain and grief and sickness and chthonic experiences that devotion to the Dark Goddess brings, I probably wouldn't continue showing up at Her gates in the underworld. But I do. I come back, and I am grateful for this gift. Just remember, the more you delve into this relationship, the less scary it will be, and the more comfort you will have dancing at the edge of the abyss.

CONNECTING WITH THE DARK GODDESS

This chapter will guide you through the mythos of many Dark Goddesses and help you align with these parts of yourself with pride, confidence, safety, and comfort. But before we get to the myth and the magick, familiarize yourself with the Dark Goddess by recognizing the ways in which Her power is already resonate within you.

One of the first steps I encourage you to take is to explore your

shadow. The concept of the shadow was coined by psychanalyst Carl Jung. It represents the aspect of self we reject, whether because of fear or trauma, societal conditioning, or our discomfort with something we recognize within ourselves, subconsciously or not. The shadow is the aspect of self that is too much or not enough, or that society deems unruly.

One easy way to meet your shadow is to spend time thinking about someone who really bothers you and annoys you and make a list of all their traits that upset you, irk you, or piss you off. When you're done, reread this list, and boom, that's your shadow . . . a simplified version, perhaps, but still a strong start. Rejecting the shadow self is your mind's attempt to keep you safe. But fracturing, compartmental-izing, and shunning your multitudes hurts the psyche. You are meant to be whole, not split into parts. This is why we do shadow work, which is healing work. This is the unveiling of the Dark Goddess.

Shadow work isn't just one thing, and it's never going to be "done." Healing is a lifelong process. Begin to cultivate a shadow work prac-tice by trying the following:

+ Work with tarot and oracle cards, the I Ching, runes, or another form of divination to peer beneath the surface of the conscious mind. Allow divination to guide you in uncovering aspects of yourself you may not be aware of.

+ Journal and free write around your fears, trauma, pain, shame, rage, anger, and all the parts of yourself you would rather reject than accept.

+ Meditate with the goal of exploring your shadow. In meditation, you can personify your shadow and talk to it; maybe it's a vampire or a crone version of yourself, a Dark Goddess, a literal shadow, or a monster. Invite it in for tea, or ask it questions. This is a con-versation with yourself. When you're done meditating, take notes in your Goddess Grimoire.

+ Try subconscious reprogramming through affirmations, hypnosis, hypnotherapy, or therapy. Because the subconscious rules so much of our mind and body (down to things like blinking, heartbeat, and breath), much of our mental programming lives here as well. Begin to release from the grasp of the shadow by repeating affirmations—which could be a phrase or a word repeated over and over—to en-courage new patterns and neural pathways in the mind. Work with hypnosis or hypnotherapy to go deeper into the subconscious, with a trained professional or prerecorded sessions on YouTube or a meditation app. A trained therapist who specializes in cognitive behavioral therapy, talk therapy, or something more specific like Eye Movement Desensitization and Reprocessing (EMDR) can help you integrate the shadow using the subconscious mind.

You also can meet the Dark Goddess in other ways, such as the following:

✦ *Meditate and contemplate.* One of my favorite ways to know the Goddess, and to live in Her space and time, is through meditation and contemplation. When I am familiarizing myself with a Goddess or energy, I like to meditate on the ways that She or it is already present in my life. To get started, identify which aspects of the Dark Goddess are already within you. Begin this meditation at night or with the blinds or curtains closed. Light some candles—black, red, or regal purple—and establish an environment that is inviting and safe. Burn incense, gather crystals (dark stones like onyx, black tourmaline, and obsidian or lapis lazuli and carnelian). Then, meditate in a way that feels right for you, whether that is by surrendering to the Dark Goddess or feeling Her supporting you in your heart. Contemplate the Dark Goddess as a path to understanding Her using the journal questions at the end of this chapter as a jumping-off point.

+ *Practice self-compassion.* One of the central aspects of Dark Goddess devotion is self-compassion. The idea of self-care is thrown around a lot in spiritual circles and the world of wellness, and it's important. Being there for yourself is a vital tool in any spiritual practice; your basic needs must be met before you can commit to self-actualization and self-inquiry through esoteric work. Self-care is radical and nuanced; it means community care, support, and access to assistance when needed, and being able to ask for it. It is never truly done alone. And although it can be as simple as taking a bath, or even taking a shower and brushing your teeth (self-care that can be difficult to maintain in the throes of some mental illnesses), it's only one part of being responsible for your health.

Self-compassion is another piece of this puzzle, and it is often harder to put into practice. Having self-compassion means that you are there for yourself in a holistic way, being gentle and caring as you would for a little sibling, a baby, or a pet. It means that you support yourself with love and kindness when you fuck up and—here's the hard part—not get angry at yourself for not being perfect. Often before you get to self-compassion, you move through shadow work, which asks you to witness your patterns and the self-talk that happens when things don't go how you expected. Without self-compassion, a simple mistake can bring to the surface anger, resentment, and embarrassment for not doing things right. This can lead to shame at the feelings themselves, which then leads to more anger at the self, creating a loop. Self-compassion intercepts this, allowing you space to be where you are without judgment. This is married with self-acceptance, the understanding that you are where you are. Use self-care and self-compassion to hold yourself accountable for your healing and not bypass it.

✦ *Try sexual exploration.* Sexual energy is life energy is creative energy. This is the vibration of initiation, of action, of metamorphosis. Sex is an alchemical act, and erotic energy has the ability to transmute and transform. This is the domain of the Dark Goddess, with Her ability to take you to new and unseen depths—those that you can't imagine but can most definitely experience.

Sex is still taboo. It is exploited and used to sell things but discouraged as a form of self-inquiry. Being sexual and claiming this, especially as a woman, is frowned upon because misogyny is a trip and the patriarchy is threatened by an empowered woman—or anyone outside the gender binary—who makes their own choices about their body. And in a world where the virgin/whore dichotomy is alive and well, rejecting that black-and-white thinking to work with sacred sex as a path of devotion and spiritual practice is your ticket to the Dark Goddess. In fact, honoring the enigma and magick of virgin/whore is integral.

Exploring your sexuality will mean something different to you than it does to anyone else. And one thing I want you to keep in mind is that this doesn't have to be a partnered practice. It may mean figuring out your sexual orientation, trying new sex toys, or exploring kink and BDSM. It may mean masturbating or making love to yourself. *The key is that whatever you do, you do it in honor of the Dark Goddess within, and/or as an offering to the Dark Goddess; this conscious intention is what makes it sacred.* Remember, your sexuality is your own, and it is simply your decision to make it sacred that makes it such.

✦ *Create your own magickal and personal set of ethics.* The Dark Goddess demands: *know thyself.* No, not just how you like your coffee. She wants you to know yourself—like *really* know yourself. One way to do this is by establishing a magickal set of ethics for shadow work and sex magick. Therapy and talking through your boundaries and ethics can launch your inquiry, but journaling is the easiest form of establishing them. When this lives in your Goddess Grimoire, it is a living document that you can engage with as your values and opinions change over time.

Start with the following questions for insight, and free journal, muse, and write to keep going. The point is to know what feels right for you, especially when it comes to sexual and romantic partners. Allow this to be a journey with no definite end.

- What sort of magick do I believe is an impeachment of another person's free will? Do love spells count?
- If I want to practice and explore sex magick with a partner, but don't want them to be involved with it and just want to raise and channel energy on my own, do I have to ask their permission? Do I have to tell them what I'm doing and allow them to give consent, even if they're not participating? How much or little do I feel comfortable sharing?
- Do I feel comfortable hexing or cursing (aka sending negative and malicious energy) others? To specific people who have caused or will cause harm? What circumstances, if any, allow for this?
- How do I feel about revenge? Does it have a place in my life and in my magick?
- How do I define right and wrong? Is it situational?

- *Honor anger, rage, and vengeance.* The Dark Goddess reminds us of the importance of honoring all your feelings, even the ones that hurt and pull at the edge of your skin. (We explored this a bit in our rage practice in honor of Sekhmet on page 57.) But you can't avoid the "bad" feelings forever. Sure, you can push them down, but they are there for a reason. Your anger, your rage, and your lust for vengeance are catalyzing you toward something. This is where having a personal set of ethics comes in handy. You may feel comfortable working magick to reclaim your power and kickstart justice, or you may not. Either way, the Dark Goddess not only can hold space as you move through these feelings, but also remind you that they are just as divine as any others.

✦ *Seek out the Dark Goddess as the Dark Moon.* One of the frameworks you can use in understanding the Dark Goddess is in Her role as the Dark Moon. By now you can recognize the way the Moon is linked to the Feminine Divine, and how her story of endless regeneration is seen in the life- and death-giving properties of the Goddess.

The Dark Moon represents both the shadow of Goddess and of humanity. During the Dark Moon, we are invited to witness the Goddess in her role as a death doula, initiating and facilitating many endings. This is the Black Crone, who receives the dead and prepares them for rebirth, just like many of the Goddesses we will discuss. During the Dark Moon, the Dark Goddess guides you through the underworld, not as a place of torture or punishment, but as a suspended space and time before rebirth—which is exactly where ritual happens. In this space, we are invited to the edges of our own body and encouraged to explore this fear, to eroticize it, and to remember that life is a gift. Here is the source of healing, regeneration, and calm before the initiation. Seek out the Dark Goddess during this lunar cycle through contemplation, meditation, prayer, sexual embodiment (or conscious cultivation of sexual energy that leads you into the body and its awareness), and divination.

———————————) ♪ ● ● ● ((———————————

THE DARK GODDESS AND THE LEFT HAND PATH

One of the concepts you'll encounter while learning about the Dark Goddess, tantra, and Western magick is that of the Left Hand Path. Originating from Hindu tantra, the Left Hand Path denotes sects that work with forbidden substances like specific wheat, meat, fish, alcohol, and sex as a means of finding the Divine in the taboo. The idea behind this is that even that which is forbidden to consume or engage with in classical Hinduism—like having sex with someone outside your caste—is of the Divine. By bridging this through ritual, the Divine is seen in all. This differs from the Right Hand Path, where these things and substances may be meditated upon and contemplated but are not engaged with directly.

In the Western Mysteries, or tradition of the occult, the Left Hand Path refers to magick that aims at liberation by becoming the Divine and embracing one's own Godliness. The Left Hand Path engages with taboo as a means of sacred transgression and as a vehicle to the numinous, often including sex, substances, and worship of the flesh and self. Whereas those who walk the Right Hand Path want to *know* God and unite with God, the Left Hand Path honors the taboo as a means of *becoming* God.

Those who honor the Dark Goddess often walk the Left Hand Path because the Dark and Divine Feminine is a force of repressed sexuality, rage, and sovereignty, something our society has regarded as impure and immoral for eons. This is innately taboo. Through walking the Left Hand Path as a means of honoring the Goddess, you can find new avenues to live in Dark Goddess energy.

———————————

FACES OF THE DARK GODDESS

Time to descend into the underworld. These Dark Goddesses from around the world have mythos and magick waiting to transport you further into your awakening. Approach them with reverence and care and as a means to know thyself with razor-sharp vision.

Kali—Hindu Goddess of Destruction, Creation, and the Void

Kali calls out with eyes aflame and skin midnight blue, reflecting the eternal abyss She comes from. Her tongue lolls out of Her mouth, reflecting Her wild and untamable nature and leading you to untangle Her magick by subversion, through the sexual or through rejecting social norms. A Goddess of Death and Rebirth, and the nonstop cycle between the two, Kali reframes your perception of linear time and what it means to exist in endless cycles of growth and transformation. She exists in paradox, another one of Her gifts, and is a loving mother to those who worship Her yet will kill Her enemies without a second thought. She is the "life and death mother, womb and tomb," the ageless crone whose wisdom exists beyond binaries. The Brahmin, the priest caste of the Hindu tradition and culture, assigned Kali's functions to the three main deities of their pantheon: Brahma took on Her role as creator, Vishnu as the preserver, and Shiva as the destroyer. But Kali holds all these dimensions in Her form as a Triple Goddess who manifests beyond space and time, the waxing, full, and Dark Moons in all their glory.

Kali's sphere is *existence*, the living flux of all that is, including death and rebirth. She rules over the margins, over the rejected, demonized, and castrated aspects of humanity that must be separated from societal order. She is pure consciousness without judgment, although those who don't understand Her often judge Her as evil. But Kali is a tantric Goddess, patron of the Left Hand Path, honoring the taboo as a means to psychic knowledge and gnosis. She lives at and is worshipped at the periphery. She "threatens stability and control" when the safety of those She loves is jeopardized. Kali exists as the void, in the liminal, as the potential for both creation and destruction, a mirror to the mysteries of the Dark Moon. She is a Goddess of Time and of Bondage, and if you find yourself in the throes of ego, She will destroy what you know so you have no chance but to see it anew.

Kali is the first of the ten Mahavidyas, the Tantric Goddesses of Hinduism. Kali Herself is one of the forbidden things, and like the Dark Moon, she represents the portal of death as the formless beginning of new life. Like Lilith, she isn't a subservient wife, but She is whole unto Herself and Her desires. She is sexual, with names including She Whose Essential Form Is Sexual Desires and She Whose Form Is the Yoni, Who Is Situated in the Yoni, Who Is Adorned with a Garland of Yonis. What is sex if not both generation and annihilation?

Kali asks you to move past the myth of duality and into the realm of union. Her four arms show the balance of destruction and creation. One right hand forms the mudra, or symbolic gesture, that says "fear not," while Her other is in a mudra offering boons or blessings to Her devotees. Her left hands hold a bloodied sword and a severed head, representing the temporality of the body and the destruction of ego. Kali's three eyes represent Her Triple Goddess aspect, and Sun, Moon, and fire, as they gaze at the past, present, and future (just like Hekate). The garland of skulls at Her neck and the skirt of severed arms around Her waist represent the destruction that happens when you solely identify with the ego. If your heart is in the right place, then this Divine Mother will protect you, nurture you, and hold you accountable to express all your depths.

To connect with Kali: Lay your ego on your altar—all aspects of the self you identify with, the form you take, the sort of love you share, what makes you special—everything. Offer it to Kali. Pray for dissolution, to return to Her void. Share offerings of blood, drawn (carefully) from your veins or your Moon blood, as an act of devotion.

Only enter this path if your mind and heart are ready, but know they never will be fully ready. Channel your anger and rage into an act of self-protection, and work with a rage practice (page 57) in Kali's honor. Practice meditation when you feel yourself dissolving into the abyss of eternity, melding into the black nothingness that *is* Kali. Spend time with Her art, Her icons, or Her mythos, and wrap yourself in Her fierce magick. Pray and worship using Her mantras, and explore the taboo in Her honor, allowing the flesh to guide you deeper into the tantric mysteries over which this Goddess presides.

Lilith—Jewish Goddess and Mesopotamian Demoness of Sexual Sovereignty

Before there was Eve, there was Lilith. Lilith was created not from Adam's rib, but from the soil of the earth. One day, Adam wanted to have sex with Lilith in missionary, but She didn't want to lie beneath him. When he refused Her wishes, She uttered the sacred name of God, sprouted wings, and flew to the Red Sea, where She lived in a cave and had sex with demons, giving birth to thousands of infernal babies.

Lilith is an enigma, an alien, vilified for Her erotic chaos and dissident spirit. She exists beyond the realm of Judaism, where She is best known, most likely originating in Mesopotamia, as Her mythos is found in Sumerian, Babylonian, Assyrian, Canaanite, Persian, Hebrew, Arabic, and Teutonic mythology. But Lilith is also a Goddess of the Desolate, of the Desert. She rejects that which is forced upon Her.

Lilith embodies everything the patriarchy hates—just as every Dark Goddess does—and the anxieties of the monotheistic Western world in particular. Lilith is a demoness screech owl, a distorted version of the ancient Bird Goddess, and a golem who mirrors the fears of society. According to the Sumerian King's List (a cuneiform tablet that states the rulers of different parts of ancient Sumer), the Hero Gilgamesh's father was a Liltu—one of the four classes of demon that Lilith belongs to. She appears as a beautiful maiden who chooses a lover and who refuses to let him go, never quite giving in to what he wants, and never truly caring for his needs. In the Old World, Lilith was a formidable demoness, waiting for men at crossroads where She would kiss them . . . only to kill them later.

Lilith encompasses society's fear of the power of sex and the potential for rejection that can happen when we give in to our desires. Lilith has sex with sleeping men, causing nocturnal emissions and mothering demon children. In Sumer, Lilith was associated with the Goddess Inanna as Her handmaiden, bringing worshippers from the street into the temple where they would honor the Goddess of Love in sexual rites with the Temple Priestess. She enjoys sex for the sake of it, outside its reproductive purposes, and in this, She represents sexual sovereignty and independence. Lilith is the destructress, the nightmarish, and the unhinged, breaking down the chains of the patriarchy by refusing to contort and conform to its will.

In esoteric Judaism, Lilith lives alongside the often-forgotten Divine Feminine, Shekinah, as the "motherless forms of the feminine that arise from the Self. They arose with the coming of the patriarchy as the embodiment of the neglected and rejected aspects of the Great Goddess. Lilith is the part of the feminine that is experienced as a seductive witch, outcast, and shadow." She is both succubus and vampire, taking selfishly and devouring, unhinged. She is the death bringer, the dark and transformational face of the Divine Erotic.

Lilith is the Goddess of Life and Death in Her younger form as Naamah, the maiden and seductress; in Her ancient or crone form as a child killer and hag; and in Her form as the mother. In all Her faces, She represents the obscurity and loneliness that comes with living by your own rules. But Lilith is only scary when you don't take the time to look Her in the eye.

To connect with Lilith: Lilith beckons you to honor the full range of the shadow, of the rejected and demonized self, because in reality there is nothing wrong with this aspect of who you are. Lilith leads you into your lust; into your dominance; and more than anything, into your erotic autonomy, revenge, and rage. To honor Lilith, go into the desert—either in the flesh or in your heart—and search for Her in the caves. Call out with your whole being that you will no longer be subservient to the desires of the patriarchy. Call back your inner demoness, and spend time dancing around a fire (a candle works, too) as you call to Her. Allow Lilith to fill you with Her power, anger, lust, and independence. Embrace your inner succubus. Spend time exploring your eroticism, figuring out what you enjoy and what you can give yourself. Don't let anyone tell you what you can and can't do with your body. Use sex and sex magick to birth magickal children— whether that's a creative project or a new, empowered state of your sexuality—that you send to support your vision, helping you summon the world you desire.

Morrigan—Irish Celtic Goddess of War, Battle, and the Earth

Morrigan exists in the vastness of the unknown, the potential for destruction and transformation latent within Her. Morrigan belongs to the Irish Celtic people, presiding over death and battle. This Triple Goddess, whose name means "Phantom Queen," was described as a demonic flying creature, frightening in Her torment but fertile in Her potential. Morrigan is one of the Tuatha dé Danann, the people of the Goddess Danu, who are considered either Gods or members of the faery race; after being conquered by the Milesians, the story goes, the Tuatha dé Danann moved into faery mounds. Morrigan may have been a real-life queen, or She may have always been a deity to her people.

Because the Celts didn't leave much written history, the best we can surmise is that Morrigan's mythos originated in Ireland during the Celtic era between 1000 BCE and 500 CE. Morrigan is a Goddess of War and Battle, yet she is also a Goddess of Creation, Preservation, and Destruction, like the Hindu Kali. There are many faces to this Goddess: Badb, Macha, and the Morrigna in particular represent Her multifaceted nature. Badb, the mother, is also known as the fighting lady, the Goddess and witch of Rage and Violence. As a prophetic Goddess, Badb tells of danger to come, and She can take the form of a carrion crow as easily as the other mother Goddesses.

The face—or sister—of the Morrigan known as Macha is depicted in Her own triplicity as prophet/warrior/matriarch who reflects the magick and connection of the Irish Celts to the land itself. Macha is the face of the Goddess who understands how to navigate the obstacles of being human, and She can be called on for restoring a sense of personal power and navigating stressful situations with confidence and perspective.

But Morrigu, or Morrigan, is the archetypal face of this Goddess—a queen among Gods, known for Her strength and Her catalytic ability in battle and war. She helps those who need it, but She refuses to show mercy to Her enemies. Like Kali, She is the Dark Mother, loving those who are devoted and true of heart, and unforgiving to those who betray Her or Her people. She prefers cooperation over violence, demands reverence for the dead, and understands how the cycles of creation and destruction, of life and death, keep things in balance. Morrigan reminds us that death is part of life, that sometimes battles simply must be fought, and that you can choose to be there for yourself with compassion through it all.

To connect with Morrigan: Spend time lingering in the shadow, in the liminal. Call out for Morrigan as you meditate in the darkness, and ask Her to lead you into the in-between and shadow realm. Honor and ponder death, strolling through a cemetery as you invite

Her to walk with you. Listen to the caws of the raven and crow, sacred animals of the Goddess, and ask them to share their secrets. Make a list of what you're fighting for, what you believe in, and what enrages you with passion, and leave it on your altar with a glass of red wine as an offering. Drive into a field and scream with bloody rage at all the ways the feminine has been vilified and demonized. Let Morrigan know this is a sacred offering of fury in Her honor. Practice the gifts of prophecy by spending time with your dreams, by reading tarot, and by meditating in the realm between sleep and waking. Invite Her power into your life by making space for the full experience of life, death, rage, and war.

Hekate—Greco-Roman Goddess of the Crossroads, Necromancy, and Magick

There's a reason that Hekate is often called the witch's Goddess. A Goddess of Magick, of Necromancy, of existing in the liminal, Hekate's lantern lights the way through the darkness for any devotee who is pure of heart and spirt. She kindly guides you past the river Styx, through the land of the dead and the living, to a place where everything is everything and magick is palpable. Originally a Titan, who was given dominion over the earth, land, and sea—the likely origin of Her Triple Goddess form—Hekate is an ancient and chthonic Goddess who can lead you into new dimensions of your truth, darkness, and power. Standing at the threshold between life and death, Hekate acts as a "protective membrane" between the human and heavenly realms, much like the Egyptian Goddess Nuit cradles the sky in Her body, separating cosmic order and chaos. In the Orphic Hymn, Hekate has the responsibility of holding the key to the universe and cosmos, and Her association with keys endures.

This lunar Goddess's three faces gaze into the past, present, and future, aware of all the possibilities of the cosmos and offering compassion without fear or judgment. This Goddess accepts the totality of Her devotees. Some of Hekate's epithets include the guide (Enodia), the guardian (Lampadios), and the gatekeeper (Kleidoukhos). Hekate holds the key that unlocks the door to personal gnosis, acting as both the road and the odyssey. The voyage isn't always easy. But as She answered Demeter's cry for help seeking Persephone, as She acted as Persephone's guide between the underworld and the human world, so, too, can she guide you in moments of grief, sadness, darkness, anger, and pain.

In Her role as guardian, Hekate protects you through underworld excursions, allowing access to the subconscious and psyche, the shadow self that must be traversed for unity and for the sake of the Great Work. As guide, She ensures you are following the path meant for you and only you. And in Her face as gatekeeper, Hekate takes on the initiating role in your magick, unlocking the transition into a new state of being, one that can only come from direct experience.

Hekate has commonalities with Selene the Moon, as the Goddess of Heaven; Artemis, the Huntress, as Goddess of the Earth; and Persephone, the Destroyer, Goddess of the Underworld. As a Goddess of Knowing and Devotion, Hekate has both the bite and love of many other Dark Goddesses. In the Chaldean Oracles, Hekate says, "if you call upon Me often you will perceive everything in Lion-form"—"lion-form" being ancient; lustful; powerful; bloodthirsty; and connected to the visceral, the potent, and the unapologetic. This protective Goddess will spill blood as an offering to what She cares about, and Her magick exists through the power of death leading to birth and vice versa. Follow Her to learn the mysteries of magick, of darkness, and of sovereignty.

To connect with Hekate: Gather your tools of magick, and spend time with them in a cemetery. Draw your cards, and spill some red wine as an offering. Lingering in the liminal, in the magick, in the palpable esoteric is a surefire way to this Goddess, as is opening a line of communication to the underworld and spirits past and present. Dogs are sacred to Hekate, and when you open yourself to their magick, whether through adoption, meditation, or spending time with your pup, you can be sure She is close by. Create an altar to this Goddess, and leave a gold key there for use in ritual or in meditation to open the way for Hekate's guidance. Leave Her food and wine at a crossroads in the forest, and meditate at this liminal place in real life or on the astral. Spend time in the darkness, and seek out the light of Hekate's torch. Spend time with Her many names to know Her personally, and trust in the unfolding of the unknowable.

Persephone—Greek Goddess of the Underworld and Spring

You've already met Persephone through the story of Her and Her mother, Demeter. Persephone, in the Hellenistic myth, was kidnapped by God of the Underworld, Hades, and taken against Her will to live as his consort and wife as Queen of the Underworld. She stayed there until Demeter rescued Her, with the help of some other Gods like Helios, Mercury, Hekate, and Zeus. Because Persephone had eaten pomegranate seeds before returning to the earth, and because pomegranates are a symbol of sexual consummation, Her marriage to Hades was insoluble. Thus, Persephone was "forced" to spend part of the year alongside Hades as Queen of the Underworld and part of the year alongside Demeter as Goddess of Spring.

But Persephone, known as Kore in Her maiden form and called

Prosperina by the Romans, has a pre-Hellenistic mythos that touches more deeply on the truth of Her sacred dualities. In this version, Persephone was with Demeter when the two of them encountered the spirits of the recently dead. Persephone was struck by this vision and expressed concern to Her mother that there was no one there to help the newly departed, to counsel them and guide them on their journey. Demeter's rulership includes the dead, but She told Her daughter that She preferred to focus on the living. Persephone saw this as an opportunity to act as an emissary to those in the underworld, welcoming the departed souls and ushering them and initiating them through this death process.

In this way, Persephone represents making the unconscious conscious, descending to the unknown, and performing shadow work as an experience of totality, of unity. Persephone, after all, is a Goddess of Springtime *and* Death. She doesn't reject Her desire to know the darkness, but rather cultivates it as a source of intelligence and fortitude.

Persephone is a Goddess who is as at home in a lush garden of pomegranates and roses and jasmine as She is in a cemetery under moonlight, lush with decay and death. She has integrated Her darkness and not rejected it. She chose Hades as much as he chose Her. Follow Her to experience transformation and renewal through radical self-acceptance. She leads by example, saying you can be goth and still like flowers, or understand the importance of death while still celebrating the joy of life. We are all Dark Goddesses *and* fecund Goddesses of the Earth, and I think that's pretty damn beautiful.

To connect with Persephone: Immerse yourself in your divine dualities by honoring both the loveable and rejected parts of yourself. Light white and black candles, and by their light alone, meditate on your personal underworld. Enter willingly, not as victim but as sovereign. Revel in your shadow, in the darkest parts of who you are, Bordeaux like wine. Eat a pomegranate, dedicating each seed as a token of devotion to honoring all your facets. Leave some seeds and red wine as an offering to Persephone. Allow yourself to think of death, and to meditate on the way this decay has the potential to transform into life. Crown yourself as royalty for your sacred magick, and invite in a Divine union—of flesh, of magick, of lover, of self—that reflects the mysteries of death and rebirth that Persephone and Hades oversee.

Nephthys—Egyptian Funerary Goddess of Magick

Nephthys is to the dusk what Isis is to the dawn. If Isis initiates life, then Nephthys guards the abyss of the afterlife and leads those who have passed through the test of Anubis and Ma'at to the other side. Nephthys—or Nebet-Het in Khemetian—never got the same amount of love or adoration as Her twin sister, but She still was widely worshipped between the Predynastic period (6000 to 3150 BCE) and the Ptolemaic dynasty (323 to 30 BCE), the latter the last dynasty to rule Egypt before the Romans took over. As the Lady of the House, the Lady of the Temple Enclosure, or Mystery of the House, Nephthys rules over those who watch over Her temples. Just as a house or temple is a haven, this Goddess protects the souls of those who worship Her. Like the temple, the tomb is a divine container, and Nephthys embraces the possibilities of a soul's evolution in this life and the next. Like Persephone, She guides souls through the death process, and one of Her titles, "friend of the dead," further exemplifies Her compassionate nature as a guide through the afterlife.

Like Lilith, Nephthys is a Goddess of the Desert, associated with ether and air. She breathed life into the body of Osiris alongside Her sister, Isis, raising him from the dead. During their heyday, Nephthys and Isis were almost always mentioned together and are depicted side by side in contemporaneous tombs and art, and their combined name, Isenephthys, can be found in the Greek Magical Papyri. They even share a lover; while Isis and Osiris fathered Horus, Nephthys and Osiris fathered the dark God Anubis. Whereas Isis represents the veil of the mysteries, Nephthys *is* the mysteries. Isis relates more to the conscious mind and to the light of the Moon; Nephthys illustrates the subconscious and the dark side of the Moon. Are these Goddesses sisters, or are they mirror-image twins?

Both are Goddesses of mourning and funerary rites, and Nephthys can hold you during moments of grief and release. She is the pitch black of midnight before the dawn, the flicker of the candle in complete darkness. Her song invites you into forgotten parts of your soul. All you have to do is listen.

To connect with Nephthys: Bless mourning beads in the name of this Goddess, and wrap them around your wrist so you always have Her protection. Call to Nephthys as you hang in the in-between of wakefulness and sleep. Nephthys is an enigma, and to know Her, you must make space for Her. Meditate in the darkness, and allow Her to penetrate the veil of illusion so you may peer into Her sanctuary. When you are mourning—no matter if what has passed are people, realities, expectations, or past selves—you may find refuge in the promise of first light. When you honor Isis, also remember that Nephthys is there, by Her side, and vice versa. Practice shadow work in honor of Nephthys, and leave offerings of snowflake obsidian on your altar, honoring the duality of darkness and light within yourself.

Inanna/Ishtar—Sumerian Goddess of Heaven, Earth, and the Underworld

How am I supposed to pay due respect to the Great Inanna, the first Goddess in recorded history, the queen of above and below who blesses us with lust and love? Inanna is the Goddess of Sumer whose story was integrated wholly into that of the Akkadian Ishtar, whose cult worshipped Her for more than four thousand years as the Queen of Heaven, Earth, and the Underworld. Her story could have just as easily fit in the chapter on Goddesses of Love because ultimately that's what She is. But She is also a Dark Goddess, and one of Her most enduring myths speaks of Her experience in the underworld. But remember: boundaries and boxes are human inventions used to contain immeasurable and unfathomable forces. Her power spans beyond our understanding.

Inanna is a Goddess of Love, Sex, War, Beauty, Heaven, the Earth, and the Underworld, whose power is continuously renewed through veneration of any Goddess of Love whose current begins with Her, including Ishtar. Although Inanna was worshipped for a thousand years before Ishtar, because Ishtar received nearly all of Her attributes (except Her consort), the Goddesses are often seen as one being. Inanna's stories survive on inscribed clay tablets, and through the work of translators, folklorists, and historians, as well as through we witches who honor Inanna and other Goddesses of Love.

Clothed in the heavens, with a crown of twelve stars for each of the zodiac signs, wearing lapis lazuli and a rainbow around Her neck and an enchanted girdle at her waist, Inanna was the original glamour queen. While She ruled as Queen of Heaven and Earth, Her sister, Ereshkigal, ruled over the underworld.

The rejected feminine is often castrated and sent away, but sooner or later, she must be reintegrated. In the myth of the Descent of Inanna, the Great Goddess of Heaven and Earth makes Her way down to the underworld for a funeral for Ereshkigal's husband, Gugalanna. Inanna tells Her attendant Ninshubur to be prepared to ask for help if for some reason She does not return to Earth; first at the temple of the God Enlil (God of Air), then to Nanna (God of the Moon), and lastly to Enki (God of Wisdom).

Inanna is stopped before She can even make Her way into to the underworld. She is told that Her sister has commanded Her to remove a piece of clothing before entering the land of the dead. At the first gate, Inanna removes Her crown. She gets to the next gate, and it happens again. Here, She removes Her lapis lazuli necklace. And then it happens again and again. At the third gate, She removes the beads around Her breast; at the fourth, Her breastplate. At the fifth gate, She removes the gold bracelet from around Her wrist, and at the sixth, the lapis measuring line and rod from Her hands. Last, at the seventh gate, Inanna's royal robe is taken from Her. She enters the underworld naked and mortal, stripped of everything that brings Her power, Her talismans and items of protection and magick.

As She enters Her sister's room, Ereshkigal turns and strikes Her. She sentences Inanna to death, and Inanna hangs on a hook, naked and unadorned, for three nights and three days. In the meantime, Ninshubur beseeches Enlil and Nanna, who both reject her plea. Finally, Enki, the God of Wisdom, agrees to help. He creates a creature from the dirt of his fingernail and breathes life into it. The creature makes its way to the underworld, where it imitates Ereshkigal in all Her woes and complaints to get on Her good side. Ereshkigal is so pleased to be seen in this way—to be completely witnessed—that She promises the being whatever it wants. What it wants, it explains, is the corpse hanging from the hook on the wall: Inanna.

But just as Inanna is about to ascend, the Annuna—the judges of the underworld—proclaim that someone must take the Goddess's place. Even the chthonic realm requires balance, after all. After visiting Earth to find a suitable replacement, Inanna notices Her husband, the shepherd Dumuzi, sitting on Her throne, dressed in his royal garb, as if nothing had happened. He doesn't care that Inanna had been gone, that She is in trouble, or that She's back. So Inanna kindly says "Fuck that!" and commands that the Annuna take Dumuzi in Her place. But Inanna is a Goddess of Love, remember, so They are able to come to a compromise. Half the year, Dumuzi would rule the underworld, and the other half the year, it would be his sister, Geshtinanna.

When Inanna returns to Earth, she rediscovers Her wholeness. She is no longer just Queen of Heaven and Earth; She is Queen of Heaven, Earth, *and the Underworld*. She contains all the dualities of life, and now She can give it or take it away. Per the translation work of Diane Wolkstein and Samuel Noah Kramer, "Her mythology revolves around the connection made between the light and dark lunar phases and the rhythmic alteration of the earth's fertility and bareness." It was Inanna's dark twin who initiated Inanna into Her wholeness. This was an ordeal process, a ritual of the edge, but to know Herself in all dimensions, She needed Ereshkigal.

(Isthar's mythos is slightly different. Instead of going to the underworld for a funeral, Ishtar descends to be with Her husband, Tammuz, who was killed by a boar. She brings him a new cycle of life, like the Moon renewing itself as a waxing crescent.)

For the fertility of the world to flourish, for the unconscious to be made manifest, you must be unafraid of traversing the depths of the psyche. We must travel through what we think we know to receive the initiation of the Goddess, which dwells on the other side of knowing, in the wild.

To connect with Inanna: Find peace being one with heaven and the earth. Spend time in a field—in your heart or in the flesh—and ponder the sweetness of existence with the bounty of the Goddess surrounding you. Honor both the angelic and heavenly self as well as the underworld and chthonic self, doing so through the body and sexuality. Under the Dark Moon, hold space for your shadow. Read translations of the Descent of Inanna, noticing the sexual and erotic language and undertones in Her story. Call out to Inanna when you are in moments of transformation and need the strength to trust in what's on the other side. Leave Her offerings of bread, wine, blood, or roses on your altar, and explore that which seems taboo. Celebrate your darkness and love, your sexuality, and your rage and vengeance, and boldly battle anything that attempts to defy your greatness.

Babalon—Thelemic and Western Goddess of the Abyss, Subversion, and Ego Death

Mother of the antichrist, deity of subversion, Red Goddess of Unconditional Lust and Love who guards the abyss and the annihilation of the known self, waiting for honest seekers to spill every last drop of their blood in Her chalice . . . Babalon is that bitch. A uniquely modern Goddess with ancient origins, Babalon first appears as the Whore of Babylon in the New Testament's book of Revelation. In Revelation 12:1, She is described as a "great wonder in heaven: a woman clothed with the Sun, and the Moon under her feet and upon her head a crown of twelve stars." A couple sentences later you are met with the consort of this woman: a seven-headed beast, the great beast, who Babalon is riding and fucking. The yet-unnamed woman is about to give birth, and the seven-headed dragon who impregnated Her is going to devour the baby, hoping to gain the power of his child. This scene foretells the End Times, the prophecy's apocalypse that marks the end of the world. And although the book of Revelation reflects the thoughts of an impending apocalypse at the time it was written, we can observe it unwind now in real time.

Clad in purple and scarlet, gold, precious stones, and pearls, Babalon is a Goddess of Luxury, exemplary of a type of woman who doesn't conform to expectations: lavish, sexual, ecstatic, clothed in the same garb as Inanna/Isthar. Written on the forehead of the Whore of Revelation is "MYSTERY, BABYLON THE GREAT, MOTHER OF THE HARLOTS AND ABOMINATIONS OF THE EARTH." Her mystery is that of orgasm. She is the Mother of Harlots because She imprints the initiations of sex and death onto those who worship Her. And as the Abominations of the Earth, Babalon—like the Dragon Goddess Tiamat who births all creation from chaos—brings a new way of being to the world by mating with the Great Beast. But hidden in the madness is a riddle, and its solution. Per Peter Grey, "Babalon and the Beast can be seen as a sexual formula to lead the aspirant to enlightenment . . . Babalon reclaims the essential primal power of Woman and Man giving birth to something entirely new."

Babalon's identity as the Goddess we know today was excavated by the talented occultist and magician Aleister Crowley in 1909, but She first reemerged in 1587 in what is now the Czech Republic, when court magician John Dee and his assistant, Edward Kelly, were performing rituals and piecing together the angelic language and system of magick known as Enochian. While Kelly was scrying into a piece of black obsidian, a young woman named Madimi, the first trace of Babalon, appeared to the duo in a vision with words that echo the gnostic poem of "The Thunder, Perfect Mind" found in the Nag Hammadi library. The name *Babylon* translated to "wicked," mirroring the biblical Whore of Babylon in Her truest form of subversion.

When Crowley enlisted his lover and magical partner, Victor Neuburg, to reenact this ritual of scrying with the aethyrs (or levels of reality in the Enochian system of angelic magick), he came into contact with the Goddess he would name Babalon, changing the *y* in Babylon to an *a* to form a connection with the number 156 using the Hebrew system of Gematria. This didn't happen, however, until Crowley surrendered his ego at the altar of the subversive and taboo by having anal sex with Neuburg, bottoming for him passively as an act of sacrifice or offering that allowed him to cross the abyss. It was this act of "transgression" that allowed Crowley to receive the teachings that Babalon had in store for him. And although Crowley may have helped conceptualize Her being to the egregore we know now, She has evolved far past this magician's Victorian ideas of receptivity, femininity, and sexuality.

As a Goddess of the Apocalypse—or the ability of orgasm to destroy and rebuild—Babalon undoes self and society by holding up an obsidian mirror to the collective. In Crowley's system of magick, Thelema, Babalon guards the abyss, or what must be crossed to get to enlightenment. Before coming face-to-face with this Goddess, you must battle your demons, and only after you have annihilated your ego can you pour your blood—all that remains of *you*—into Her chalice, fulfilling Her prophecy; only then can you cross the abyss and truly experience ego death and enlightenment.

Like the rest of Her Goddess cohort, Babalon is a creator and destroyer who loves and lusts unconditionally, without expectation of anything back, to a point of annihilation. Babalon challenges our outdated ideas of what it means to be corporeal. She is a divine temptress, asking you to surrender all your hang-ups to experience what the body has to offer. She starts with silence and moves to ecstasy as a means of transformation. Babalon's sexual hunger represents the power of surrender to reach altered states of spirit, mind, and being. She is a Goddess of BDSM, Queer Sex and Love, Sex Workers, the Holy Whore, and the Sacred Slut. She is a Goddess of Glamour, Sex Magick, and the Illicit.

To connect with Babalon: Write a list of your characteristics that you identify with and then burn the list in the name of Babalon. Leave a chalice of red wine on your altar in Her honor, and pour drops of your blood into this (safely). The way to know Babalon is through the path of the subversive, so spend time with your eroticism, with your sexuality, with your fetishes and kinks. Allow the Red Goddess to help you explore erotic destruction and spiritual domination in the name of ego death. Meditate on what you consider your vices and virtues, and let Babalon dissolve all boundaries between "good" and "bad." Dress in scarlet and purple, layer gold jewelry in Her name, and ask that Babalon bless your flesh with Her lust and love. Leave fresh red roses on Her altar, and use roses in spellwork after dedicating them to Her. Your sexuality is a path to your most sacred magick, so dedicate the journey to Babalon as She guides you through the abyss back into the numinous. Indulge in the sensual, indulge in pleasure, indulge in the flesh in Her name, and always invite Babalon to destroy the binaries that keep you in fear. Offer your sexual exploits and orgasms to Her.

A SHADOW MAGICK RITUAL
FOR EMBRACING THE DARK GODDESS WITHIN

Using the framework of the Goddess's journey, as She travels to the underworld and comes back transformed, you will create your own

Dark Goddess mythos for embracing this journey in your own life. There's no rush to do this ritual, and I implore you to try it only when you feel ready and after you have done shadow work to begin healing and integrating your underworld experience. You can call on a Dark Goddess, or the Great Mother Goddess if you wish, but again, I suggest forming a relationship with this deity first.

This ritual can take place whenever you need it, but it is especially potent during the Dark Moon, new Moon, or waning Moon—the times of the Dark Goddess and Her descent into the underworld.

You will need: A black candle (can be a chime candle, a taper, or a five- or seven-day candle), a candleholder, oil for protection such as black tourmaline oil or olive oil, a lighter or matches, your Goddess Grimoire, a pen or pencil, an offering that you will eat and share on the altar, supplies to craft something that will represent your under-world journey in whatever medium you prefer (a sigil, a piece of art, a poem, a song, a dance, etc.).

Optional: Herbs or resin to burn for sacred smoke such as mugwort (connected to the Moon; assists psychic downloads and inner know-ing), lavender (ruled by God of Communication Mercury; heals and relaxes), sweetgrass (calls in loving energy and spirits), or frankincense and myrrh (ruled by the Sun and Venus, respectively; cleanses and clears energy), crystals, or sex toys and lube for sex magick.

Read through the entire ritual a couple times to get familiar with it, and prepare your evocation/prayer in advance.

Step 1: Set up your altar and shrine
Before you begin, set up your altar however you'd like, perhaps clean-ing and cleansing it with rose water and sacred smoke (page 88).

Step 2: Ground and call in guidance
Before you ground, you may use sacred smoke to lift the vibration of

your space by cleansing and clearing any negative or stuck energy. If you are using a resin, be sure you have a firesafe dish, a piece of activated charcoal, and a lighter or matches. Light the charcoal until it sparks, wait for a minute or two, and then drop a bit of the resin on top. If you are cleansing with sacred smoke, light the herbs until they flame and then gently blow or fan them out until they're smoldering. Cleanse your space—including the corners of the room and of course your altar and tools—and yourself, making sure to get the palms of your hands, the bottoms of your feet, between your legs, your arms and legs, your torso, your throat, and the back of your head. As you do this, declare that *"All negative, unneeded, stuck, and stagnant energy is cleared, cleansed, and banished from this sacred space and from myself."* You can sprinkle rose water, Moon water, or Florida water in every direction and on your altar and tools, and anoint yourself at your third eye, your throat, the back of your head, and your heart.

When you feel that the energy of the room is supportive and ready for ritual, ground and center (page 12).

Stay here as long as you need and then call upon a specific Goddess, the Dark Goddess, or the Great Goddess of Life and Death to guide you in this shadow experience. You may read a prayer or evocation (which is calling forth the Goddess to communicate with Her, whereas an *in*vocation is inviting the Goddess *in*to you). You also may read and adapt the following to suit your needs:

Dear Goddess, Dark and Divine Feminine, I call upon You now to assist me in this journey of mythologizing and activating the Dark Goddess energy within me. May Your loving presence support and guide me, and may your Love hold space for me as I integrate and alchemize this journey. Thank You, thank You, thank You, and so it is.

Step 3: Journal and mythologize

Remove any and all ideas of your mortality and your humanity. From this moment on, you have crossed the threshold from human to Divine. You *are* a Goddess. And it is from this place, from the framework of the descent of the Goddess into the underworld, that you will be examining your own underworld journey. This could be a single experience, a collection of experiences that marked a specific point in your life, a moment when you were struggling, or whatever else constitutes an underworld journey *for you*. You may have had many, but for now I want you to pick the one that you feel the most comfortable writing about and that you've already done some healing around; be sure the wound is not too fresh because you are going to be performing shadow work with it.

When you've picked a moment, answer the following questions from the perspective of a Goddess. If you want to add dramatic flair, go ahead. Ask yourself *What would the Dark Goddess do?* and answer from this place. The point of this aspect of the ritual is to untangle and contextualize your experience by connecting it to the mythos of the Feminine Divine.

What was my underworld journey?

What was my experience? What trials and tribulations did I have to move through?

What was I like before this?

What was I like after this? What changed? What has changed since?

What have I been resistant to integrating and accepting from this practice?

What did this awaken in me? In my magick?

What do I want to take from this? What do I want to let go?

Take as much time as you need, and if you wish, rewrite your answers in a story form, casting yourself as the Goddess who moves through this journey. (Or return to this later.) Before moving on, write a concise but descriptive paragraph about your underworld journey, what you learned, and, after your ascent and return, what kind of Goddess you are. As Inanna becomes the Goddess of Heaven, Earth, and the Underworld after Her trip, something has been born within you after your own journey. Use the template below to get started, and fill in the details with your own experiences, preferences, and correspondences.

Your Dark Goddess declaration:

I have undergone the Goddess's journey. I have made my way through the darkness of the underworld, where I experienced [write your experience] *and moved through* [write what you had to go through]. *It was painful and scary and dark, but through it, I found a part of myself. When I returned from these depths, I came out transformed. I was changed and found myself* [how this journey changed you]. *Before I was just* [your name], *but now I am* [your name], *Goddess of* [whatever you're the Goddess of] *because* [what initiated this transformation for you].

This might look like the following:

I have undergone the Goddess's journey. I have made my way through the darkness of the underworld, where I experienced pain, a collective death process, and anxiety and moved through a year of intense awareness of mortality, loneliness, and separation from community. It was painful and scary and dark, but through it, I found a part of myself. When I returned from these depths, I came out transformed. I was changed and found myself more connected to the Goddess, more in tune with my magick, and more aware of my energy. Before I was just Gabriela, but now I am Gabriela, Goddess of Lust, Love, and Magick because I had the time to sit with my purpose and what matters to me.

Step 4: Meditate and create

Whew! Take a deep breath. Drink water. You're doing magnificent work, beloved. Now you are going to meditate and hold space for all of it. If there's a part of your underworld journey that you are having trouble accepting or integrating, *especially* hold space for that. You don't have to fully accept it right now, at all, or ever. You still can practice this ritual without being okay with what happened to you. But by holding space for this shadow, and even talking to it, you will penetrate deeper into the medicine. Meditate on this in whatever way feels right.

Now, if you feel called, create something for the Goddess and for yourself. You can draw a sigil or symbol of your declaration, or you may make a piece of art inspired by your time below, write a poem, dance a dance, sing a song, read a hymn—however you can express what you've moved through and learned.

Step 5: Activate the Dark Goddess wisdom

After you've made your art, turn off the lights or dim them if you like. You can dress your black candle, which represents the illumination that comes after the darkness, with protective oil, moving from the middle of the candle to the ends to banish any unnecessary or negative energy.

Take a moment to breathe as you make your way to the altar, making sure to bring your declaration. Light the candle, noticing how it illuminates the room and your altar. Then read your Dark Goddess declaration out loud, and add the following to close it out and activate this essence in you, rewriting or sharing your own version:

Through this underworld journey and through the spiral of the Dark and Divine Feminine, I have been reborn as myself, as a Goddess. And it's on this [date of the day you're performing the ritual, zodiac season, and phase and sign the Moon is in] *that I activate the Dark Goddess essence within me. I activate the strength, erotic magick, transformative power, and potent alchemy of the Dark Goddess within me. I declare it. I activate it. I will it so. This or something better for the highest good of all involved, so it is and it is done.*

You may find yourself giggling or crying or tingling—allow it to move through you! You may sing or dance or jump around. You also may practice sex magick here, raising the energy and sending it through the crown of your head at the peak or climax of this experience. Express yourself in whatever way feels right.

Step 6: Give gratitude, close the ritual, and record
Find a comfortable meditative posture. Close your eyes and feel the energy swirling within you, noticing anything that feels different without trying to analyze it. Thank the Goddess and any of Her faces you may have called in, using the following or whatever words flow from your heart:

Dear Goddess, Dark and Divine Feminine, I thank You for Your assistance and support in helping me in this journey of mythologizing and activating the Dark Goddess energy within me. Thank You for Your presence, support, and guidance. Thank You for Your Love and for holding space for me. Thank You, thank You, thank You. The ritual is done, and You are free to leave. So it is, and so mote it be.

After Goddess is thanked, close and ground (page 13). Then record your experience in your Goddess Grimoire: what you felt, what you noticed, and what came up. You also may record any initial thoughts and feelings and plan to return to it in a few days for a more detached and detailed run-through.

Step 7: Conclude the ritual

Set out some edible offerings for the Goddess on your altar, take a moment to send energy to them, and then eat these same offerings and feel their blessing move through you. Also be sure to drink plenty of water! Enjoy this activation and rite as it expands your perception of yourself.

Allow the candle to burn all the way down, leaving it in a sink if necessary. If you have to snuff it out, use a candle snuffer, a fan, or your fingers; don't blow it out. Relight the candle when you can and reconnect to this intention. If there's any excess candle wax, dispose of it at a garbage can at an intersection. And so it is!

JOURNAL QUESTIONS

Continue your dance with the Dark Goddess with these questions, which will help light the path to your shadow, to the subconscious, to the underworld. Many times, the Goddess comes through in unexpected ways, so part of this work is to be open and perceptive. This is an ever-evolving unfolding, one that reaches into the aspects of humanity that many are too afraid to wander through. You are here. You are doing the work. You are worthy, and you are welcome. Use the steps on page 34 to get as much out of this journaling experience as possible.

- What does the Dark Goddess mean to me? How would I describe Her energy? What does She feel like in my body? Taste like? Smell like?
- What Dark Goddess am I drawn to? What do I know about Her factually? Intuitively?
- How does the Dark Goddess reflect my own sacred depths? How does She help me understand my shadow?
- What is my intention in starting a journey with the Dark Goddess? What can I offer Her? What do I hope She offers me?
- What underworld journey have I gone on recently that reflects my experience with the Dark Goddess? What did I learn?
- What offerings—both physical and energetic—can I share with the Dark Goddess that both inspire me and share my devotion?
- What aspects of myself am I most afraid to confront? How can I do this alongside the Dark Goddess, as an offering to both Her and myself?
- How does my sexuality connect me to the Dark Goddess? How does my pain? My shadow?

AFFIRMATIONS

To look your shadow in the eye, to take the path of the Dark Goddess, to initiate yourself in the language of the underworld . . . this is power. But you are also human, and that means sometimes you won't feel as confident as you'd like. As a devotee of the Goddess, you're already one step ahead because you know the gift of your words and intentions. Whether you're in the pits of the underworld or wading through shadow work that never ends (spoiler alert: it literally never ends), turn to affirmations for support. Work with them as anchors and signposts in your journey through the realms of the subconscious.

Use the steps on page 38 to make your affirmation practice as powerful as possible.

- I claim my sacred depths, no matter how dark.
- I surrender to the darkness and find myself whole through the journey.
- I am a Dark Goddess, rooted in all expressions of my soul.
- I surrender to the Dark Goddess and allow Her to guide me through the darkness.
- I integrate my shadow with compassion and tenderness.
- I own my desires and find space to explore them.
- My sexuality is sacred, my eroticism is sacred, and my subversion is sacred.
- I honor pleasure as a path to my fullest expression.
- I am a vessel of Divine deviance and sacred subversion.
- I integrate my shadow by releasing shame, guilt, and fear around my truth.

+ I am Queen/ King/ Muse of Heaven, Earth, and the Underworld.
+ I am safe and whole unto myself.
+ The Dark Goddess holds me, cares for me, and loves me, even
  when I feel unworthy.

A TAROT SPREAD FOR COMMUNING WITH AND EMBODYING THE DARK GODDESS

I can't stress enough how helpful it is to have a variety of tools and systems of support as you're embracing the Dark Goddess. Embodiment practices like movement and dance, journaling, affirmations, daily devotional practices, prayer, and spellwork are potent support systems. This is especially true of tarot when it comes time to mythologize and understand your personal Goddess journey, how Dark Goddess energy plays into this, and what you're meant to retrieve from the underworld to bring back as wisdom. Work with this tarot spread to awaken this knowledge.

Use the steps on page 42 to prepare yourself for this reading.

Card 1: How is the Dark Goddess awakening me right now?

Card 2: How is She calling me into myself and my power?

Card 3: What am I meant to learn from the underworld journey?

Card 4: What am I meant to integrate upon my return?

Card 5: How does the Dark Goddess want me to ritualize this?

6

Embracing the Goddess Within

Well, Goddess, if you've made it this far, I want to congratulate you. (Even if you've skipped ahead, the sentiment stands.) Your commitment to awakening the Divine Feminine is not one to be overlooked or understated.

This chapter is a little bit different from the previous ones. Instead of focusing on different kinds of Goddesses, it's time to turn the mirror so you can witness *the Goddess within yourself.* In my experience, this is the component that really changes it all.

**When you are able to remember,
to know, to experience, to *feel* yourself
as a sublime emanation of the Goddess, and
when you're able to treat yourself as such,
that's when you not only can "get"
Goddess energy but *embody* it.**

Instead of something you relate to in your mind, you feel Goddess energy as a resonate truth. And that's power.

Throughout this chapter, I will share an array of methods to connect to the Goddess within, so you can infuse Goddess energy into everything you do, whether it's through embodiment practices like beauty that lead you further into your body's wisdom, by calling the Goddess into your flesh, or via astrology. When you live in Goddess time and on Her frequency, you can finally remember that you are the Goddess incarnate.

BRINGING THE GODDESS
INTO THE EVERYDAY

As you continue spiraling through your relationship with the Goddess, there are a few things I've hope you've been able to realize. One is that your relationship with the Goddess will be intensely personal; it will mirror your heart, your most sacred treasure trove. Also, your connection to the Goddess is the most potent when it's woven into your life and not fragmented throughout it. What I mean by this is that the upgrade comes when *everything* is a ritual to the Goddess, not just a discrete practice you do once a week. In my books *Inner Witch* and *Bewitching the Elements*, I share that the magick comes through living your life through the lens of the witch. You're not only a witch when you perform a ritual or cast a spell; your life changes when you become a witch because it defines the way you move through the world. This is also true when it comes to Goddess energy and being a devotee of the Divine Feminine. The clarity and inner knowing comes when you let it course through you, surging like a sea of expression and art and love.

This takes time! The Goddess reminds you that there's no rush, ever—just as the Moon cycles through death and rebirth each month, so will you throughout your life. Commitment and devotion are important, but the process of becoming is one that will be as unique as your journey.

Some ways to begin seeing your life as an expression of Goddess energy include the following:

+ As you put on clothes in the morning, think of yourself dressing the Goddess and draping Her in finery.
+ As you wash your face and brush your teeth, offer this up, knowing that taking care of yourself is a commitment to Her.

- Put on cologne or perfume as you say an affirmation to yourself and your beauty, knowing this holds a mirror up to the Goddess.
- As you put on makeup and feel yourself submerge into your beauty, remember that this is the Goddess's way of speaking to you.
- Bless your food and water in the name of the Goddess, holding your palms above them and feeling Divine white light moving through your body into them. Charge them with gratitude for the bounty of the Goddess and the earth, sending thanks to all the farmers, workers, drivers, and people who have brought your food to you.
- As you interact with friends, strangers, and loved ones, remember they're also made in the image of the Divine, and that you are all embodiments of the Goddess.
- When you wash your hands, visualize rinsing them with white, healing light that the Goddess sends to release anything that's physically, spiritually, mentally, or emotionally keeping you from aligning with your truth.
- If you feel sad or angry or upset or horny, remember that these are reflected in the Feminine Divine, too, and that working through them instead of rejecting them is the holiest thing you can do.
- As you breathe, notice how good it feels, allowing each breath to be a prayer of clarity and gratitude for this life. With each inhale, draw in life-giving awareness, Goddess energy, and consciousness, and with each exhale, release worry, tension, and anxiety.
- Take a walk or spend time in nature as you honor the Goddess of the Earth. Speak to Her. Make an effort to feel the sunshine or wind on your skin every day if you can. Remind yourself that you are a fractal of the universe.
- See taking care of yourself as an act of service to your higher self and the Goddess. When you exercise or make supportive choices

about how you feed and nurture your body, you are reaffirming to the Feminine Divine that you *are* Her. Taking care of yourself is also taking care of the Goddess. Allow this to inspire you and to guide your decisions when it comes to health, healing, and self-care.

+ When you feel safe and in your body, thank the Goddess of Protection and Healing.
+ When you feel love, when you notice your heart growing, or when you feel soft and tender, thank the Goddess of Love.
+ When you notice your rage and anger as catalysts to true transformation, thank the Dark Goddess.
+ In moments of ecstasy, joy, play, gratitude, love, or happiness, thank the Goddess! Your full-bodied awareness and presence is a prayer and a cry of thanks to this life you get to live and an immersive experience of cocreating with the Sacred Feminine.

EMBODIMENT AS A PATH TO GODDESS ENERGY

Because the Goddess is of the flesh, and because Goddess energy is immanence and not just transcendence, the self becomes a sacred temple to this energy. Your body isn't dirty, or perverse, or sinful. Your body is perfect just as it is, and it's a reflection of the Goddess's infinite guises.

Some pillars of embodiment in the Goddess path are glamour and rituals of self-adornment, invoking or drawing the Goddess into your body during ritual, and moving and feeling into your body as a path to Her vital essence. Keep in mind that embodiment isn't confined to just these three things, but is an array of experiences that helps you feel that the Goddess dwells in you. As the feminine face of God in mystical

Judaism is called Shekinah, which means "indwelling," you can know the face of the Goddess by the way you experience Her energy within.

THE GLAMOUR OF THE GODDESS

The word *glamour* comes from the Scottish *gramarye*, meaning "magick," "enchantment," or "spell." This isn't far off from our meaning here, although its definition is twofold. In an esoteric sense, a glamour conceals or veils that which dwells beneath it. A glamour shifts the way something is seen through mindfulness and/or adornment. It is a layer of conscious transformation. When you swipe on red lipstick or declare a charm of beauty or confidence, you are casting a glamour. When you wear red to attract passion, desire, and action, or black to melt into the shadows, you are casting a glamour. When you wear something that makes you feel fabulous as fuck, you are casting a glamour. Welcome to the world of fashion alchemy. We don't have cookies, but we have great style. Glamour is adornment, but it is also our day-to-day version of sculpted elegance with a healthy dash of je ne sais quoi, à la Dita Von Teese. Those we tend to describe as "glamorous" have an air of mystery and breathtaking beauty that seems to lift them up to the realm of the Divine. Glamour and the Goddess are inextricably linked.

The glamour of the Goddess is veiling yourself with reverence and devotion so you can draw in Her energy, as a path to live in Her honor and claim your own divinity. Channel this when you work with glamour, whether you're doing so to put on your best face for a date, to move through an anxiety-inducing situation, or to worship the Goddess. Your end goal may be unrelated to beauty itself; you may wear rose perfume to live with Venus energy or all white for cleansing and healing. You may wear a talisman for luck or heirloom jewelry to honor your ancestry. Glamour is *intention*, and adorning yourself this way means reclaiming how you're seen and how you move through the world, both by your will and that of the Goddess.

Magick transforms you from the inside out. Glamour transforms you from the outside in. Combine the two, and you get a truly alchemical ritual, shifting your internal and external states at once. Seeing yourself as a living, breathing Goddess means treating yourself as such, giving yourself permission to be expressed in any way that aligns with who you are. If you're ready to answer the call of the glamour of the Goddess, start here:

+ *Allow the Goddess to guide you through Her energy, magick, and correspondences.* Because this isn't just glamour but *Goddess glamour*, turn to the source (aka Goddess) for inspiration. Allow Her correspondences to guide you. What is She associated with wearing? Maybe its Inanna/Ishtar's and Venus/Aphrodite's girdle, or maybe She dons a lunar crown like Hathor, or perhaps She is seen with flowers like Xochiquetzal.

Take into consideration Her color associations. What colors is She pictured in? Are there colors that are sacred to Her? Look for scent and herbal correspondences, too, and seek out matching perfume or oils. Because scent is a stronger tie to emotion and memory than any other sense, this can be an advantageous association, especially in ritual. You may dedicate an oil or perfume to the Goddess or a specific Goddess, wearing it in ritual and in real life whenever you want to align with Her.

By taking a look at what the Goddess wears in Her art and icons, you also can get a clue as to how to dress in Her honor. Researching what Her priests and priestesses wore to worship Her is a road into Her glamour mysteries.

+ *Wear the symbols and correspondences of your Goddess for protection and connection.* Work with the symbols and correspondences to craft talismans and glamour rituals. If you're worshipping a lunar Goddess like Artemis/Diana, you could wear silver, which is associated with the Moon, or a crescent Moon on your jewelry or clothing. If you're worshipping the Morrigan, wear a necklace with a crow on it, or something with black feathers. The symbols of the Goddess are pathways to your own holy associations. Even the planetary, elemental, and astrological correspondences of your Goddess can guide you to Her; wearing them will change how you feel and perceive yourself, which will then change the way others are affected by you. Wearing yellow and gold for a solar Goddess like Sekhmet or Amaterasu will feel different from wearing the black of a Saturnian Goddess like Kali, or the green and copper associated with Venus or Green Tara. Keep a note of all the correspondences you come up with in your research, *as well as any which you come to through meditation, ritual, communication with the Goddess and personal gnosis.*

+ *Envision yourself as your chosen Goddess.* Ask yourself, *What do I want to wear? How do I feel in my body? How do I embody and express*

PLANETARY, METAL, AND COLOR CORRESPONDENCES		
PLANET	METAL	COLOR
Saturn	Lead	Black
Jupiter	Tin	Blue
Mars	Iron	Red
Sun	Gold	Yellow
Venus	Copper	Green
Mercury	Mercury	Orange
Moon	Silver	Purple

my power? How do I want to be worshipped? What excites my senses? What do I feel, and how can I bring this down to Earth?

Fashion, beauty, and adornment are vital pathways to magick *because you have to wear clothing every day anyway* (unless you live in a nudist colony, which, hello, I'm jealous!). Wearing clothing is just a reality of life. But when you add reverence and intention to picking out your clothes, jewelry, and makeup; to bathing yourself and doing your skin-care routine; or to painting your nails, you're adding a mystical and spiritual layer to your day.

Creating a glamour practice to the Goddess isn't vain or shallow. In fact, it's quite the opposite. Priestesses of the Goddess of Love have adorned Her statues with sacred oils and dressed them in Her likeness. Ancient erotic votaries would make themselves beautiful to receive guests in the temple of the Goddess of Love while embodying the magick of this face of the Divine. As astrologer and mystic Manly P. Hall stated, "The garments and ornamentations supposedly worn by the gods are keys, for in the Mysteries clothing was considered as synonymous with form," and it's only through form—and embodiment—that the Goddess lives among us in the earthly realm.

)) ● ● ● ((

CREATING TALISMANS OF GLAMOUR

One of my favorite ways to connect to the Goddess is by wearing my prayers to Her in talismans I consecrate and charge in Her honor. A talisman is an item infused with sacred intention and magick to bring something toward you, whether it's love, money, beauty, or devotion. An amulet, on the other hand, is infused with sacred intention and magick to keep something away, such as bad luck, death, or negativity. You can charge amulets and talismans in the same way, changing your wording and associations as you do so. Talismans don't have to be something you wear either. They can be made of paper, wood, metals, or other materials that you keep on your altar or in your home, purse, or car. For example, you could call on Frigg to charge a talisman for blessing your Divine union with your partner, or to charge an amulet to protect you from negative influences that will drive you and your partner apart.

There are many ways to charge talismans or amulets, and this is just one. You may find another way that works better for you. The goal is to begin embellishing yourself in magickal items that draw you closer to the Goddess. Although you can use anything you want to make a talisman, I've written this spell for jewelry. Adapt it as you wish, and remember that your jewelry doesn't have to be expensive to be a talisman. What matters is that you like wearing it and find it aesthetically pleasing and/or that it has significance. This heart-centered connection will draw in the Goddess.

You will need: The jewelry you'll be charging; the more associations it has with Goddess, the better. Herbs or incense for sacred smoke, water (Moon, rose, or Florida) or oil, your grimoire, a pen or pencil, an offering. Optional: crystals.

Before you begin, get clear on your intention. Ask yourself why you're creating this talisman, what this piece of jewelry means to you, what Goddess you're calling in (or you can always just work with the Goddess or Great Mother), and what qualities of Hers you want to grow. When you know these answers, perform the ritual.

Perform this ritual at a new, waxing, or full Moon for a talisman and at a waning or Dark Moon for an amulet.

Step 1: Set up the space, ground, and center
When you've decided on your intention, follow the instructions on page 12 to set up your space and ground and center.

Step 2: Invite in the Goddess, and share your intention
Use a prayer you've written to Her, a hymn, or a poem you've written. Feel free to write your own or use the following invitation:

> *Great Goddess, Divine and exalted feminine,*
> *Goddess* [name of the Goddess you're inviting], *I invite you now into this ritual.*
> *I call upon your* [list the qualities of this Goddess you're wanting to draw into this talisman] *and your Divine essence to be infused into this talisman for* [read/state your intention with this talisman]. *With this sacred container upon my flesh and heart, may I embody Your energy and draw You closer to me.*
> *I ask for Your blessing, for Your support, and for Your guidance as I proceed in the charging of this talisman.*

Step 3: Cleanse and consecrate
Place your talisman before you, and sprinkle it with water—just a bit, rubbing it off when you're done if it's not supposed to interact with water—or dab a little oil on it as you say the following or your own declaration:

In the name of the Goddess, in the name of [name of the Goddess
you're working with], *I cleanse this talisman of any negative
energies, of any energies that don't belong to me, of any energies
that don't vibrate in 100 percent Divine light. May the sacred waters
wash away what's no longer serving me.*

Put down your water, and light your sacred smoke. Then say the
following or write your own declaration:

In the name of the Goddess, in the name of [name of the Goddess
you're working with], *I consecrate this talisman. May this talisman
draw this intention to me, quickly, easily, and continuously, as this
smoke infuses it with this desire and carries this message to the
cosmos effortlessly.*

Step 4: Charge your talisman

Charge the talisman with your desire. Perform an invoking ritual like
a pentagram or a hexagram ritual that corresponds with the planetary energy of your Goddess if it's familiar. You also can work with sex
magick if it's in your practice.

Hold your intention in mind and heart as you rub your palms together, breathing into this, feeling the heat grow and grow. When it
gets too hot to handle, slowly pull apart your palms, feeling a ball of
energy forming between them. Then hold your palms above your talisman as you feel the healing and protective light of the cosmos and the
Goddess moving through your palms and into the talisman. Read the
following out loud, or write your own declaration:

In the name of the Goddess, in the name of [the Goddess you're
working with], *I now charge my talisman with my desired intention.
This talisman helps me embody Goddess energy and Goddess*

consciousness, and through this talisman I [read your intention for your talisman out loud]. *Every time I wear this talisman, it continues to draw my intention to me. Through the will of the Goddess, through my will, the blessing is done and the talisman is charged. This or something better for the highest good of all involved. And so it is!*

Infuse the talisman with your energy for as long as you'd like and then put it on.

Step 5: Thank the Goddess, and close the ritual

Find a comfortable position sitting up or lying down. Feel the profundity of this work, of charging your talisman in the name of the Goddess. Thank the Goddess, and let Her know that the working is done and you're grateful She joined you. You may say the following, adapting and rewriting as you wish:

Goddess [name of the Goddess you're inviting], *I thank You now for joining me in this ritual.*
I thank You for caring for me, for helping me charge this talisman, for assisting me in attaining my desired intention. I am grateful and filled with love. Thank You, thank You, thank You. You are dismissed and may leave if you wish. So mote it be.

Close and ground (page 13). Then leave an offering to the Goddess—like wine, food, incense, flowers, or sweets—on your altar alongside your talisman, placing any crystals on your talisman to further imbue it with energy. You also can write a prayer or an affirmation that you repeat to yourself whenever you put on your talisman.

You may wish to find a space on your altar—or erect a new altar—for your talismans to charge, keeping certain crystals or icons nearby to further them with Goddess energy when you're not wearing them. When in doubt of how best to wear and care for your talisman, ask the source directly! Wear or hold the talisman in your hand as you call to the Goddess in meditation or prayer, and ask how She'd like you to work with it. You may receive clear guidance, a feeling, an emotion, or an inner knowing, or you may receive something else completely. Follow your intuition and psychic senses, recording your experience in your Goddess Grimoire.

THE INVOCATION OF THE GODDESS

Because embodiment is of the body—literally, practices that lead you into the body's wisdom and foster this—and because invocation is drawing a deity, spirit, or archetype into your body, it felt right to include invocation in this section. Invocation has different correspondences: it can mean identifying with and then calling down an archetype, it could be when you are possessed by a deity, or it could be drawing this spirit into your circle or sacred space for the performance of a specific task. Invocation is a way not only to be *in* Goddess energy, but also to connect your consciousness with that of the Goddess, either the Goddess as Her role as the Great Goddess or a certain face of Hers.

In a pagan and theurgic sense, invocation means bringing the consciousness of a deity within your being. The problem with that is that deity and Divine consciousness are *big* and humans are small. The idea of filling ourselves with the consciousness of spirit seems a little silly, so I see it as less bringing the Divine into my physical body and more allowing my consciousness to be a part of the Divine consciousness I'm invoking and drawing *that* into my body. It's less trying to fill a chalice with the ocean and more swimming in its waves. It is usually done in a ritual setting, where you ask, or declare, that the Goddess be invoked into your being. I don't like to use the word *command*, but many practitioners say they "command spirits." I have too much love, reverence, and appreciation for the Goddess to command Her to do anything. I request or invite.

It is possible to lose track of yourself and get lost in the Goddess soup, but you don't have to worry about this if you're intentional and if you invoke deities you already have relationships with. Like any form of occultism or magick, there is potential for danger or to get fucked up, but that's why we're going to outline safe practices.

For one, I don't suggest invoking a Goddess you've never worked with. Instead, pray to Her, leave Her offerings, and meditate with Her. Once you've formed a relationship with Her, then you can invoke Her. And I suggest *e*voking before you *in*voke. Evocation is communicating with the Goddess, drawing Her into the sacred space to pray to Her, honor Her, and bring Her energy within your heart but not actually draw Her *into* you. If invocation is swimming in the ocean of the Divine, evocation is more like meditating on the shore;

you still feel the waters swirling around your feet, but you're not submerged.

Both evocation and invocation are embodied states of Goddess worship. You don't need to draw in the Goddess to feel Her presence and love. Praying or talking to the Goddess also can bring them about. Some of my most memorable visions and experiences with the Goddess haven't been when I invoke Her but when I feel Her in my heart, either in meditation, in the bath, or in ritual. There's a time and place for invocation—to allow Her to fully embody you—but sometimes you don't have the time for a whole ritual and need Her strength ASAP.

Invoking the Goddess

Before I share my own form of invocation, I want to mention a couple things. First, you may have a totally different practice for invoking a deity, and that's beautiful! Please use what resonates. Beyond that, you may invoke your deity at a different point of a ritual than when I do. When I'm performing rituals, and when I write and teach, I use the following framework, which I will expand upon later in this chapter to help you form your own devotionals and rituals with the Goddess.

A note: I work within the structure of Hermetic Qabalah, and you will see rituals like the Lesser Banishing Ritual of the Pentagram and the Lesser Banishing Ritual of the Hexagram in the following pages. These are rituals that work with the symbolic power of the pentagram and hexagram for grounding and protection. You can add them to your Goddess energy repertoire if you're familiar with them, but if not, you may wish to check out the 22 Teachings School of Hermetic Science and Magical Arts as well as *High Magick* by Damien Echols for more.

1. Set up myself, my space, and my intention. Adorn myself, gather supplies, ensure my phone's off, and light candles and incense.
2. Collar myself to the Goddess.
3. Perform the Lesser Banishing Ritual of the Pentagram.
4. Perform the Lesser Banishing Ritual of the Hexagram (optional).
5. Cleanse with water.
6. Consecrate with smoke.
7. Ground and center.
8. Declare the intention for the working to the Goddess I'm invoking.
9. Prepare candle magick.
10. *Invoke the Goddess and then meditate with Her.*

11. Practice sex magick, divination, and/or meditation.
12. When I feel the ritual is complete, thank the Goddess and dismiss Her from my body.
13. Close and ground.
14. Perform Lesser Banishing Ritual of the Pentagram.
15. Perform Lesser Banishing Ritual of the Hexagram (if I did it in opening).
16. Thank the Goddess again.
17. Put out my candles.
18. Record the results in my Goddess Grimoire.
19. Leave an offering for the Goddess on my altar.

You may invoke the Goddess first or dismiss Her last. You may do magick after you invoke Her and not before. Again, this is *Goddess energy*, and She should be the one to guide you. If in doubt, ask Her what She wants; pull tarot cards or free write to download Her desires.

When it comes to the invocation, I invite you to write your own to the Goddess you're invoking, work with an Orphic or Homeric Hymn, or use an invocation or poetry that speaks to you. I have found that channeling invocations to the Goddesses I'm devoted to has been useful and beautiful. You may use the following as a guide, filling in the blanks to the Great Mother Goddess or a specific Goddess you are calling into your body.

I love to chant and dance to invoke the Goddess. Try something like this:

[Name of Goddess]
[Name of Goddess]
I invoke Thee
I invoke Thee

Into me, into me
[Name of Goddess]
[Name of Goddess]
I invoke Thee
I invoke Thee
Into me, into me

Saying this rhythmically as you dance and move and build energy is so simple but so effective. I get faster and faster as I chant, dancing ecstatically until I collapse into a pile on my meditation cushion and begin breathing into the Goddess within me.

Invocation for the Goddess

Before you begin, you may want to practice the following visualization. See yourself in space, and allow yourself to slowly dissolve into nothingness. From here, feel yourself re-formed in the vision of your Goddess, *as* your Goddess. Allow this to take as much time as you want, and as you're embodied in Goddess energy, say the following:

O Great Goddess [name of Goddess]
She of [love and lust, death and rebirth, magick and
    mysticism, etc.]
I call upon Thee through my flesh
I call upon Thee from the heavens into my being
On all planes and in all ways
I invoke Thee
I invoke Thee
I invoke Thee
O [name of Goddess]

To whom I honor in this ceremony tonight
I breathe You through my heart
I breathe You through my soul
I breathe You through myself
Until we are one in Divine union
O Goddess of [name some attributes of the Goddess or some
    of Her epithets]
On the day of this ritual for [name the purpose of this ritual]
You and I are one
So You may know the beauty of the body
And so I may know the powers of Goddess consciousness
For the highest good of all involved
You and I are one
You and I are one
You and I are one
And so it is

When you've said your invocation, breathe Goddess energy through your being. Allow Her to bubble through you like a volcano or an earthquake. It may be slow, and you may not feel anything at all. It may be intense, and you may get the spins. You may feel a vibration or buzzing, or you may feel slightly stoned. You may feel all of this or none of this. Be gentle with yourself and remember, *this is a practice.* The more you do magick, the more you train yourself, your subtle body, and your nervous system to get into these modes of consciousness. With the Goddess, the more you show up to Her, the more She will show up to you. Don't be discouraged if you don't feel anything at first; it takes time. I still don't always feel a huge shift. Sometimes it's just not the best day for it!

And an incredibly important note: If something doesn't feel right—

if you start having a panic attack, for example, or feeling sick or overwhelmed—*remember that you are in control, and you can dismiss the Goddess whenever you want.* Use the following dismissal if you want to be formal, or just thank the Goddess in your own words, let Her know the ritual is closed, She is dismissed from your body, and She is able to return to where She is meant to be.

To Dismiss the Goddess

O Great Goddess [name of Goddess]
She of [love and lust, death and rebirth, magick and
     mysticism, etc.]
I have called upon Thee
Through my body
And now the time has come to close the ceremony
O Goddess,
Thank You for Your energy
I dismiss Thee
I dismiss Thee
I dismiss Thee
From my being
From my body
This invocation is complete
And now I dismiss Thee
I dismiss Thee
I dismiss Thee
With perfect love
And perfect trust
You may leave with peace
So mote it be

When you're done, breathe into the Goddess and feel Her energy dissolving, returning to the realm from which it came. Take as much time as you want, thanking Her as you do so.

If you did the visualization before the invocation, now do the opposite: visualize the Goddess dissolving and see yourself re-forming in your image instead. You can perform the following chant to finish the dismissal of the Goddess, moving and ecstatically dancing once again:

[Name of Goddess]
[Name of Goddess]
I dismiss Thee
I dismiss Thee
I dismiss Thee
Leave with peace, leave with peace

[Name of Goddess]
[Name of Goddess]
I dismiss Thee
I dismiss Thee
I dismiss Thee
Leave with peace, leave with peace

Whether or not you closed with the chant, remember to close and ground as on page 13 and do whatever you need to do to finish your ritual, including leaving offerings that support your desired intention with this ritual.

Understanding and working with a traditional invocation is important, but I also want to invite you to expand the idea of what it means to invoke the Goddess. Why can't you invoke Her when you're walking to your car at night and feel unsafe? Or when you're going through something tough in your home life but still have to dominate a work meeting? Or when you're grieving and lonely and want to give yourself permission to feel whatever it is you're experiencing? Invoking the Goddess means experiencing Her in an embodied state. It can be through dance, or prayer, or whenever you invite Her into your heart. Remember that you can call Her power into You whenever you want and need.

YOUR BIRTH CHART

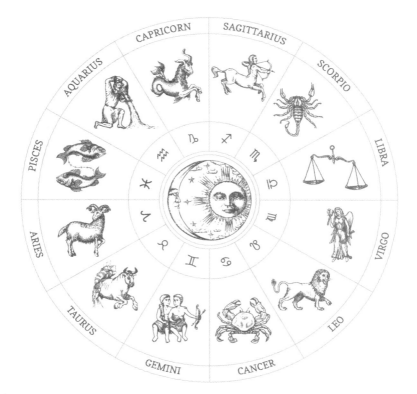

If you want to know about how the Goddess shows up within you, in your life, in your energetic field and cosmic potential, then all you have to do is look at the stars. Well, more accurately, all you have to do is look at your birth, or natal, chart. Your birth chart is your personal cosmic blueprint to your greatest potential, and it acts as a snapshot of the locations of the planets at the time of your birth. The 360-degree wheel, known as the zodiac or zodiacal wheel, is broken up into twelve sections, or houses, each of which is ruled by a different zodiac sign. Each of the planets falls into one of these houses, and the planet is colored by the house and sign it's in. Think of the planets as the actors, the signs they're in as their roles, and the houses as the scenes. Each zodiac sign is ruled by a different planet, adding another nuance to the mix. The relationships these celestial bodies have with one another are called aspects; some are harmonious and supportive (like trines), some are challenging or activating (like squares), and some are intensifying and amplifying (like conjunctions).

Your birth chart is a complex puzzle that can help you understand and live your soul's potential. Looking at both its individual pieces and as a whole will help you understand and integrate the lessons you're meant to learn in this life and shine a light on the challenges, struggles, lessons, and moments of growth and expansion you're meant to face. Calculate your birth chart using websites like astro .com and apps like TimePassages (my favorite astrology app).

The Divine Feminine will show up in your birth chart in a few ways. First, look for the sign that the Moon and Venus are in. The Moon represents the unconscious, the intuitive, and the feeling, and here it represents your inner nature and the way you need to be nurtured and cared for. Venus represents sex, love, glamour, wealth, receiving, and beauty, and your relationship to all these facets. The Moon reflects the subconscious and mysteries of the Goddess, and the Goddess in Her guise as the Lunar Queen. As the Goddess of Love, Venus illuminates your relationship to sexuality, love, and what femininity means to you.

Checking the locations of the Moon and Venus in your birth chart, and what aspects they make, can clarify how the Goddess shows up in your life. A trained astrologer will be able to add more granularity to your reading, but even just knowing the sign that the Moon and Venus are in can be educational in terms of how you receive love and give love, and the way you move through the world living in Goddess energy.

Next, look for which houses Venus and the Moon are in. For example, if you have Venus in the third house, which is the house of Gemini ruled by Mercury, you'll find a motif of duality because Mercury is the Divine messenger; the God of Magick; and the deity who can travel between the underworld, the earth, and the heavens at will. Because the third house rules over communication, information, and travel, Goddess energy may manifest as being inspired by Goddesses of knowledge, such as Athena, or through Goddesses who express those dualities, such as Persephone. Or maybe you're deepest in Goddess consciousness when you're teaching what you believe in, when you're traveling to new places and learning about other cultures, or when you're writing or creating something to share.

The two signs, and their respective houses, that also can reveal how the Goddess shows up in your chart are earth sign Taurus and air sign Libra because both are ruled by Venus. Taurus rules the second house, which is all about money, wealth, possessions, and personal security but can really point to what you value. Libra rules the seventh house, which contains partnerships of all kinds (including business and romantic), marriage, and social contracts; the seventh house is all about collaboration. Likewise, seeing what's in either

Taurus or Libra can help you engage with how Venusian energy appears in your life. If you have a lot of planets in Libra or Taurus, or a lot of planets in the second or seventh house, this also can help you understand how to nurture the Goddess within yourself and lead the way in knowing how to worship Her. Finally, look at the fourth house, ruled by Cancer and the Moon, which encompasses home, family, and your relationship with your mother, as well as the way the feminine influences your internal world.

ASTEROIDS

The discovery of planetary bodies in modern astrology often correlates to shifts in human consciousness. The discovery of Neptune in 1846 came alongside the Victorians' reawakened interest in the spiritual, reflected in philosophies like transcendentalism and in movements like spiritualism, and Pluto was discovered in 1930, at the precipice of World War II and the heightened tensions of the Atomic Age. So, too, the discovery of asteroids reflects the collective ambiance, specifically through the lens of the feminine.

Alongside the Moon and Venus, asteroids are a cosmic window into the forces and forms of the Divine Feminine in the birth chart. Discovered in the early 1800s, asteroids are smaller planetary bodies that are contained mostly between the orbits of Mars and Jupiter. This was around the time that women's societal roles began changing in a big way. The first four asteroids discovered were named after Great Goddesses: Ceres/Demeter, Athena/Minerva, Juno/Hera, and Vesta/Hestia. Each one, like the Goddess it's named after, has specific characteristics and associations that are affected by its house, sign, and aspects. But there are more than a thousand asteroids, each with a name and a number, including Aphrodite, Isis, Babylon, Artemis, Medusa, and Pythia, as well as for Gods like Apollo, Osiris, and Eros. Like the planets, the asteroids personify human traits and characteristics and allow greater understanding of self through the natal chart.

Some of the main Goddess asteroids are listed in the following pages. Use a website like astro.com and its Extended Chart Selection tool to pick the asteroids whose placements you want to review in your natal chart.

Ceres

#1
Associated zodiac sign: Cancer

Ceres—the Roman equivalent to Demeter—was the first asteroid ever discovered, and it's technically a dwarf planet, which is the largest object in the asteroid belt. It's a fitting name and discovery, seeing as the influence of Ceres/Demeter was so profound on the ancient world. With major Queen of Pentacles energy, Ceres is the asteroid that represents the universal mother, the maternal aspect of the self, mainly through the way you support and nourish others. As Persephone's mother, Demeter expressed Her unconditional love, and this same energy is found in this asteroid. As the corn mother, bringing the harvest and providing sustenance, Ceres also represents the ways in which you feed and care for yourself and your body and keep yourself safe in the material plane.

Pallas Athene

#2

Associated zodiac sign: Libra, Aquarius, Leo

Pallas Athene resonates with the mythos of the Greek Athena and Roman Minerva, the Goddess of War, Wisdom, and Justice, and it can help you articulate how these values manifest in your life. As an asteroid, Athena can reveal the ways you can take charge while holding your vision close to your heart. This is discernment, sharp as a sword, showing you that you are capable of making the wisest choice possible. Asteroid Pallas Athene is also wildly creative and, depending on its location, can tell you what you can manifest through visualization. Per astrologer Demetra George, Athene "embodies the magical will that enables us to create and control our own reality" and the placement of this asteroid can pin down where you have the most influence over shifting this reality.

Juno

#3

Associated zodiac sign: Libra, Scorpio

In Greek mythology, Juno is Zeus's wife, and She embodies devotion and love in committed relationships. The asteroid Juno speaks this same language, highlighting the role of the feminine in sacred union and divine partnerships. Juno speaks of merging with another, and of the fears that can often come with commitment: the fear of betrayal, the fear of sexuality, and the fear of abandonment. In this same way, it highlights the power of marriage, of commitment, of devotion to another as life-changing and -enhancing. Autonomy is required to merge with another without losing the self. This asteroid can clarify your story and patterns in relationships, whether romantic or any kind of union. Juno is a guide in creating healthy templates for conscious relationships, not by avoiding the shadowy or scary or intimidating bits, but by embracing all the self as an offering to the beloved to maintain a balanced and loyal partnership.

Lilith

#1181

You have met Lilith, the Goddess of the Untamed Feminine who refuses to be subordinated. In the birth chart and as an asteroid, Lilith represents power, repressed anger, lust, and the ability to voice one's needs and desires. Lilith represents independence and, depending on placement, how this is channeled and expressed. In the birth chart, She can mean the "perception of the feminine as evil," the potential for sexual assault or abuse, or imbalanced power dynamics. Working with this energy in a personalized way through the birth chart can be an experience of claiming and liberating your sexuality and embracing the Dark Goddess of Love within.

Dive deeper into Goddess energy with these asteroids by taking into consideration the way they dance with the other pieces of your birth chart. They can help you understand Goddess energy in a way that feels embodied and unique because you can see how their influence plays out for you personally. Allow this short guide to be a starting point in your personal explorations.

CREATING YOUR OWN GODDESS CORRESPONDENCES TO WORK WITH

Beyond working with your birth chart, you can internalize, understand, relate to, and honor the Goddess with a personalized set of correspondences. Correspondences are objects—like plants or herbs, planets, colors, numbers, and sounds—that are associated with a particular vibration, deity, or spirit. They have an energetic link to a specific archetype, and in this way, they are shorthand for calling on it. They can't replace the thing itself, but they act like a number you can dial to get ahold of their frequency.

In my own practice, I work with the correspondences laid out by The Hermetic Order of the Golden Dawn and later Aleister Crowley through his book *777*, which also follows the tradition of Hermetic Qabalah. This places the planets on the Qabalistic Tree of Life, alongside tarot cards, crystals, colors, numbers, notes, animals, and Goddesses for each of the ten spheres and twenty-two paths of the tree. For example, roses, chocolate, honey, and red wine are all linked to Venus and Aphrodite, the Roman and Grecian Goddess of Love, and this is reflected in the classic Valentine's Day gifts. Other associations for Venus are the number seven, copper, lynxes, dolphins, and roses. If you need luck, you could look to associations like Jupiter, the number four, the color blue, and mint. (I highly recommend *777* and *Llewellyn's Complete Book of Correspondences* for more specifics in using correspondences in ritual, ceremony, spellwork, and devotion.)

You also can concoct your own system of correspondences. One of the secrets of magick is feeling—feeling into what you're doing, raising an emotion associated with your intention or goal, and using this to heighten the sensation and experience in the ritual space. When you begin to generate your own chain of correspondences while working with the Goddess, you are infusing your personal being, heart, and soul into this work. Use the established correspondences as a starting point, and take note of what makes you feel Goddess energy when you see it. Maybe there's a certain flower your mom always bought for your birthday, or an herb your grandma tended to. Maybe there's a specific color you love to wear that makes you feel like the Goddess incarnate, or a scent that transports you back to the first days you were exploring magick.

What I'm trying to get at here is the power of *your own personal set of correspondences that connect you to Goddess energy.* Make a list in your Goddess Grimoire, perhaps allocating space to each of the Goddesses explored in this book—Goddesses of the Earth, Goddesses of Healing and Protection, Goddesses of Love, Dark Goddesses—and whatever other sections you want to include. Because we are modern witches, we also can include modern-day correspondences in our workings: artists you associate with the Goddess or a certain movie, director, city, or song. Consider including colors, numbers, herbs, crystals, trees, scents, artists, words, oils and incense, animals, metals, and foods. As always, your heart and feeling are your lodestar. Use these correspondences to honor the Goddess and the Goddess within yourself.

Get creative; there's no right or wrong. There's just what's right and true for *you,* and that's what will generate an even more personal relationship with the Goddess.

TABLE OF CORRESPONDENCES

Elemental Correspondences

ELEMENT	DIRECTION	ARCHANGEL	SENSE	HERBS	
Earth	North	Uriel/Ariel	Touch	Rosemary, frankincense, bay leaf, oak, daisy, clover	
Air	East	Raphael	Smell	Lavender, eucalyptus, rosemary, dandelion, mugwort, honeysuckle, nettle, thyme, sandalwood	
Fire	South	Michael	Sight	Cinnamon, basil, carnation, clove, vanilla, vervain, tobacco, cumin, devil's shoestring, cayenne, mandrake, dragon's blood, Saint-John's-wort, deer's tongue	
Water	West	Gabriel	Taste	Rosemary, apple, chamomile, catnip, poppy, ginseng, rose, gardenia, jasmine, birch, watercress	
Spirit	Up	Metranon		Doesn't have as clear associations; aphrodisiacs, pomegranate, butterfly pea, rose, nettle, ashwagandha	

CRYSTALS	COLORS	MAGICK	ZODIA SIGNS
All crystals because they come from the earth, but especially black tourmaline, onyx, hematite, obsidian	Green, black, brown, gray, the colors of the earth, neutrals	Wealth, abundance, prosperity, boundaries, protection, grounding, commitment, loyalty, home	Capricorn, Taurus, Virgo
Selenite, clear quartz, smoky quartz, sodalite, celestite, fluorite, lapis lazuli, lepidolite	Yellow, white, silver, iridescent, gossamer	Business, legal problems, communication, travel, inspiration, knowledge, breathwork, astral travel, divination	Aquarius, Gemini, Libra
Carnelian, citrine, orange calcite, pyrite, tigereye, bloodstone, garnet, ruby, peridot	Red, orange, yellow, gold	Transformation, initiation, sexuality, the erotic, passion, confidence, release, adventure, banishment	Aries, Leo, Sagittarius
Amethyst, blue lace agate, jade, moonstone, pearl, topaz, malachite, rhodonite	Blue, purple, indigo, silver, white, light pink	Divination, shadow work, love, healing, self-love, karmic and ancestral healing, pleasure, intuition, sensuality, psychic work, dream work	Pisces, Cancer, Scorpio
Clear quartz, labradorite, charoite, Herkimer diamond, selenite	Silver, gold, the rainbow	Spiritual development, connecting to your intuition, karmic untangling, past life work, enlightenment, channeling and working with deities	

TABLE OF CORRESPONDENCES

Herbal Correspondences

PROPERTIES	HERBS
Love	Herbs of Venus, acacia flower, jasmine, lavender, mistletoe, myrtle, valerian, vervain, violet, rose, gardenia, apple, cinnamon
Protection	Basil, feverfew, hyssop, laurel, motherwort, nettle, juniper, yerba santa, mullein, cascarilla (powdered eggshells), patchouli, rosemary, rowan, sandalwood, frankincense, myrrh, cinnamon, bay leaf, vervain
Healing	Lavender, carnation, rosemary, gardenia, garlic, ginseng, hops, mint, saffron, rowan, rue, eucalyptus, peppermint, lemon balm
Psychic work	Dragonwort, mugwort, ginseng, laurel leaves, saffron, chamomile, dandelion, skullcap, catnip, clover, mint, nutmeg, rosemary, lavender
Manifesting	Bamboo, beech, dandelion, ginseng, pomegranate, mint, rosemary, sandalwood, violet, walnut
Creativity	Laurel, lavender, cinnamon, myrtle, valerian, orange
Banishing/binding	Cascarilla, nettle, devil's shoestring, bamboo, benzoin, cayenne, rosemary, frankincense, mandrake, peppermint
Wealth	Balm, High John the Conqueror root, lavender, mandrake, oak leaf, saffron, valerian, mint, cinnamon, citrus

TABLE OF CORRESPONDENCES

Color Correspondences

COLOR	MEANING
Red	Passion, sexual love, vitality, heat, attraction, fire
Pink	Love, femininity, nurturing, protection of children, healing, sensuality, the heart, tenderness, feeling, bliss
Orange	Encouragement, creativity, stimulation, warmth, attraction, power, motivation, direction
Yellow	Confidence, inner strength, power, vitality, will, vigor, self-awareness, happiness, energy, masculinity
Green	Finance, luck, wealth, prosperity, abundance, healing, heart opening, the energy of the earth, love, fertility, grounding
Blue	Tranquility, patience, healing, surrender, the ocean, the subconscious, dreams, relaxation, safety
Purple	Royalty, magick, power, ambition, business progress, spirituality, connecting to your third eye and higher self, psychic awareness
Black	Absorbing negativity, darkness, night, shadow work, banishing
White	Attracting positivity, healing, light purity, the energy of the cosmos, cleansing, protection
Silver	Celestial energy, the Moon, protection, the unconscious, the heavens, the Divine, the angelic sphere
Gold	Wealth, abundance, radiance, victory, money, power, security, the Sun

CREATING RITUALS WITH THE GODDESS

Share your love and devotion to the Goddess and Her energy by creating rituals for Her and yourself. By now, you understand what a ritual format looks like, and this is especially true if you came into this with your own practice already established. Use the framework that follows for inspiration, or make your own. Take what serves you, and leave the rest. From here, allow the Goddess to guide you, and trust in Her to show you what you need, even if it's not what you want.

Use the following steps to begin customizing your Goddess rituals.

STEP 1:
GET CLEAR ON YOUR INTENTION
Think of what you want, whether it's to heal, invoke, banish, call in, inspire, or give an offering.

STEP 2:
DECIDE WHICH FACE OF THE GODDESS YOU WANT TO CALL ON
Do you want to call on the Goddess in Her face of maiden? Mother/queen? Crone? Do you want to call on the Goddess of Love or the Goddess of Protection and Healing? The Dark Goddess? A specific Goddess like Kali or Persephone? Get clear on what Goddess energy you're connecting with.

STEP 3:
DETERMINE WHAT RITUAL STRUCTURE
BEST SUPPORTS YOUR GODDESS AND YOUR INTENTION
Do you want to dance as an offering to death and rebirth to Kali? Do

you want to do sex magick to reach out to Venus? Do you want to do automatic writing to meet Thoth? Is something more formal and structured going to align with your working, or is something more intuitive and flowing going to support you more?

STEP 4:
DECIDE ON TOOLS AND CORRESPONDENCES
What do you need for this ritual? What correspondences, like colors, oils, herbs, etc., can you work with to form an association to the Goddess? Use the tables on pages 248–51 and your own list of correspondences to assist in this.

STEP 5:
ESTABLISH THE ASTROLOGICAL SUPPORT YOU WANT
Think of what Moon phase would work for this ritual. Also consider the sign the Sun and Moon are in and what the day of the week or what planet they're ruled by. If you want to get specific, use an app like Time Nomad to pinpoint a supportive planetary hour for this ritual.

STEP 6:
FIGURE OUT HOW TO EMBODY AND HONOR THE GODDESS
Now comes the fun part: how do you want to honor the Goddess in this ritual? You can try the following:

+ Dance
+ Invoke or evoke
+ Pull oracle or tarot cards
+ Create art: write a poem, paint, knit, draw, take photos, etc.
+ Adorn yourself through glamour and clothing

- Sing or chant
- Pray
- Meditate
- Practice sex magick
- Work with candle magick

You also can work with the elements to guide you in this work:

Earth: Rituals around grounding, protection, and safety
Air: Rituals around speech, inspiration, and breath
Fire: Rituals around passion, sexuality, strength, battle, and
   anger
Water: Rituals around love, healing, shadow work, and opening

STEP 7:
CONSIDER HOW YOU WANT TO CLOSE, AND DECIDE ON OFFERINGS

If there's a specific prayer or affirmation you want to say to close your ritual, now is the time to decide on it. It's also the time to choose whatever offerings you want to leave.

STEPS FOR A DIY RITUAL

The following is an example of a ritual structure I work with, which may help you incorporate the above:

1. Gather supplies (step 4).
2. Ground and center.
3. Open the circle/Lesser Banishing Ritual of the Pentagram.
4. Make your statement of intention, or why you're performing the ritual (step 1).

5. Invoke, evoke, or invite in the Goddess (step 2).
6. Perform magick and raise the energy (step 6).
7. Send the energy to your intention.
8. Thank the Goddess and dismiss Her.
9. Close the circle.
10. Ground and close.

CREATING LONG-FORM DEVOTIONALS TO THE GODDESS

Spells and rituals are a staple in any witch's routine, yet one of the most transformational and potent tools I have discovered when working with Goddesses is long-form devotionals.

A devotional is a magickal working extending a certain number of days that's dedicated to an intention—in this case, to meet a Goddess, to get to know Her better, or to explore a specific energy or quality. You can perform a devotional to a specific Goddess, to a specific face of the Goddess like the Dark Goddess, or to the Goddess energy within you. Devotionals extend a ritual or spell over time; instead of doing a spell and being done with it, you come back to the devotional practice every day for the allotted number of days. This regular practice, in service to a Goddess or the Goddess, colors your life with its frequency. When you transform your day-to-day into a ritual for the Divine Feminine, its power truly cannot be overstated.

For the last sixteen months, while I have been writing this book, I also have been practicing long-form devotionals from new Moon to new Moon. For this time, I dedicate myself to an intention, an exploration, or a Goddess. I have done devotionals for longer, spanning months, and shorter, spanning days or a couple weeks, and I prefer the month-long format because it coincides with the lunar cycle. Because I already have an established daily magickal practice, it's not difficult for me to commit. When you are deciding to embark on a long-form devotional, I recommend starting small and making sure you can commit every day. It's better to be honest and commit to a week, if you know that you can achieve it, than to commit to a month and forget the practice for multiple days. You always can extend the devotional practice if you feel called.

The center of this long-form practice is the Goddess or a Goddess. You will use this container to meet Her every day. You can have a formal declaration and opening of this ritual, or you can meditate and let the Goddess know you are committing to Her in this way. In this same vein, when you end the devotional, you may do so formally or through meditation.

Here are some questions and guidelines to plan a devotional to Goddess:

+ *When will my devotional start? How long will it last?* Take into consideration what lunar phase you want to begin and end in and what sign the Sun and Moon are in. You can do a devotional for three days, five days, thirty days, or ninety days—again, whatever works for you without feeling overwhelming.
+ *What Goddess is this in devotion to?* If not the Goddess, then maybe one of Her archetypal faces like the Goddess of the Earth, the Goddess of Love, etc.?
+ *What is my intention?* For example, to connect with a specific Goddess, to embody Goddess energy, or to feel the Goddess of Healing or Love or a Dark Goddess.

+ *What magickal or spiritual act can I commit to every day to honor this? Can I start with one thing for a few days, add another thing, and then add another?* Make a schedule for yourself if this is useful.
+ *Can I name my devotional?* For example, maybe Devotional to the Dark Goddess, Devotional to Goddess Energy, or Devotional to the Divine Erotic?
+ *How will I open this or close it? How can I formalize this ritual, using the steps in the section on creating rituals with the Goddess* (page 252)?

Some of the activities you may choose to work with every day in your practice include the following:

+ Meditation
+ Prayer
+ Lighting a candle
+ Leaving an offering
+ Reading about the stories, mythology, or symbols of your Goddess
+ Sex magick (Check out my book *Sacred Sex* for a step-by-step guide to creating a devotional to the Goddess using sex magick.)
+ Creating art as an offering
+ Divining with an oracle or tarot deck and journaling the results
+ Dancing, singing, or playing music
+ Repeating an affirmation or mantra

Tailor a ritual of devotion to a Goddess of your choice, and use the outline of a ritual format on page 252 to help. You are held, protected, and guided on this path, and you deserve to bask in it. And so it is!

———) ◗ ● ● ◖ (———

A SELF-INITIATION/DEDICATION RITUAL
FOR THE GODDESS PATH

Self-initiations or dedications hold major power. They mark a transformation of self through commitment, either to the path or to a specific face of the Goddess. When you perform a ritual to mark your devotion, you are affirming to the Goddess that this is something you choose, are willing to engage with deeply, and dedicate yourself to.

This self-initiation ritual can be done in one of two ways: you may work with it as an initiation into the Goddess path and into the Goddess religion, dedicating yourself to the Divine Feminine, or you may adopt it to devote yourself to a specific face of the Goddess, like Venus or Athena.

Either way, there is no rush. You will know when you're ready, even if you never feel 100 percent there. If you are devoting yourself in service to a Goddess, this is a big step in and of itself. Spend time with Her in meditation, in divination, and in long-form devotional ritual to ensure this is something you are both ready for. When you feel you are sure, then take the leap. Know this requires responsibility, especially if you are devoting yourself to a specific Goddess. You will need to honor Her regularly and commune with Her often. If you are not ready for this commitment, then I suggest holding back for now. You always can honor Her through rituals, meditation, and long-form devotionals instead.

Keep in mind that dedicating yourself to a Goddess is not infinite. You can formally end this period of devotion by adopting this same ritual and letting the Goddess know that the relationship is called to be transformed and that is no longer serving both of you to be dedicated to Her in this way.

You will need: A chalice of water; herbs to burn for sacred smoke and something to burn them in; a lighter; something to represent the Goddess or the Goddess you're devoting yourself to (a statue, an image, jewelry, or a candle); something to represent your devotion to the Goddess (a song, art, jewelry, a poem, a candle you carve and anoint, a crystal, another talisman that's meaningful, or a cord or string to tie to represent this bind); and an offering like roses, honey, milk, bread, or incense.

Optional: Sex toys and lube for sex magick.

In this ritual, you will be cleansing and clearing yourself so you can be reborn as a devotee of the Goddess, or as a devotee to the Goddess of your choosing. You will be spending time in creative ritual, in service to Her. Before you begin, you may wish to take an Epsom salt bath in the dark, an expression of the womb, to represent being rebirthed on this path. You also may wear something that makes you feel beautiful and in Goddess energy, whether this is leather, red lipstick, or nothing but your favorite perfume.

A note: If you are dedicating yourself to a Goddess, replace Goddess in the following with the name of your specific Goddess. You may write your dedication to the Goddess (step 6) before you begin.

Step 1: Set your intention and your space

As always, ask yourself why you're doing this ritual. What do you hope to get out of this initiation? What do you hope it will change or transform? How do you plan to carry forth this Goddess energy into your daily life? Spend time in contemplation, getting clear on who or what you're dedicating yourself to and why.

Now get your space ready, following the instructions on page 12. Be sure you have all your supplies. Set up your altar with representations of your Goddess, with water and herbs to either side and whatever represents your devotion nearby.

Step 2: Ground and center
Ground and center (page 12). Perform any other opening rituals in your practice.

Step 3: Cleanse yourself with water
When you feel present within yourself, dip your fingers in your water, touch the top of your head, and say:

I open myself to the Divine consciousness of the Goddess.

Dip your fingers in your water, touch your third eye, and say:

I see the Goddess and Goddess energy everywhere.

Repeat, touching your throat chakra as you say:

I speak love and radiate the truth of the Goddess.

Dip your fingers again, touch your heart, and say:

My heart is open and overflowing with the love of the Goddess.

Now repeat and touch your solar plexus, above your belly button, as you say:

I am fueled with the power and lust of the Goddess.

Dip your fingers in the water and touch your sacral chakra, under your belly button, as you say:

I am alive with the radiant sensuality and eroticism of the Goddess.

Finally, dip your fingers in the water, touching your root chakra, right above your pubic bone, and say:

I am grounded in the power of the <u>Goddess</u>, from the highest above to the lowest below. I am cleansed in the name of the <u>Goddess</u>. And so it is.

Take a second to feel cleansed and held.

Step 4: Cleanse yourself with smoke

Light your herbs and blow them out so they smolder. Pass this smoke around you clockwise to draw in the protection of the Goddess as you say the following:

I am enlivened and alive with the power and radiance of the <u>Goddess</u>. I am imbibed with the magick of the <u>Goddess</u>. I consecrate myself in the love of the <u>Goddess</u>. And so it is.

Step 5: Evoke the Goddess

Call the Goddess into your circle to declare your devotion to Her. Use the following, write your own evocation, or say one you've used before:

O <u>Goddess</u>
I evoke Thee in this sacred space
With perfect love and perfect trust
May You fill my heart and circle
in all planes and in all ways with Your grace
O <u>Goddess</u>
I call upon Thee at this time,
So You may hear my sacred plea
So You may hear the song of my heart and soul
So I may dedicate myself to Thee.
O <u>Goddess</u>,
I evoke Thee, I evoke Thee,

Come to me, come to me.
O Goddess,
I evoke Thee, I evoke Thee,
Come to me, come to me.
O Goddess,
I evoke Thee, I evoke Thee,
Come to me, come to me.
So mote it be.

Step 6: Devote yourself to the Goddess

Write something, or speak from your heart. Use whatever you brought to signify your devotion. Dance, write a song, or meditate with a crystal that expresses your intention. It's a time to speak, to cry, to commune. You may tie a string, either a bracelet or anklet to wear or a knotted cord, to represent binding yourself to the Goddess. Say or adopt the following and then spend time in devotion:

O Goddess, o unyielding power of the Divine Feminine,
On this [day/month/year] in the season of [whatever zodiac season
you're in], I officially and with nothing but perfect love and
perfect trust, devote and dedicate myself to You.
O Goddess, I officially declare myself on the path of the Feminine
Divine, rebirthed through Goddess energy. I serve You, and
honor You, and remember the power and expression of the
Goddess within me as I do so. I initiate myself on this path, as
part of the Goddess religion. I open my heart and soul to Your
initiations, knowing they will keep me safe in my body and in
harmony with my truth.
May this resonance of Goddess energy and Goddess consciousness
be awakened and reawakened in me, on all planes and all
ways.

If you are tying a cord or bracelet, now is the time to do so.

As aligned with my True Will, for the highest good of all involved, so it is, the initiation is done.

Spend time with the Goddess however you want. Pray to your Goddess, meditate, or dance. If you wish, practice sex magick to raise and send out this energy to your initiation and to Her.

Step 7: Dismiss the Goddess
When you're ready to close the ritual, dismiss the Goddess, adapting the following:

O Goddess
Thank You for entering this space
With perfect love and perfect trust
You have filled my heart and circle
in all planes and in all ways with your grace
O Goddess
I dismiss Thee at this time,
You have heard my sacred plea,
And now I dismiss Thee with peace.
May You return to the realm from which You came,
Filled with love and adoration, and gone on Your own sacred way.
I thank Thee,
I thank Thee,
I thank Thee,
I am devoted to Thee.
So mote it be.

Say whatever else you need here to finish the ritual.

Step 8: Close, ground, and leave offerings
Close and ground (page 13). Then, leave offerings on your altar, which you may eat to further infuse yourself with Goddess energy. Record how you feel in your Goddess Grimoire. What feels different? Inspiring? What within you feels more devoted or transformed? Spend time here in contemplation, and remember to eat something and drink plenty of water.

Mazel tov! You have just undergone an incredible initiation. Allow this to move through your day-to-day, and know this is a responsibility you must keep to yourself and the Goddess. And so it is!

JOURNAL QUESTIONS

Use the following journal questions to create embodiment practices and rituals for feeling the love and support of the Goddess within. As they move you deeper into the mystic waters of the feminine, allow them to act as methods of self-inquiry and self-discovery that lead you into new modes of being in Goddess energy. Use the instructions on page 34 to create a journaling ritual that feels supportive and nurturing. You may wish to move your body through dance, yoga, or stretching before you begin to relate to the Goddess within.

+ How do I embody Goddess energy and Goddess consciousness in my day-to-day life?
+ How does this come through in my magickal and spiritual practices?
+ How does my devotion to the Goddess reflect my devotion to myself?

- What can I wear that makes me feel like a Goddess, that reminds me of Her power?
- How can invoking the Goddess help me understand what She feels like in my body?
- What does it feel like when I am present to the Goddess, within and outside of myself?
- How does surrendering to the Goddess guide me onto a path within myself?
- In what sign and what house is my Venus in? My Moon? What does this mean to me?
- What signs are asteroids Athene, Ceres, Juno, and Lilith in? What does this express itself as to me?
- What rituals do I practice, or want to practice, in honor of the Goddess?
- What devotionals am I inspired to create and practice in honor of Goddess energy?
- What has shifted for me since my self-initiation onto this path?

AFFIRMATIONS

As always, these affirmations will help you absorb all the lessons from this chapter. They are here to remind you of your Goddess consciousness; to help you dive into Goddess energy; and to call your attention to your sexual sovereignty, love, and power. You can follow the steps to working with affirmations on page 38, or you may want to practice these a bit differently. Chant them, say them out loud as you dance around, write them over and over in your Goddess Grimoire, or make art with them. Remember, *you are a Goddess*. Turn this into as much of a ritual as you wish.

- I am a vision of the Goddess.
- I am art incarnate.
- I am a Goddess.
- I am a living incarnation of the Divine Feminine.
- I come back to Goddess consciousness over and over.
- I honor myself as a temple of the Goddess.
- I honor my body as an altar of the Goddess.
- I adorn myself as a vessel for Goddess energy.
- I move my body as an offering to the Goddess.
- My birth chart leads me deeper into Goddess energy.
- I am healed, held, protected, and guided by the Goddess on all planes and all ways.
- I awaken the frequency of the Goddess within me.
- I am devoted to the love and power of the Goddess.

A TAROT SPREAD FOR LIVING IN GODDESS CONSCIOUSNESS

Use the tarot as a tool for swimming in the vibration of the Goddess, for knowing Her within yourself, and as a guide when it comes to creating rituals and practices that remind you of your Divinity. This simple four-card spread is for exploring yourself as a Goddess, guiding you in ritualizing this and remembering your sovereignty. Use the steps on page 42 to read the cards and unfold into the truth of the Goddess within you.

Card 1: How is the Goddess showing Herself to me right now?

Card 2: How can I live in Goddess energy?

Card 3: How can I ritualize this?

Card 4: What do I need to remember to allow myself to dwell in Goddess consciousness?

GO INTO GODDESS ENERGY

Well, dear Goddess, the time has come. Our journey ends, but your time with the Goddess is just beginning. I want to take a moment and say thank you for being here. Writing this book and sharing my devotion to the Goddess is something I don't take for granted a single bit. It is an honor to help reawaken the Divine Feminine through myth and magick, and with you being here, you also are doing this sacred work.

My hope is that by this point, you've already begun embracing the Goddess. You've already seen the ways Her energy and love are woven into your life. You've already felt Her transforming you, initiating you into new modes of being and consciousness, more aligned with your truth, your heart, your journey, and your being. My hope is that by now, you've begun to take note of and develop relationships with certain faces of the Goddess, inviting them into your life and spiritual practice.

There is no one way to be a Goddess, to be a Goddess devotee, to be "in the feminine." There is no one mode of being that is required on this wild ride. As long as you show up true to yourself, without judgment, with compassion, and with your vision held firmly in your heart and soul, the Goddess will be there. May you remember that

you are of Her sacred essence, a reflection of Her divinity, walking the earth as a creatrix made in manifest.

If you want more support on your journey, please check out the Bibliography as well as my other books: *Inner Witch*, *Bewitching the Elements*, and *Embody Your Magick* for general witchiness; *Sacred Sex* for becoming the sex Goddess of your dreams; and *Goddess of Love Tarot* for working with the Divine Feminine through divination and self-inquiry.

Sending you so much love, lust, and magick on your path!

XOXO,
Gabriela Herstik

ACKNOWLEDGMENTS

I want to thank the Goddess for the gift of sharing Her energy with me and for allowing me the privilege of writing this book. Thank you to the Goddess of Love and Lust, to whom I have devoted my heart and life—I hope this book makes You proud.

Infinite thank-yous to my amazing team for supporting my vision and helping bring this book to life. To my agent, Jill Marr at Sandra Dijkstra Literary Agency, for always having my back and for supporting my dreams. So much gratitude to my incredible team at TarcherPerigee: to Nina Shield for being the best editor a girl could dream of and for seeing my heart and my magick in its infinity. Thank you to Hannah Steigmeyer, Katie Macleod-English, and everyone else at TP for helping weave this book into its final expression.

Thank you so much to my family for your support and for seeing the Goddess in me. To my twin sister, Alexandra, for the coffee walks and love and incredible photos woven through this book. I love you, Yaya, and couldn't have done this without you to watch horror movies with, vent to, and smoke weed with. To my incredible father, Ron, the best rabbi I have ever met, whose love, compassion, and connection to the Divine never ceases to inspire me. Thank you to the OG glamour queen and Goddess, my mom, Silvia, who has always supported my exploration of the esoteric and mystical. Thank you for showing me how much beauty is available through spirit and the heart. Thank you to my Abuelita Anita, the best tita and grandma, whom I love infinitely and whose support allows me to be here. You will never stop inspiring me. Thank you to my Grandma Rose, for continuing to guide me through the spirit realm, and to all my ancestors who have supported me—Grandpa Harry, Tito, Grandpa Jose, Vanessa, Lorraine, Poochy, and to all the other ancestors, spirits, and angels, your guidance has never failed me.

I would not have been able to write this book without the teachers, friends, lovers, witches, and Goddesses in my life who have reflected Goddess energy to me and held me in its loving embrace. To Marissa, my star twin and soulmate, who has seen the Goddess in me, even when I couldn't. Thank you for your sacred chaos. I love you to the Moon and beyond. To Amelia, the best magickal partner a witch could ever need, who has been there for me through gratitude and pain and whom I love endlessly. To Goddess Daddy, who has been a sacred emissary to the Dark Goddess of Love for me, whom I adore so deeply, and whose support and devotion I am overwhelmed to receive. To Cory Russell for being a sacred example of the Divine Masculine for me, and for reflecting my divinity to me. To Ashley Laderer for being there for me and loving me through thick and thin, and for being the best bestie ever. To Isabelle Kohn for supporting me in my sacred exploration of sluttery in devotion to the Goddess. To Toska for being a part of this beautiful journey of the Holy Whore and for the art and ritual and love that has fueled my soul. To Amanda Sharpley for loving the darkness and singing to the void with me. To Sade de Amor for showing me new expressions of the Goddess and for being the best cocreatrix of Kink Coven I could have dreamed. To Gabi for being a Venusian queen, inspiration, and a fresh breeze of Goddess energy. I am so thankful to know you and have you in my life. To Olive, Iris, and Violet for seeing me through all my expressions of sluttiness for the Goddess. And to all my lovers who have helped me embrace the Dark Goddess of Love within me.

Thank you to this life for this gift and to the Goddess for guiding me through it all.

NOTES

1: The Goddess Is (Re)Awakening

1. **Many of us were taught that the body is sinful and separate from "God":** Anne Baring and Jules Cashford, *The Myth of the Goddess: Evolution of an Image* (London, UK: Penguin Arkana, 1993).

3. **The Goddess doesn't smite you to atone for "sins" or supposed wrongdoings:** Doreen Valiente, *The Charge of the Goddess: The Poetry of Doreen Valiente* (Sussex, UK: The Doreen Valiente Foundation, 2014).

4. **It's hard to imagine that there was a time before:** Baring and Cashford, *The Myth of the Goddess*.

6. **There is evidence of worship of the Great Mother Goddess since the Paleolithic era:** Elinor W. Gadon, *The Once and Future Goddess: A Symbol for Our Time* (San Francisco, CA: HarperSanFrancisco, 1989).

6. **The well-known handheld statues of Goddesses, exuberant in their curves:** Baring and Cashford, *The Myth of the Goddess*.

7. **As the Neolithic people grew and harvested their own food:** Baring and Cashford, *The Myth of the Goddess*.

8. **And in Islam, the "three daughters of Allah":** Janet Farrar and Stewart Farrar, *The Witches' Goddess: The Feminine Principle of Divinity* (Blaine, WA: Phoenix Publishing, Inc., 1987).

20. **Psychoanalyst Carl Jung, who proposed the idea of archetypes:** Marion Woodman and Elinor Dickson, *Dancing in the Flames: The Dark Goddess in the Transformation of Consciousness* (Boston, MA: Shambhala, 1996).

22. **The Triple Goddess emerged in Anatolian society:** Gadon, *The Once and Future Goddess*.

24. **Meanwhile, the Greek Goddess Hekate:** Barbara G. Walker, "Trinity," in *The Woman's Encyclopedia of Myths and Secrets*, 1018–20 (San Francisco, CA: HarperSanFrancisco, 1983).

24. In Greek mythos, the Triple Goddess is represented by the three Fates, the Moirai: Walker, "Fates," in *The Woman's Encyclopedia of Myths and Secrets*, 302–3.

2: The Goddess of the Earth

43. In *The Woman's Encyclopedia of Myths and Secrets*, Barbara Walker describes: Walker, "Goddess," in *The Woman's Encyclopedia of Myths and Secrets*, 346–7.

44. The earth itself isn't an inanimate entity made of rocks and water: James Lovelock, "Overview" (1974). Accessed November 6, 2020, from https://wholepeople.com/gaia-theory.

44. Honoring the children of the earth by working with her living creatures is another access point: Baring and Cashford, *The Myth of the Goddess*.

47. The divine life cycle is still revered: Baring and Cashford, *The Myth of the Goddess*.

47. Artemis also demonstrates the power of harnessing fear: Baring and Cashford, *The Myth of the Goddess*.

50. They are sassy and all-knowing, weaving, measuring, and cutting: Demetra George, *Mysteries of the Dark Moon: The Healing Power of the Dark Goddess* (San Francisco, CA: HarperSanFrancisco, 1992).

50. Demetra George explains, "Earlier images described them as dwelling amidst": George, *Mysteries of the Dark Moon*.

50. The Anglo-Saxons called the Fates the Wyrd: George, *Mysteries of the Dark Moon*.

51. who tended the World Tree and controlled the living earth: Shahrukh Husain, *The Goddess: Power, Sexuality, and the Feminine Divine* (Ann Arbor, MI: University of Michigan Press, 2003).

51. In Hindu mythology, the spider is the spinner of fate known as Maya: Walker, "Spider," in *The Woman's Encyclopedia of Myths and Secrets*.

51. The Moirai are not outward forces controlling our lives: Demetra George, "Fate, the Unconscious and Karma," in *Mysteries of the Dark Moon*.

56. Sekhmet in Her mutable form takes on a role of divine healer: Normandi Ellis, "Sekhmet, Bast, and Hathor: Power, Passion, and Transformation through the Egyptian Goddess Trinity," in Patricia Monaghan, ed., *Goddesses in World Culture*, 201–214 (Santa Barbara, CA: Praeger, 2011).

60. Water is intuitive and psychic, and many ancient temples: Gaia, "Sacred

Space and the Healing Power of Resonance," accessed November 16, 2020, https://www.gaia.com/video/sacred-space-and-healing-power-resonance.

60. Goddesses of Love associated with water and the ocean include: Baring and Cashford, *The Myth of the Goddess*.

61. Lakshmi rules over four kinds of wealth: Constantina Rhodes, "Lakshmi: Hindu Goddess of Abundance," in Monaghan, ed., *Goddesses in World Culture*.

61. Instead of the beauty-bestowing Lakshmi: Rhodes, "Lakshmi: Hindu Goddess of Abundance," in Monaghan, ed., *Goddesses in World Culture*.

65. There is evidence that this High Priestess: Merlin Stone, *When God Was a Woman* (United Kingdom: Harcourt Brace Jovanovich, 1978).

65. Power and property were passed down through women: Stone, *When God Was a Woman*.

65. It allowed them to track their periods and pregnancies,: George, *Mysteries of the Dark Moon*.

67. As astrologer Demetra George says: George, *Mysteries of the Dark Moon*.

74. and in the New Testament's book of Revelation: Walker, "Sun Goddess," in *The Woman's Encyclopedia of Myths and Secrets*.

76. Both were widely worshipped for millennia: Farrar and Farrar, *The Witches' Goddess*.

77. Unlike Her great-grandmother Gaia: Baring and Cashford, *The Myth of the Goddess*.

79. My favorite aspect of this story isn't one I have seen discussed often: Baring and Cashford, *The Myth of the Goddess*.

81. From then on, Osiris is King of the Underworld: Baring and Cashford, *The Myth of the Goddess*.

83. Instead, all animals are direct reflections of the Goddess: Baring and Cashford, *The Myth of the Goddess*.

84. This form, or the "vessel of the fish": Walker, *The Woman's Encyclopedia of Myths and Secrets*.

84. When Aphrodite, Venus's Greek counterpart: Walker, *The Woman's Encyclopedia of Myths and Secrets*.

85. Bird motifs are found in shamanistic practices: Walker, "Birds," in *The Woman's Encyclopedia of Myths and Secrets*.

85. The bird links dimensions and is a sacred messenger: Baring and Cashford, *The Myth of the Goddess*.

85. The dove, an emblem and emissary of Aphrodite and Venus: Baring and Cashford, *The Myth of the Goddess*.

85. The Sumerian Goddess Inanna, like the Dark Goddess Lilith: Joshua J. Mark, "The Queen of the Night," *World History Encyclopedia*, February 19, 2014, https://www.ancient.eu/article/658/the-queen-of-the-night.

86. They're emotional animals: McKernan, Dan, "The Science of Cow Friendship—Cows Have Best Friends!" Plant-Based News, September 28, 2020, https://plantbasednews.org/culture/the-science-of-cow-friendship -cows-have-best-friends.

86. In the Vedas—the oldest of Hindu scriptures: Kimberly Winston, "The 'Splainer: What Makes the Cow Sacred to Hindus?" November 5, 2015, https://religionnews.com/2015/11/05/splainer-makes-cow-sacred-hindus/.

86. Egyptian cosmology features Hathor, the cow-headed Love Goddess: Walker, "Gaea," in *The Woman's Encyclopedia of Myths and Secrets*.

87. In Crete, honey was used to preserve the bodies of the dead: Baring and Cashford, *The Myth of the Goddess*.

87. Jaguars were central to the Mesoamerican culture of the Maya: Joshua J. Mark, "The Mayan Pantheon: The Many Gods of the Maya," *World History Encyclopedia*, July 7, 2012, https://www.ancient.eu/article/415/the-mayan -pantheon-the-many-gods-of-the-maya.

87. The Hindu Goddess Durga is depicted astride a lion: Miranda Shaw, "Tara: Savior, Buddha, Holy Mother," in Monaghan, ed., *Goddesses in World Culture*, 115–28.

3: The Goddess of Protection and Healing

105. Green Tara sits on a lotus with her right leg extended: "Tara," *Encyclopedia Britannica*, last modified October 31, 2017, https://www.britannica.com /topic/Tara-Buddhist-goddess.

106. Tara refused, saying She would continue incarnating exclusively: Lama Tsultrim Allione, "Tara, the First Feminist," Lion's Roar, August 18, 2016, https://www.lionsroar.com/tara-the-first-feminist.

106. This is a Goddess of the Left Hand Path: Allione, "Tara, the First Feminist."

106. A potent way to do so is by repeating: Thomas Ashley-Farrand, *Shakti Mantras: Tapping into the Great Goddess Energy Within* (United Kingdom: Random House Publishing Group, 2009).

107. They adopted some of these Goddesses of the Earth and Love: Raphael Patai, *The Hebrew Goddess* (Detroit, MI: Wayne State University Press, 1990).

107. **Although She is not mentioned in the Old Testament:** Patai, *The Hebrew Goddess.*

107. ***Shekinah* means "indwelling":** Patai, *The Hebrew Goddess.*

107. **Shekinah also expressed an equilibrating and "punitive power":** Patai, *The Hebrew Goddess.*

108. **Guanyin, also spelled Kwan-Yin, Kuan Yin, and Guan Yin:** Maria Reis-Habito, "The Bodhisattva Guanyin and the Virgin Mary," *Buddhist-Christian Studies* 13 (1993): 61–69.

109. **By the fifteenth century BCE, the indigenous shamanic religion of China:** Reis-Habito, "The Bodhisattva Guanyin and the Virgin Mary."

110. **We know Her as "just" the mother of Jesus:** Baring and Cashford, *The Myth of the Goddess.*

110. **Mary is in the New Testament's book of Revelation:** Reis-Habito, "The Bodhisattva Guanyin and the Virgin Mary."

110. **During the last thousand years, there have been 21,000 visions of the Virgin Mary:** Baring and Cashford, *The Myth of the Goddess.*

110. **Catholic women who want to have a child pray to Mary:** Reis-Habito, "The Bodhisattva Guanyin and the Virgin Mary."

111. **It is in Her role as the Black Madonna:** Baring and Cashford, *The Myth of the Goddess.*

111. **In 1531, the Virgin Mary showed herself to a man named Juan Diego:** Susan D. Buell, "Our Lady of Guadalupe: A Feminine Mythology for the New World," *Historical Magazine of the Protestant Episcopal Church* 51, no. 4 (1982): 399–404, http://www.jstor.org/stable/42973919.

112. **When you want to invoke this powerful manifestation of the Goddess:** Forrest, M. Isidora. *Isis Magic: Cultivating a Relationship with the Goddess of 10,000 Names.* (St. Paul, MN: Llewellyn Publications, 2001).

113. **Bastet, like Sekhmet, is the daughter of Ra:** Ellis, "Sekhmet, Bast, and Hathor," in Monaghan, ed., *Goddesses in World Culture.*

114. **It is Mercury's ability to transform that marks him:** "Mercurial," Online Etymology Dictionary," accessed December 28, 2020, https://www.etymonline.com/search?q=mercurial.

115. **The priests who presided over Aphrodite's Cyprian temple wore:** Walker, "Hermes," in *The Woman's Encyclopedia of Myths and Secrets.*

115. **It's even said that Hermes invented masturbation:** Neel Burton, "A Brief History of Masturbation," *Psychology Today*, October 15, 2017, https://www.psychologytoday.com/us/blog/hide-and-seek/201710/brief-history-masturbation.

115. **Thoth is the ancient Egyptian God of Words and Writing:** Walker, "Thoth," in *The Woman's Encyclopedia of Myths and Secrets*.

4: The Goddess of Love

134. **Their cultivation goes back five thousand years:** Peter Grey, *The Red Goddess* (London, UK: Scarlet Imprint, 2007).

139. **Venus is a Goddess of Love and an alchemical Goddess:** Jean Shinoda Bolen, *Goddesses in Everywoman: Powerful Archetypes in Women's Lives* (New York, NY: Harper & Row, 1984).

139. **This trinity presided over love and war, lust and rage:** Bettany Hughes, *Venus and Aphrodite: A Biography of Desire* (New York, NY: Basic Books, 2020).

140. **She also is venerated as Aphrodite Pandemos:** Baring and Cashford, *The Myth of the Goddess*.

140. **Aphrodite also was called Ephistrophia, the deceiver:** Hughes, *Venus and Aphrodite*.

140. **Venus, meanwhile, was Venus Genetrix:** Brittany Garcia, "Venus," *World History Encyclopedia*, August 27, 2013, https://www.ancient.eu/venus.

141. **This is a Goddess who is a patron of sex workers and rough sex:** Garcia, "Venus."

141. **She is a Goddess of Beauty, Desire, and Adornment:** Hughes, *Venus and Aphrodite*.

142. **A Goddess of Love and Wisdom, Mary Magdalene is a facet of the Divine:** Jean-Yves Leloup, *The Gospel of Mary Magdalene* (Rochester, VT: Inner Traditions, 2002).

143. **of the Emerald Tablet of Hermes Trismegistus:** "The Emerald Tablet of Hermes Trismegistus," Cabinet, June 2018, https://www.cabinet.ox.ac.uk/emerald-tablet-hermes-trismegistus.

143. **Magdalene is a Goddess of Illumination, of the Heart:** Tricia McCannon, *Return of the Divine Sophia: Healing the Earth through the Lost Wisdom Teachings of Jesus, Isis, and Mary Magdalene* (Rochester, VT: Bear & Company, 2015).

144. **It's said that Magdalene grew so horny for Her deceased beloved:** Susan Little, "Mary Magdalene: Tradition, Myth, and the Search for Meaning," in Monaghan, ed., *Goddesses in World Culture* 2, 69–81.

145. **She also embodies the archetype of the maiden:** Evan Meehan, "Xochiquetzal," *Mythopedia*, November 29 2022, https://mythopedia.com/aztec-mythology/gods/xochiquetzal.

145. Her name comes from the Nahuatl words: Meehan, "Xochiquetzal."

145. Her spirit is said to have taken the form of a dove: Meehan, "Xochiquetzal."

145. For the Aztecs, flowers were associated with the vulva: Meehan, "Xochiquetzal."

146. There is power in leading alongside a loved one: "Frigg," *U*X*L Encyclopedia of World Mythology*. Encyclopedia.com, May 28, 2018, https://www.encyclopedia.com/history/encyclopedias-almanacs-transcripts-and-maps/frigg.

146. As a patron of marriage, and a Goddess concerned with the order of contracts: Alice Karlsdóttir, *Norse Goddess Magic: Trancework, Mythology, and Ritual* (Rochester, VT: Destiny Books, 2015).

147. This is a potent spell and devotional act when shared with family: Karlsdóttir, *Norse Goddess Magic*.

147. She sees the future with a form of prophetic magick called seidr: Karlsdóttir, *Norse Goddess Magic*.

147. But after the trickster God Loki exposed the Goddess's indiscretions to Odur: Michelle Skye, *Goddess Aloud! Transforming Your World through Rituals and Mantras* (Woodbury, MN: Llewellyn Publications, 2010).

149. The Egyptian Hathor has been worshipped for more than six thousand years: Eillis, "Sekhmet, Bast, and Hathor," in Monaghan, ed., *Goddesses in World Culture*, 201–214.

149. As a Goddess of the Sky, Heavens, and Cosmos, Hathor birthed the world: Eillis, "Sekhmet, Bast, and Hathor," in Monaghan, ed., *Goddesses in World Culture*, 201–214.

150. As a Goddess associated with the dead: Joshua J. Mark, "The Coffin Texts," *World History Encyclopedia*, March 8, 2017, https://www.ancient.eu/article/1021/the-coffin-texts.

152. The Homeric Hymns were written by different authors in dactylic hexameter: Susan C. Shelmerdine, *The Homeric Hymns* (Newburyport, MA: Focus Publishing, 1995).

152. The Orphic Hymns are a collection inspired by the (perhaps) mythological hero Orpheus and the mystery religions: Apostolos N. Athanassakis, trans., with Benjamin M. Wolkow, trans., *The Orphic Hymns* (Baltimore, MD: Johns Hopkins University Press, 2013).

5: The Dark Goddess

182. This is the Black Crone, who receives the dead and prepares them for rebirth: George, *Mysteries of the Dark Moon*.

184. Her tongue lolls out of Her mouth, reflecting Her wild and untamable nature: David R. Kinsley, "Kali: The Black Goddess," in *Tantric Visions of the Divine Feminine: The Ten Mahāvidyās*, 92–112 (Berkeley and Los Angeles, CA: University of California Press, 1997).

185. She is the "life and death mother, womb and tomb": Walker, "Kali Ma," in *The Woman's Encyclopedia of Myths and Secrets*.

185. The Brahmin, the priest caste of the Hindu tradition and culture: Walker, "Kali Ma," in *The Woman's Encyclopedia of Myths and Secrets*.

185. She lives at and is worshipped at the periphery: Kinsley, "Kali."

185. She "threatens stability and control": Kinsley, "Kali."

186. She is sexual, with names including She Whose Essential Form Is Sexual Desires: Kinsley, "Kali."

186. Kali's three eyes represent Her Triple Goddess aspect: Kinsley, "Kali."

187. In the Old World, Lilith was a formidable demoness: Patai, *The Hebrew Goddess*.

188. Lilith lives alongside the often-forgotten Divine Feminine: Barbara Black Koltuv, *The Book of Lilith* (Berwick, ME: Nicolas-Hays, Inc., 1986).

188. In all Her faces, She represents the obscurity and loneliness: Koltuv, *The Book of Lilith*.

189. Because the Celts didn't leave much written history: Courtney Weber, *The Morrigan: Celtic Goddess of Magick and Might* (Newburyport, MA: Weiser Books, 2019).

190. Badb, the mother, is also known as the fighting lady: Weber, *The Morrigan*.

191. Originally a Titan, who was given dominion over the earth, land, and sea: Cyndi Brannen, *Keeping Her Keys: An Introduction to Hekate's Modern Witchcraft* (Alresford, UK: Moon Books, 2019).

191. In the Orphic Hymn, Hekate has the responsibility of holding the key: Brannen, *Keeping Her Keys*.

192. Some of Hekate's epithets include the guide: Brannen, *Keeping Her Keys*.

192. And in Her face as gatekeeper, Hekate takes on the initiating role in your magick: Brannen, *Keeping Her Keys*.

192. Hekate has commonalities with Selene the Moon, as the Goddess of Heaven: Walker, "Hecate," in *The Woman's Encyclopedia of Myths and Secrets*.

192. In the Chaldean Oracles, Hekate says, "if you call upon Me often you will perceive everything in Lion-form": Sorita d'Este and David Rankine, *Hekate Liminal Rites: A Study of the Rituals, Magic and Symbols of the Torch-bearing Triple Goddess of the Crossroads* (London, UK: Avalonia, 2009).

193. Because Persephone had eaten pomegranate seeds before returning to the earth: George, *Mysteries of the Dark Moon*.

194. Persephone saw this as an opportunity to act as an emissary to those in the underworld: George, *Mysteries of the Dark Moon*.

195. Nephthys—or Nebet-Het in Khemetian—never got the same amount of love or adoration as Her twin sister: Joshua J. Mark, "Nephthys," *World History Encyclopedia*, March 13, 2016, https://www.ancient.eu/Nephthys.

195. Like Persephone, She guides souls through the death process: Mark, "Nephthys."

196. During their heyday, Nephthys and Isis were almost always mentioned together: Mark, "Nephthys."

196. Isis relates more to the conscious mind and to the light of the Moon: Ellen Cannon Reed, *Ancient Egyptian Magic for Modern Witches: Rituals, Meditations, and Magical Tools* (Newburyport, MA: Weiser Books, 2021).

197. How am I supposed to pay due respect to the Great Inanna, the first Goddess in recorded history: Diane Wolkstein and Samuel Noah Kramer, *Inanna: Queen of Heaven and Earth* (New York: Harper & Row, 1983).

197. Clothed in the heavens, with a crown of twelve stars for each of the zodiac signs: Wolkstein and Kramer, *Inanna*.

199. "Her mythology revolves around the connection made between the light and dark lunar phases": Wolkstein and Kramer, *Inanna*.

200. In Revelation 12:1, She is described as a "great wonder in heaven": Grey, *The Red Goddess*.

201. Per Peter Grey, "Babalon and the Beast can be seen as a sexual formula to lead the aspirant to enlightenment": Grey, *The Red Goddess*.

202. The name *Babylon* translated to "wicked": Temple of Our Lady of the Abyss, "Who Is Babalon?" accessed March 8, 2021, https://www.templumabyssi.com/who-is-babalon.

6: Embracing the Goddess Within

225. Planetary, metal, and color correspondences: Aleister Crowley, *777 and Other Qabalistic Writings of Aleister Crowley* (Newburyport, MA: Weiser Books, 1986).

225. astrologer and mystic Manly P. Hall: Manly P. Hall, *The Secret Teachings of All Ages*.

242. The discovery of Neptune in 1846 came alongside the Victorians' reawakened interest: Demetra George and Douglas Bloch, *Asteroid Goddesses: The Mythology, Psychology, and Astrology of the Re-Emerging Feminine* (Lake Worth, FL: Ibis Press, 2003).

243. *Associated zodiac sign*: George and Bloch, *Asteroid Goddesses*.

243. Ceres—the Roman equivalent to Demeter—was the first asteroid ever discovered: "Ceres," NASA, Solar System Exploration, March 22, 2023, https://solarsystem.nasa.gov/planets/dwarf-planets/ceres/overview.

243. Ceres is the asteroid that represents the universal mother: George and Bloch, *Asteroid Goddesses*.

243. As the corn mother, bringing the harvest and providing sustenance: "Ceres," Empress Atlantis, accessed March 30, 2021, https://www.empress atlantis.com/asteroid/ceres.

244. Asteroid Pallas Athene is also wildly creative: George and Bloch, *Asteroid Goddesses*.

244. Athene "embodies the magical will that enables us to create": George and Bloch, *Asteroid Goddesses*.

244. Juno speaks of merging with another: George and Bloch, *Asteroid Goddesses*.

245. In the birth chart, She can mean the "perception of the feminine as evil": George and Bloch, *Asteroid Goddesses*.

BIBLIOGRAPHY

Allione, Lama Tsultrim. "Tara, the First Feminist." Lion's Roar, August 18, 2016. https://www.lionsroar.com/tara-the-first-feminist.

Andrew, Scottie. "The Moon Is About 85 Million Years Younger than We Thought, New Study Finds." CNN, July 16, 2020. https://www.cnn.com/ 2020/07/16/world/moon-85-million-years-younger-scn-trnd/index.html.

Ashley-Farrand, Thomas. *Shakti Mantras: Tapping into the Great Goddess Energy Within.* United Kingdom: Random House Publishing Group, 2009.

Athanassakis, Apostolos N., trans., with Benjamin M. Wolkow, trans. *The Orphic Hymns.* Baltimore, MD: Johns Hopkins University Press, 2013.

Auryn, Mat. *Psychic Witch: A Metaphysical Guide to Meditation, Magick & Manifestation.* Woodbury, MN: Llewellyn Publications, 2020.

Baring, Anne, and Jules Cashford. *The Myth of the Goddess: Evolution of an Image.* London, UK: Penguin Arkana, 1993.

Bolen, Jean Shinoda. *Goddesses in Everywoman: Powerful Archetypes in Women's Lives.* New York, NY: Harper & Row, 1984.

Brannen, Cyndi. *Keeping Her Keys: An Introduction to Hekate's Modern Witchcraft.* Alresford, UK: Moon Books, 2019.

Buell, Susan D. "Our Lady of Guadalupe: A Feminine Mythology for the New World." *Historical Magazine of the Protestant Episcopal Church* 51, no. 4 (1982): 399–404. http://www.jstor.org/stable/42973919.

Burton, Neel. "A Brief History of Masturbation." *Psychology Today*, October 15, 2017. https://www.psychologytoday.com/us/blog/hide-and-seek/201710 /brief-history-masturbation.

Campbell, Joseph. *Goddesses: Mysteries of the Feminine Divine.* Edited by Safron Rossi. Novato, CA: Joseph Campbell Foundation, 2013.

Cartwright, Mark. "Aphrodite." *World History Encyclopedia*, October 24, 2018. https://www.ancient.eu/Aphrodite.

"Ceres." Empress Atlantis. Accessed March 30, 2021. https://www.empressat lantis.com/asteroid/ceres.

"Ceres." NASA, Solar System Exploration, March 22, 2023. https://solarsys tem.nasa.gov/planets/dwarf-planets/ceres/overview.

Crowley, Aleister. *777 and Other Qabalistic Writings of Aleister Crowley.* Newburyport, MA: Weiser Books, 1986.

d'Este, Sorita, and David Rankine. *Hekate Liminal Rites: A Study of the Rituals, Magic and Symbols of the Torch-bearing Triple Goddess of the Crossroads.* London, UK: Avalonia, 2009.

Farrar, Janet, and Stewart Farrar. *The Witches' Goddess: The Feminine Principle of Divinity.* Blaine, WA: Phoenix Publishing, Inc., 1987.

Forrest, M. Isidora. "Hathor, Lady of Heaven." In *Isis Magic: Cultivating a Relationship with the Goddess of 10,000 Names,* 35–37. Portland, OR: Abiegnus House, 2013.

Fortune, Dion. *The Mystical Qabalah.* Newburyport, MA: Weiser Books, 2000.

"Freyja." *Encyclopedia of Religion.* Encyclopedia.com, May 21, 2018. https://www .encyclopedia.com/environment/encyclopedias-almanacs-transcripts-and -maps/freyja.

"Frigg." *U*X*L Encyclopedia of World Mythology.* Encyclopedia.com, May 28, 2018. https://www.encyclopedia.com/history/encyclopedias-almanacs-transcripts -and-maps/frigg.

Gadon, Elinor W. *The Once and Future Goddess: A Symbol for Our Time.* San Francisco, CA: HarperSanFrancisco, 1989.

Gaia. "Sacred Space and the Healing Power of Resonance." Accessed November 16, 2020, https://www.gaia.com/video/sacred-space-and-healing-power -resonance.

Garcia, Brittany. "Venus." *World History Encyclopedia,* August 27, 2013. https:// www.ancient.eu/venus.

George, Demetra. *Mysteries of the Dark Moon: The Healing Power of the Dark Goddess.* San Francisco, CA: HarperSanFrancisco, 1992.

George, Demetra, and Douglas Bloch. *Asteroid Goddesses: The Mythology, Psychology, and Astrology of the Re-emerging Feminine.* Lake Worth, FL: Ibis Press, 2003.

"The Gospel According to Mary Magdalene." The Gnostic Society Library. Accessed March 14, 2021. http://gnosis.org/library/marygosp.htm.

Gray, David B. "Tantra and the Tantric Traditions of Hinduism and Buddhism." Oxford Research Encyclopedia of Religion, April 5, 2016. https://oxfordre .com/religion/view/10.1093/acrefore/9780199340378.001.0001/acrefore -9780199340378-e-59.

Grey, Peter. *The Red Goddess.* London, UK: Scarlet Imprint, 2007.

Hughes, Bettany. *Venus and Aphrodite: A Biography of Desire*. New York, NY: Basic Books, 2020.

Husain, Shahrukh. *The Goddess: Power, Sexuality, and the Feminine Divine*. Ann Arbor, MI: University of Michigan Press, 2003.

Karlsdóttir, Alice. *Norse Goddess Magic: Trancework, Mythology, and Ritual*. Rochester, VT: Destiny Books, 2015.

Kinsley, David. "Kali: The Black Goddess." In *Tantric Visions of the Divine Feminine: The Ten Mahāvidyās*, 92–112. Berkeley and Los Angeles, CA: University of California Press, 1997.

Koltuv, Barbara Black. *The Book of Lilith*. Berwick, ME: Nicolas-Hays, Inc., 1986.

Kushner, Dale M. "Understand Your Dreams by Using Jung's 'Active Imagination.'" *Psychology Today*, October 23, 2016. https://www.psychologytoday.com/us/blog/transcending-the-past/201610/understand-your-dreams-using-jungs-active-imagination#comments_bottom.

Kynes, Sandra. *Llewellyn's Complete Book of Correspondences: A Comprehensive and Cross-Referenced Resource for Pagans and Wiccans*. Woodbury, MN: Llewellyn Publications, 2013.

Lawler, Lillian Brady. "The Dance in Ancient Greece." *The Classical Journal* 42, no. 6 (1947): 343–49. http://www.jstor.org/stable/3291645.

Leloup, Jean-Yves. *The Gospel of Mary Magdalene*. Rochester, VT: Inner Traditions, 2002.

Lesko, Barbara S. *The Great Goddesses of Egypt*. Norman, OK: University of Oklahoma Press, 1999.

Mark, Joshua J. "The Coffin Texts." *World History Encyclopedia*, March 8, 2017. https://www.worldhistory.org/article/1021/the-coffin-texts.

Mark, Joshua J. "The Mayan Pantheon: The Many Gods of the Maya." *World History Encyclopedia*, July 7, 2012. https://www.ancient.eu/article/415/the-mayan-pantheon-the-many-gods-of-the-maya.

Mark, Joshua J. "Nephthys," *World History Encyclopedia*, March 13, 2016. https://www.ancient.eu/Nephthys.

Mark, Joshua J. "The Queen of the Night." *World History Encyclopedia*, February 19, 2014. https://www.ancient.eu/article/658/the-queen-of-the-night.

McCannon, Tricia. *Return of the Divine Sophia: Healing the Earth through the Lost Wisdom Teachings of Jesus, Isis, and Mary Magdalene*. Rochester, VT: Bear & Company, 2015.

McKernan, Dan. "The Science of Cow Friendship—Cows Have Best Friends!" Plant-Based News. September 28, 2020. https://plantbasednews.org/culture/the-science-of-cow-friendship-cows-have-best-friends.

Meehan, Evan. "Xochiquetzal," *Mythopedia*, November 29, 2022. https://mythopedia.com/aztec-mythology/gods/xochiquetzal.

"Mercurial" Online Etymology Dictionary. Accessed December 28, 2020. https://www.etymonline.com/search?q=mercurial.

Monaghan, Patricia, ed. *Goddesses in World Culture*. Santa Barbara, CA: Praeger, 2011.

"Muse." *Encyclopedia Britannica*, February 15, 2023. https://www.britannica.com/topic/Muse-Greek-mythology.

Patai, Raphael. *The Hebrew Goddess*. Detroit, MI: Wayne State University Press, 1990.

Reed, Ellen Cannon. *Ancient Egyptian Magic for Modern Witches: Rituals, Meditations, and Magical Tools*. Newburyport, MA: Weiser Books, 2021.

Reis-Habito, Maria. "The Bodhisattva Guanyin and the Virgin Mary." Buddhist-Christian Studies 13 (1993): 61–69.

Roland, James. "Why Do We Dream?" Healthline, August 22, 2017. https://www.healthline.com/health/why-do-we-dream.

Shelmerdine, Susan C. *The Homeric Hymns*. Newburyport, MA: Focus Publishing, 1995.

Skye, Michelle. *Goddess Aloud! Transforming Your World Through Rituals and Mantras*. Woodbury, MN: Llewellyn Publications, 2010.

Stone, Merlin. *When God Was a Woman*. United Kingdom: Harcourt Brace Jovanovich, 1978.

"Tara." *Encyclopedia Britannica*, Updated October 31, 2017. https://www.britannica.com/topic/Tara-Buddhist-goddess.

Temple of Our Lady of the Abyss. "Who Is Babalon?" Accessed March 8, 2021. https://www.templumabyssi.com/who-is-babalon.

Valiente, Doreen. *The Charge of the Goddess: The Poetry of Doreen Valiente*. Sussex, UK: The Doreen Valiente Foundation, 2014.

Walker, Barbara G. *The Woman's Encyclopedia of Myths and Secrets*. San Francisco, CA: HarperSanFrancisco, 1983.

Weber, Courtney. *The Morrigan: Celtic Goddess of Magick and Might*. Newburyport, MA: Weiser Books, 2019.

Winston, Kimberly. (2015, November 05). "The 'Splainer: What Makes the Cow Sacred to Hindus?" Accessed October 23, 2020. https://religionnews.com/2015/11/05/splainer-makes-cow-sacred-hindus/.

Wolkstein, Diane, and Samuel Noah Kramer. *Inanna: Queen of Heaven and Earth*. New York, NY: Harper & Row, 1983.

Woodman, Marion, and Elinor Dickson. *Dancing in the Flames: The Dark Goddess in the Transformation of Consciousness*. Boston, MA: Shambhala, 1996.

ABOUT THE AUTHOR

Gabriela Herstik is an angelic succubus residing in the City of Angels. She is the author of *Inner Witch: A Modern Guide to the Ancient Craft*; *Bewitching the Elements: A Guide to Empowering Yourself Through Earth, Air, Fire, Water, and Spirit*; *Embody Your Magick: A Guided Journal for the Modern Witch*; *Sacred Sex: The Magick and Path of the Divine Erotic*; and *Goddess of Love Tarot: A Book and Deck for Embodying the Erotic Divine Feminine*. Gabriela's work lives at the intersection of the erotic and esoteric, and she has written for outlets such as *Vogue International, Glamour, i-D, Cosmopolitan, Dazed Beauty*, Taschen's *Witchcraft, The Library of Esoterica*, and the anthology *Becoming Dangerous: Witchy Femmes, Queer Conjurers, and Magical Rebels*. Gabriela has headed columns for *NYLON, High Times*, and *Chakrubs* on the intersection of glamour, sexuality, and the Feminine Divine, and she writes the monthly essay series "Diary of a Sacred Slut" on Patreon. Gabriela has also been featured in publications around the world such as *The Guardian, LA Weekly, Tattler Asia, The Atlantic, USA Weekly*, and *Vogue Spain* for her contribution to the occult milieu. Gabriela leads kinky rituals and sex magick discussion circles and creates erotic art and performance rituals inspired by the power and magick of the flesh. Gabriela has been a practicing witch since the tender age of thirteen and is a devotee of the Goddess of Love and Lust. She believes magick is for everyone. You can keep up with her at gabrielaherstik.com and on Instagram and Twitter at @GabyHerstik.